Raelyn

Moose Skow...

Jim McDevitt

Tony Johnson

Alex Wright

John...

Frank Brown

John A. Dale

Pete Carpenter

Bob Breault

Jeff "Tico" Tice

Lance & Alois,
To longtime friends, and with respect to
a fellow service man. Many miles and
many memories ago.

Terry

ON THE WINGS
OF GEEZERS

LIFE LESSONS FROM OLD PILOTS

First person stories of growing up flying in the old days - the early years of the military and civil aviation and lessons learned living through it. Stories from the lives of the Friday Pilots of Tucson, Arizona. Come lunch with us and listen to lies, laughs and lessons. We're old and we know things. You'll enjoy the wild ride!

EDITED BY DON SHEPPERD

authorHOUSE®

AuthorHouse™
1663 Liberty Drive
Bloomington, IN 47403
www.authorhouse.com
Phone: 833-262-8899

Published by AuthorHouse 03/30/2021

ISBN: 978-1-6655-1976-2 (sc)
ISBN: 978-1-6655-1975-5 (e)

Library of Congress Control Number: 2021905299

Print information available on the last page.

CONTENTS

ABOUT THE COVER

This is an iconic cover. Most readers look at a cover once. We guarantee you will look at this one, front and back, several times. It contains aviation symbolism. The cover was designed by award winning aviation artist, writer and filmmaker, John Mollison, as an homage to the influences he had as a "plane crazy" little boy. The stories of famous aviators and their machines helped to shape his deep respect for the American story, sense of personal responsibility and appreciation for how studying history is crucial for the success of future generations. The cover design contains fourteen objects and symbols that have been important to the stories of aviators. See if you can find them on the cover, an aviation treasure hunt. The objects, on front and back pages, are circled with explanations on the next page.

KEY TO THE COVER

The cover circles contain: 1. A four-ship of fighter aircraft flying a "missing man" formation with #3 pulling up out of the flight towards the heavens as a tribute to a fallen comrade, 2. "Three linebackers" symbolizing B-52 flights in Operation Linebacker I and II in the Vietnam War, 3. An airline captain's hat, 4. A POW/MIA flag symbolizing the suffering of our POWs in all wars, 5. A "Jolly Green Giant," symbolizing the heroism of the HH-3E Jolly Green helicopter crews that performed daring and miraculous rescues of downed pilots in Vietnam, 6. An SA-2 Surface to Air (SAM) Missile prevalent in the Vietnam War, 7. Army helicopter wings "hovering" over the grass, 8. Marine/Navy wings, 9. USAF wings, 10. "Dead bug," symbolizing an Air Force bar game - someone yells "DEAD BUG" and everyone hits the floor - last man standing buys the bar, 11. A "nickel on the grass," - a symbolic gesture of throwing a nickel on the grass to commemorate the loss of a comrade, 12. The moon, honoring our astronauts, 13. An old geezer telling a story and..., 14. A young mind taking it all in.

How to contact John Mollison

john@johnmollison.com
www.oldguysandtheirairplanes.com

DEDICATION

To our fellow pilots who made these stories possible, those who are with us and those who aren't. Several members of our Tucson Friday Pilots slipped the surly bonds of earth before publication of this book – may a good and gracious God hold them and their families in the palm of His hand until we meet again. Rest in peace, our dear brothers and sisters.

Norm Sandell
Jim Record
"Dusty" Showen
Louis L. Wilson
Al White
"Boris" Baird
Tunis Parsons
Eric Erickson
Gordy Williams
Bob Dundas
Frank Morton
Lew Daugherty

We know we are geezers. We know we've lived longer than we were supposed to especially doing what we have done - fly old airplanes for a long time all over the world, day and night, in all kinds of weather, some of it in wars. Flying has taken a toll on our bodies, but it has filled our memories. Few have experienced the full life we have all enjoyed because of aviation and because of each other. We meet every Friday at Hacienda del Sol for lunch. Some have asked, "Why would you meet every Friday at the same place with the same people?" Our answer - "If you have to ask, you wouldn't understand." As Shakespeare wrote, "We few, we happy few, we band of brothers." - **The Friday Pilots**

QUOTATIONS

God does not subtract from man's allotted time the hours spent while flying, but He exacts harsh penalties for those who do not learn to land properly.

The difference between fear and terror: fear is when your calculations show you may not have enough fuel to make it to your destination. Terror is when you realize you were right.

I wore my mask while pulling 9 Gs, checking six, pumping out flares, telling #2 to "BREAK LEFT!", selecting auto guns, locking up a bandit, selecting the Aim-9, keeping visual while gaining a tally, getting a 1500 MHz tone, watching my altitude, planning an egress, shooting the bandit, telling #2 to "bugout south", reforming into tactical formation, pushing it up, taking it down, short range radar, and resetting the CAP….and all you gotta' do is pick up a gallon of milk.

Mommy, I want to grow up and be a pilot. Honey, you can't do both.

When you see a tree in the clouds, it's not good news.

Heaven is crowded with civilian pilots who did not get their Instrument Rating.

Aviation's greatest invention was the relief tube.

My junior high school teacher told me no one would pay me to look out the window. Now I'm an airline captain.

The older I get, the better pilot I was.

We're at the age when we realize the best thing about flying fighters was free oxygen.

Takeoffs are optional, landings are mandatory.

Never fly the "A" model of anything.

Because I'm the Captain, that's why!

Pilots - looking down on people since 1903.

There are three simple rules for making a smooth landing. Unfortunately, no pilot knows exactly what they are.

The average fighter pilot, despite a swaggering personality and confident exterior, is capable of feelings such as love, affection, humility, caring and intimacy. They just don't involve others.

When everything else is going against you, remember an aircraft still takes off into the wind.

Friday Pilots Pat Halloran and Tom Keck in their SR-71s, "Yeah, though I fly through the valley of the shadow of death, I fear no evil, for I am at 80,000 ft. and climbing."

An idiot can get an airplane off the ground, it takes a pilot to get it back in one piece.

Pilot dictum: remember, in the end, gravity always wins.

You can only tie the record for flying low.

Black boxes may be replacing pilots, but pilots can be maintained easily and produced by unskilled labor.

Many young, inexperienced pilots have delusions of adequacy.

Flying is the art of learning to throw yourself at the ground and miss.

Richard Reid forced us to remove our shoes in the TSA line. Thank goodness he wasn't the "underwear bomber."

Elderly lady to airline captain, "Are you sure you are safe to fly?" Answer, "Lady, how do you think I got this old?"

Optimists invented the airplane. Pessimists invented the parachute.

Scientific fact: the rings of Saturn are composed of lost airline luggage.

Newton's Law: What goes up must come down. Squadron Commander's Law: What comes down better be able to go up again!

I was 14 when I wanted to be a pilot. I'm now 80 and still want to be a pilot, but I'd rather be 14 again.

Ladies and gentlemen, this is the Captain speaking. This was the First Officer's leg and he made that landing you just experienced. I have asked him to stand at the door and receive your comments.

Passenger to Flight Attendant: "John Wayne didn't use a seatbelt." Flight Attendant: "John Wayne isn't going to New York with us and neither are you unless you buckle up!"

Icarus could have flown if he picked a cloudy day.

You've never been lost until you've been lost at Mach 3 - SR-71 pilot.

As George Carlin said, "If black boxes survive crashes, why don't they make the whole airplane out of that stuff?"

Soldier to a pilot: "Why didn't you join the Army?" Pilot's answer, "I found out that good food and clean sheets were readily available on nearby Air Force bases."

"Roger" - a term used by pilots when they can't figure out what else to say.

"Cone of Confusion" - all radio terminology on JFK ground control.

"Balls-to-the-wall" - FULL THROTTLE, or an extremely bad landing.

Kennedy Ground Control to female pilot. "I told you to turn on Alpha!" Female pilot, "Don't be angry, I didn't understand you!" Controller, "Are you my ex-wife?"

Beer was invented to make pilot stories more interesting.

Pilots have to be brave so they don't get scared when they can't see at night, or inside of clouds, or when a motor or wing falls off.

You have never lived until you have almost died. Life has a special flavor the protected will never know.

Helicopter pilots are different from airplane pilots. Airplane pilots are open, clear-eyed, buoyant extroverts. Helicopter pilots are brooders, introspective anticipators of trouble. They know if something bad has not happened, it is about to.

Death is God's way of telling pilots to watch their airspeed on final.

You can't fly unless you can land, but you can't land unless you can fly. So, which is it?

What is the worst thing that can happen when you are flying? - running out of airspeed, altitude and ideas all at the same time.

All engine sounds are magnified over the ocean.

What do you do when you are in trouble flying? Call for help. What if no help is available? Then, no sense calling.

What do you do if you don't like your boss? Go flying. What if he won't let you go flying? Go anyway, he won't be your boss for long.

We are reaching the age where "life sentence" is less of a threat.

FAA motto for pilots: "We're not happy unless you're not happy."

Airline pilots must learn to land because some passengers have low pain thresholds.

ACKNOWLEDGEMENTS

This book would not have been possible without Hacienda del Sol and its staff. Hacienda del Sol is a Tucson resort, hotel and restaurant with a storied past. Spencer Tracy and Katherine Hepburn were amongst the famous of old-time guests. They would have fit right in with us. We would have invited them to our table. We gather every Friday, 20-30 of us, for lies, laughs, lunch and stories. Our favorite waiter is Preston. He waits on us and puts up with our stupid questions, poor hearing, bad eyesight and requests to repeat the day's special once again.

Special thanks to renowned aviation artist, John Mollison, for our cover design and to Chris Vasquez for the use of his high quality photos.

Russ Violett is our, "el jefe," one of the longest-term members of the group. He makes policy calls, of which there are few, if any.

Thanks to Andy Muscarello for thankless years of managing the lunch call-in numbers and thanks to Dan Moore for taking over the reins.

Thanks to Rose "Rosie the Riveter" Shepperd for editing, advice (some welcomed), proof reading and not yelling, "GET OFF THE COMPUTER!" too often during the long, aggravating assembly and publication process of an edited book with numerous authors.

Thanks to Bill Pitts, Claudia Johnson and Rob Van Sice for additional proof-reading assistance.

Thanks to Tyler, Rebecca and Christian Shepperd for their computer advice, ideas and assistance.

Thanks to our families who stayed with us through the rough years that produced our stories.

Thanks to the leaders in our Air Force, Army, Navy and Marines who trained us, put up with us and helped us live to tell these stories.

Thanks to the authors of the stories in this book. This is our second book. Writing is hard. Writing, when you are elderly, is REALLY hard, but we did it. Part of the proceeds to every book goes to the Fisher House military charity at the VA Hospital in Tucson.

Thanks to the America we love. You have changed since we first knew you, but rest assured we will be with you to the end of our lives. We are no longer tan, fit and ready. We are now old, gray and grizzled, but if you ever need us again, we'll be there. You can bet on it.

FOREWORD

Walk into Hacienda del Sol on a Friday noon and you will see a table of anywhere between 20-30 men. They are geezers, the youngest late 60s, most late 70s to late 80s, six over 90. Bald heads, hearing aids and canes abound. Laughter and camaraderie is their most noticeable contribution. These guys like each other. They laugh repeatedly at each other's jokes, many of them the same told the previous week. The four members over 90 are still surprisingly vital. They live in their own homes, drive their own cars and write their own stories.

The stories in this book are worth reading. They are filled with lessons learned, some obvious, some vague and embedded, but they all come from flying airplanes long ago. The lessons come from the old America in which these geezers lived.

The stories in this book come from an exceptional group of men. They are pilots, old pilots, that flew in the old days, in the old airplanes and the early jets. They sat nuclear alert in the Cold War. They have been to war. Some have crashed and burned. Some have been shot by AAA, MiGs and SAMs. Some were hit and parachuted into enemy jungles. They evaded and ran from the enemy. Some were captured. They endured torture and imprisonment in North Vietnam, some for almost six years. Some were part of rescue forces who tried desperately to rescue them. Some flew helicopters into intense gunfire to insert troops and came back to pick up the wounded. Some have ridden huge rockets into space and orbited the earth. Some flew the Lunar Lander. Some have run large companies. Some have been rich and many started out poor. They have all been married, some divorced. They have had successful children and some have lost children. Some have lost wives. There are pilots who finished their careers as generals, colonels, lieutenant colonels and majors, captains, even lieutenants, and Navy jocks as Navy Captains. There are fighter pilots, bomber pilots, airline pilots, corporate pilots and astronauts, even some who have owned airplane companies and been senior executives of corporations and on boards, and men who have landed on Navy carriers in pitching seas at night.

Listen closely. The stories are often about their flying days, their wars and emergencies. Absent are stories about heroism. It's a foreign word to them. They did it, they watched it, but none will use the word. It was just what happened because they were there. The conversation is about the latest University of Arizona decision to postpone the sports seasons into 2021, a huge bummer. They are Wildcat football and basketball fans, and lately women's basketball. COVID has brought another temporary disappointment - many are not meeting because they have underlying conditions and until the COVID statistics alter dramatically downward, they won't attend lunch. It may be next year before most feel comfortable. They are all hoping for a vaccine that works. But, there is good news - it gave the geezers time to write this book.

These men do not look impressive, but they are the REAL DEAL. They are geezers and these are their stories and the lessons they learned living through them.

The Friday Pilots

INTRODUCTION

Here was the introduction to our **"first"** book, The Friday Pilots: It seems everyone at some point in life wants to write a book. There appears to be a desire to leave something for posterity, for one's family, for the grandchildren. Maybe it's as simple as wanting to say, "I was there. I did things. I mattered." Most leave photos, but few actually write a book. It is hard work and most people are not good writers. It is even harder to get published.

The Friday Pilots did something almost everyone talks about and few do: they wrote down their memories for their kids, grandkids, families and friends. These men reached back decades into history, times in our nation that were both difficult and different. Life and airplanes were hard. Some of the stories evoke joy and laughter; some bring back memories better left unvisited. The authors overcame addled memories, arthritic fingers and steam driven computers to write their stories. Strap in, hold on and you'll enjoy a look at aviation history through the eyes of those who lived it.

The idea for this book came at one of our Friday lunches in Tucson, Arizona. We meet every Friday and we kid each other, we laugh, we tell stories, some even true. We have become legends in our own minds. We decided to write a book, a collection of first-person stories. Some will write about life, some about flying. Unless one is an author, he does not keep copious notes, but we all have memories. These are our memories. Enjoy.

And, here is our **"second"** book, "On the Wings of Geezers - life lessons from old pilots." We know we are geezers. Some people look at us with pity. None of us ever wanted to be this old until recently. We assure you WE ARE FOR REAL. Our poster would read, "BEEN THERE, DONE THAT." We think we've seen it all by this time in our lives: war; peace; recession; plenty; protests, riots, terrorism. Our world has changed and those in it. We want to pass on to you our stories and impressions of the world from which we came. It has not all been easy. We call this "life lessons." Others might call it "advice." Ignore us at your peril. If you are lucky like us, some day you too will be old and can write your own book.

BECAUSE WE FLEW...

Once the wings go on, they never come off whether they can be seen or not. It fuses to the soul through adversity, fear and adrenaline, and no one who has ever worn them with pride, integrity and guts can ever sleep through the call of the wild that wafts through bedroom windows in the deep of the night.

When a good flyer leaves the job and retires, many are jealous, some are pleased and yet others, who may have already retired, wonder. We wonder if he knows what he is leaving behind, because we already know. We know, for example, that after a lifetime of camaraderie that few experience, it will remain as a longing for those past times.

We know in the world of flying, there is a fellowship which lasts long after the flight suits are hung up in the back of the closet. We know even if he throws them away, they will be on him with every step and breath that remains in his life. We also know how the very bearing of the man speaks of what he was, and in his heart, still is.

Because we flew, we envy no man on earth.

Author Unknown

Poster purchased from Leanne Flannery's Gallery on Etsy.com

CHAPTER ONE

1,989 DAYS CAMPING OUT IN HANOI

by Bob Barnett

I found myself in the "ropes." The guards had cinched me down so I could barely breathe, stuck a dirty rag in my mouth, and then walked out of the "Knobby Room." The room had seen many indescribable torture sessions of my fellow Nam-Pows. It had rock-like plaster bumps on the ugly green walls. The color was described as looking like bile.

So, here I was, in the "ropes" again. The first time was after I was captured in a jungle area approximately 15 miles northeast of Haiphong Harbor. I had been shot down on my 43rd mission by a surface-to-air missile six days before. With any luck at all I would have been picked up, but the fickle finger of fate came into play since a navy pilot had been shot down moments after me. The rescue helicopter picked him up and then was too low on fuel to come back for me.

I evaded capture for two days and nights. On the third day I was tracked down by a dog, who bit me on the shoulder, and then was captured by a group of ten men, some of them wearing loincloths. I was taken into a village and put on display for a throng of people looking at me as if I were a creature from Mars. They beat me and put me in the body-crushing ropes when I would not answer their questions. They threatened that they would break my arms and my legs, and then kill me if I didn't talk to the rescue airplanes and lead them into an ambush.

Thankfully, I was able send a false code and rescue attempts were ended. My captors then tied me up and sat me on a fuel tank in the bed of a truck and drove me into Hanoi to Hoa Lo prison, also known as the Hanoi Hilton.

I was taken immediately to the Knobby Room and forced to sit on a low stool. I hadn't slept for six days. Even though mosquitoes were biting me, I couldn't stay awake, so I climbed up on a table that was covered with a blue tablecloth and fell asleep. Suddenly the door opened, I was put in the ropes again, and they left me on the floor in terrible pain. My hips were pulled out of the sockets, and my shoulders were stressed. After an interminable amount of time they returned, untied me, and resumed the interrogation.

North Vietnam had signed the Geneva agreement for the treatment of Prisoners of War. However, they did not comply with their obligation saying that since there was no declaration of war, we were considered "War Criminals," "Blackest Criminals" and "Air Pirates."

When my initial interrogations were over, I was moved into a small solo cell. They brought me pajamas, a mat and a water jug. I remember saying to myself, "I guess I'm going to stay." I had very little to eat until this point. My first meal after my stint in the knobby room was a bowl of raw sugar.

I have not been a very religious person, but when I was under intense pressure I started saying over and over, "Yea, though I walk through the valley of the shadow of death, I will fear no evil." It is amazing to me that when it seemed that I was at my wits-end and felt that it couldn't get any worse, I fell back on praying to God and it seemed that He was there. It was all so surreal. I kept asking myself, "What did I do to deserve this?" It is an enormous adjustment to go from being a free, happy man to being locked up in a dirty, small cell halfway around the world.

In the early days, every contact I had with the Communist Vietnamese was hostile and threatening. I was told that I would be tried as a war criminal. Furthermore, they said I had a bad attitude and would never go home. My name was not released as a POW, and I remained as Missing in Action for two and one-half years. I received no mail for three years. But, I was not alone. All of us that were being held had to deal with this. Many were tortured to make audio tapes saying they were receiving good treatment.

I had spent my first month in solitary at the Hilton, then I was moved blindfolded and cuffed to a camp we called the Zoo. It was about 12 miles southwest of Hanoi. We were moved into a new area called the Zoo Annex.

There was a lot of bombing going on, and the POW population was growing rapidly. The move took place at night, and I had no idea where I was going or where I was.

When I got to the Zoo, they put me in a room. I had to put my hands on the wall while they took off my blindfold. As I turned around I saw that I had three cellmates, Don "Digger" Odell, Jim Clements, and Wayne Waddell. All had been F-105 pilots. Digger and Jim had been shot down after me and Wayne had been there for 14 weeks. I looked at Wayne and was amazed that he was still alive after 14 weeks. The military can be a small place sometimes. Both Digger and Jim had been at Korat with me. Jim had been in my flight. Digger had lived in the other half of a duplex many years ago when he was going through F-86D training, and I was an instructor at Perrin Air Force Base. It seems that we always know somebody or know somebody that knows somebody.

The four of us lived in this dark, windowless cell for six months. I was the Senior Ranking Officer (SRO) and every so often, I was taken out for a quiz to be threatened in order to improve "my attitude." Fortunately, it went no farther than that. The first winter was tough. We had very little clothing and the temperatures were near freezing. We went six weeks without a bath. A bath consisted of throwing a bucket of freezing water over you and drying off with a hand towel.

We would get rice and a bowl of soup made of pumpkin, cabbage or something we called green weeds or whatever was in season. We had a bucket to do our business, it had a rusty rim that caused nice red circles. After a year or so dealing with the rusty bucket rim, I got a new cellmate. When he needed to use the bucket, he set his sandals on the rim and sat down. I was amazed! It was like inventing the wheel! So, the next time I needed to use the bucket, I put my sandals on the rim, just like him, and one of my sandals promptly fell in the bucket. I needed training. I had diarrhea most of the time.

Digger had suffered what proved to be a broken neck and his hands were useless due to the ropes. He occasionally would start to pass out and had to lie down. He would often look at me and say, "What a predicament!"

After about six months, the door opened and we got a new cellmate, Navy Lieutenant Commander Ed Martin. The Vietnamese would say that we had no rank, but they knew everyone's rank. I was always with what we call O4s (Majors and Navy Lt. Commanders) for the first few years. Ed outranked me and we had a change of command. The next time the guards came for an "attitude check," they took Ed out.

Ed had heard about the "tap code." He took a piece of brick out and we wrote it on the floor. With that we were able to make contact with the next cell for the first time. Being able to communicate with our fellow POWs in the next cell was a very big deal!

It was always impossible to figure out what the NVA would do next.

We moved around from one cell to another which seemed to be their way of breaking up communication between cells. If we were caught communicating, the penalty was severe.

Unexpectedly, in the spring of 1968, we were moved and there were nine of us in the same cell, all O4s. We were together for about a month. Almost every day we had an altercation with the guard since we didn't bow properly. Among my new cellmates was Dwight Sullivan, "Sully." He had been Digger's flight lead. Digger had been hit and had a midair with Sully. But, Digger hadn't realized it until we made contact with Sully. After a month, we were all marched out of our cell in the Annex and moved into two-man cells in the main camp.

Dwight Sullivan became my cellmate. Our cell was approximately 10' by 10'. There were two vents about 10' high and close to the ceiling. We had a board-bed and a bucket. Sully and I were in this cell for over a year. In the summer it was like an oven and the mosquitoes were after us all the time. We had nothing to read and were locked up 24 hours a day. Once or twice a week we would go out to a well, throw a bucket or two of water on ourselves and wash our shorts and pajamas the best we could.

I had learned the tap code and with Sully "clearing," we communicated with the cells next to us. We began learning the names of the other POWs in the Zoo. We tried to remember names of capitols, presidents, etc. We walked around in circles for hours at a time in order to exercise and to pass the time. I would guess that we walked from Los Angeles to New York more than once.

I had a lot of outstanding cellmates, but Sully was my favorite. Sully was courageous, loyal, even-tempered, and dependable. He never complained. When Sully lost weight because of an ulcer, he was given extra milk and cookies. Sully refused to drink the milk or eat the cookies unless I would too. My friend Sully passed away 12/8/19. GBU, Sully.

One day the guards came and had us roll up our worldly possessions in our badly stained mats, and we moved to what we called the Pig Sty. We had names for all the buildings in the camp, none more colorful than the Pig Sty. It was summer, and I had a terrible case of heat rash with pus blisters over my arms and the back of my legs. That summer Sully and I were separated, not to see each other again until we got on the airplane to go home over three years later.

In 1970, I was moved in with four Navy pilots and an Air Force pilot. We were together for nine months. I have often thought how tough, how strong, how brave, my cellmates were. We were randomly shot down and were a cross-section of all military officers flying in North Vietnam. Every one of my cellmates had resisted to the best of their ability and never lost faith in our fellow prisoners and our GREAT COUNTRY.

I was a prisoner for 1,986 days, but because I was able to evade capture for three days, I was actually in North Vietnam for 1,989 days. Thankfully, I didn't know that I was going to be there nearly FIVE AND ONE HALF years. When I would say "woe is me," I was quick to remind myself that when I got to Hanoi, there were those that had already been there for two and a half years.

I'm often asked how I dealt with this nightmare. My method was to think that the war was going to end in three months and that we would be going home. This actually worked for quite a while, but in November 1970, the US sent a force of heroes to Son Tay where prisoners had been known to be held. However, the NVA had actually closed the camp a couple of months earlier. The result was that all of the 340 or so POWs were moved from all the camps into the Hanoi Hilton, and we were all held together in an area we called Camp Unity. I had a period of depression when I realized that if the U.S. would go to such an effort, then the war was not going to end anytime soon.

I stayed at the Hilton for nine months. All 340 of us were in big cells for the first time. I was in a cell of 26. We were sleeping on a cement slab that was in the middle of a large room. We organized and had all kinds of classes on all kinds of subjects. Since I had learned Spanish during my tour as an Advisor to the Ecuadorian Air Force, I had a group of Spanish students. We had no books, so everything was done by memory. One never knows when a talent or a skill will come in handy.

I was again moved back to the Zoo and remained there until May 1972. All bombing of the northern part of Vietnam had stopped in the Spring of 1968. So, when we heard air raid sirens and anti-aircraft guns being fired, it was the first positive sign we had had in years. After the bombing started, the guards moved all POWs who were in the Zoo back to the Hilton. We were there for two weeks when one night, about 220 of us were blindfolded, handcuffed, and stuffed into canvas-topped trucks and we departed Hanoi. After a while, they took off the blindfolds, and I peeked through the canvas tarp and saw a sign that said Lang Son. I knew this was on the border with China. I thought we were going to China. Instead, we turned west and when it became light, they parked all the trucks under the trees, and we stayed there all day. When it was dark, we continued west until we came to a group of buildings that had been unoccupied. We were by the city of Cao Bang, a few miles from the Chinese border. It was pouring rain when we arrived after midnight.

We were divided into groups of 12 or so. Each building had two large connecting rooms. Our room had a current of water running through it. In one room they found a cobra. There was no electricity or running water, just camping out. The best thing was, they left us alone. I, along with several cellmates, started an intense exercise program. We were doing over 500 pushups a day, and I started walking around on my hands and doing things I hadn't done since high school. We had public speaking classes, movie night, story time, church services, and I had my group of Spanish students. We were writing letters home occasionally, but none of them were ever sent. They were hiding us.

In October 1972, we were all moved around and ended up in rooms with those that had concurrent shoot down dates. Our hopes soared that something was happening. Then one day, the guards came with a tape recording telling us that the obdurate, bellicose United States had sabotaged peace talks. Downer, again. For the first time, the US, under President Nixon, dispatched our B-52s to Haiphong and Hanoi. North Vietnam capitulated and a peace agreement was signed. The release of the POWs was a big part of the agreement. Every ex Nam-Pow that I know is eternally grateful to President Nixon for his brave decision. We are indebted to the courageous B52 crews, many of whom lost their lives, so we could come home.

In January, we were bussed back to Hanoi, no cuffs and no blindfolds. I ended up in a place we called the Plantation in downtown Hanoi. There were about 110 of us, all within the same shoot down dates. The first group left on February 12th, 1973. They flew out of Hanoi on C-141s. We would never have guessed that that would be the way we would go home. My turn came on March 14th when my group left Hanoi and flew back to Freedom. It seemed like a dream. We landed at Clark Air Base in the Philippines. There we were debriefed, received medical checkups, showered in hot running water, flushed toilets, ate ice cream, drank milk and had meat. Each of us had an escort officer. My escort, Neil, arranged for me to call home and talk to Anita. She, along with the rest of my family, had suffered beyond words and now I was free. After three days, we flew back to the good old USA with a stop at Hickam Field. It seemed like thousands of people met us at 3:00 am cheering our arrival. We then flew on to March Air Force Base, CA where I was met by Anita and our daughter, Lori. My sister, Doreen, my brother, Don, my sister-in-law, Carol and many other family members and a host of friends were there to welcome me home.

I was FINALLY FREE!

That was on St. Patrick's Day, 1973. What a life it has been since then. I look at my wonderful grandchildren and great-grandchildren and realize that they would not be on this earth if I had not survived and made the choices I made. I graduated with a Masters Degree from the University of Arizona, was the Professor of Aerospace Studies at the U of A, and started and developed an airplane business. I sold the business and spent another 20 years flying and teaching Learjet Pilots.

My wife, Anita, passed away on Christmas Eve in 2012. We had been married over 60 years. Another pivotal life changer. Then, another miracle. I found Suzanne Purcell. Her husband had been a Nam-Pow and passed away in 2009. We are soulmates and travel the world together. There is always another rainbow - Suzanne is my rainbow.

What has the POW experience taught me?

MY LESSONS LEARNED

I had hours, days, months and years to review every aspect of my life. I was unable to answer the age-old question of why we are here and where we are going. Much smarter people have been unable to answer that. My overriding goal, along with my fellow POWs, was to come Home With Honor. I felt that I would have rather died than carry the burden of failing at that promise. I feel I fulfilled that objective. I do not have any nightmares about Vietnam and never dream about it. We had to adapt and adjust to this horrible situation. We kept our minds busy and exercised when we could. I learned the tap code and communicated with fellow prisoners almost daily during our early years in the Zoo. We trusted and cared for each other. That carries over to this day. I thank God for each day.

And, almost every Friday, I have lunch with the same kind of outstanding men that I knew in the prison camps of Vietnam, The Friday Pilots.

If the reader is interested, I refer you to an in-depth story of my shoot down, evading, and capture. Just Google, 2005 Air Power Archive, Spring Volume 52, Number 1, "Ozark Lead is out of the airplane," written by Howard Plunkett. Also, Google "Veterans Tributes." Select "View Tributes," Scroll to Air Force or Coast Guard and find Robert Barnett.

CHAPTER TWO

THE BOY, THE MAN, THE FAILURES, THE GOOD THINGS

by Dr. Robert P. Breault, alias "The Lieutenant"

Let me start from the very beginning. It was hot. I remember there was pain. Excruciating pain. My whole body hurt. It came from every direction. Then, there was a burst of light and the pain was gone. I was born. Those are the first thoughts that I remember. I am saying that I remember my birth. For years later up to age 33, I would have a recurring nightmare of the event. A doctor told me that there is some decent percentage of people who do.

I was born at home in Naugatuck, Connecticut in 1941. My two sisters were also born at home. My Ukrainian immigrant grandmother, Boona, actually "delivered" me as Dr. Williams was scrubbing down in our kitchen. He supposedly said "Mrs. Swiska, just hold him until I wash up. I'll be right with you." It was the perfectly natural way.

I was a devil of a child for my mother to care for. At four years old, I would climb out windows to "escape." I once rode downhill standing up in my Red Flyer wagon, hit a bump, fell backwards and got a concussion. I would tie snow sleds together and slide down streets. As a 10-year-old, I climbed to rooftops of two-story houses without a ladder. But, I was a good boy, with a lot of spirit.

From about 1951 to flying fighter planes out of Phan Rang in 1967, I built complex solid based rockets from scratch. I do mean scratch. In the early '50s they did not have rocket kits for kids, but I did have a chemistry set. I was able to purchase potassium nitrite from the drugstore in quart sized jars. If you add sulfur and charcoal in the right amounts, you get either gunpowder or rocket fuel. You'd better test it in small amounts before you load your rocket. I always did. Nevertheless, I did have one "rocket test capsule" blow up and fly as shrapnel over a two-story garage, a parking lot, and a two-story house before landing on a neighbor's second-floor porch. I did successfully launch rockets across my hometown over multiple churches and houses, very small rockets. At Phan Rang, I launched a three-stage rocket from the hooch area by the O-Club onto the road adjacent to the ammo dump. I had five Bird Colonels that witnessed that flight. I even launched one from underwater. I did enough through grammar school and college that I got a call from Gus Grissom when I was a Freshman at Yale.

For years as a young boy, I hunted down crystalline rocks in the Connecticut woods and studied them. By 7th grade I was reading college textbooks. It was in the summer of 1954 (three years before Sputnik) that I decided to go to college and get a degree in Mathematics, and then go into the USAF to become a fighter pilot, and then get a PhD from the University of Arizona, and then enter my career doing spaced based research. I had never yet traveled far from Connecticut. Hey space, here comes your scientific space explorer. This is so documented in my high school and college yearbooks - you plan and then execute.

I graduated from Yale in '62, BS in Math, barely. I went to Officer Training Scholl (OTS), received a Regular Commission and was assigned to Vance AFB Class 64E for pilot training. I was lucky. My vision was 20-30. I had reading glasses but was able to see and memorized the eyechart instantly. "TECFOXIDPNH." But, after seven flights of filling the white bag, I was put on probation so I could be "washed out." Every time I got sick it was JUST before returning to land. I could perform all the maneuvers, all the flight join-ups, touch-and-go landings, the spin tests etc. without getting sick. Only when I was instructed to head back to the base for final landing, did I get sick. Classmates, Capt. Hanna and Capt. Heizer, did some fast-talking on my behalf, and I was re-accepted into the class with a new instructor, Capt. Tom Wiley, a soothing teacher. He calmed my anxiety almost immediately. I got over getting sick on my second flight with him, and then, never got sick in a plane again. I graduated near the top of the 64E class and got one of the two fighter assignments. I went to Luke for F-100 training, then was assigned to the 614 TFS, Lucky Devils, at England AFB, LA. I went to Alaska doing Polar Strike as an Umpire, then TDY to Misawa, Japan and Kunsan, Korea.

I was the only lieutenant in the 614th but was a "hotshot" kid. My performance earned me the distinction of being flight lead qualified at 300 hours in the F-100. That led to an F-100 Wild Weasel assignment in 1965. F-100 Weasels were the pioneers. I was the only first lieutenant in the program. I have often been called out as "The Lieutenant." In Korat, Thailand in early January 1966, we had only seven F-100 Wild Weasel aircraft, and 12 F-100 pilots. By early February, we were down to two F-100 Wild Weasel flyable planes and seven pilots, all combat losses. I was sent back to the 614th TFS. In 1967 the 614th deployed to Phan Rang, Vietnam and its aluminum planking runway (lots of stories to tell).

March 27, 1967, my 6:30 a.m. takeoff: On a most beautiful morning at Phan Rang, I experienced the most exciting four seconds in my life. It was when I was in an F-100. It was when my F-100 blew its engine apart on takeoff.

I had an early morning takeoff time. I was loaded with two cans of napalm and two 500lb. bombs. The sun was just coming up through a broken cloud bank over the ocean to the east of Phan Rang. The temperature was cool. It was such an inspiring morning, and I took the time to take pictures of the plane with the sunrise as a background. I even took time to position my helmet on the canopy rail and re-shoot the picture. I was in a happy mood and feeling the thrill of being a fighter pilot.

I was flight lead. We taxied to the runway and received clearance for takeoff. I rolled into position. I stopped and pressed hard on the brakes as I pushed the throttle to full power. I performed my instrument check, RPM, oil pressure, exhaust gas temperature and all read normal. I released brakes and lit the afterburner. I felt normal acceleration pushing me back into the seat as I enjoyed the view and the thunderous sound of engine thrust.

As I accelerated, I had a wonderful feeling, realizing the plane was in perfect shape as I rolled down the runway centerline. I remember thinking, "It doesn't get better than this. This is one of the most beautiful moments in my life, a near virgin concrete runway and the perfect plane on a magnificent day."

Check speed was good and as I accelerated towards 200 knots, I pulled back on the stick lightly and the plane lifted free of the runway, about

7,000 ft. down the 10,000 ft. strip. I reached for the gear handle to raise the gear and suddenly there was a huge explosion all around me. Surprisingly, I was still alive. In a glance, I saw all my engine indicators drop. I had no power. To successfully eject from an F-100 you needed to be above 200 kts. and above 200 ft. for safe ejection, parachute deployment and most importantly, for safe landing (maybe). I was at 200 kts. and four ft. off the ground. If I pulled up, I would lose airspeed and probably die if I ejected.

In a half a second, I determined that I might have a slim chance. I lowered the plane back down onto the runway approaching the 9,000-foot marker. I had two seconds to stop a 15-ton aircraft moving at 200 knots from running off the end of the runway and into a minefield that was there to protect the base from enemy infiltration. Under these circumstances, the minefield was not likely going to finish me off. Past the overrun, there was a four-foot drop that would have collapsed my nose gear and I would have tumbled and gone up in one spectacular ball of fire, napalm, bombs, full load of fuel and the mines. It would have been a spectacular sight to remember - for the men in the tower and firemen watching.

I carefully lowered the nose back down onto the runway. Then instinctively, I pulled the drag chute with my left hand and simultaneously hit the tailhook release with my right hand. This was not protocol. It was never something we practiced. I also pressed as hard as I safely could on the brakes avoiding a skid and blown tires.

It occurred to me that if I approached the end of the cement paved runway there would be a heavy-duty cable designed for "barrier" engagement. Beyond that, there was a webbing that might stop a slow-rolling F-100, but I would probably tear through that like a red-hot knife in butter. I had only one slim hope. When I dropped the tailhook, I glanced up and saw the cable that I had to hook, just going under my view under the nose of the plane. I was hoping the hook had not bounced over the cable as it was often known to do. The runway was new, smooth and flat. The cable was new and as strong as it would ever be, but I wondered if it could withstand a carrier type landing with a full load of fuel and my weapons. I didn't know the answer, but I would soon find out.

The overrun was only a few hundred feet long. I sped towards the end pressing ever harder on the brakes. Nothing happened. There appeared to be no decrease in my speed. I felt that there were now only fractions of a second left in my life. I had done all that I could. About halfway down the overrun, I sensed a rapid deceleration, but would the cable hold or snap apart? I was still going pretty fast but decelerating ever more rapidly as the hydraulics pulled harder with every foot forward. I remember sitting back in my seat, very relaxed, being very composed and I remember twiddling my thumbs round and round exactly three times asking myself, "Did I catch it, or am I a hamburger? Did I catch it, or am I a hamburger? Did I catch it, or am I a hamburger?" Time dilation is very real.

Finally, I sensed I would stop before the end of the overrun. I now had just one more problem. The brakes were going to heat up and possibly explode setting the plane on fire, along with the napalm and bombs. I had to get out. I opened the canopy and a crew chief was already there with a ladder on the plane for my escape. I got out safely and got away quickly. The firemen put cages on the wheels in case they exploded and sprayed a mist of water on the brakes to cool them down. A short while later a crew chief came over to me and said, "Sir, you set a record. You pulled all 1,738 ft. of a 1,740 ft. cable. You are a lucky man."

The officer in the tower and the fire crew on duty that witnessed it all, told me later that they thought my bombs had exploded on takeoff. From their perspective, it appeared that as I lifted off, my plane had been engulfed in flames. I never saw any flames. They were all behind my canopy.

Upon review and inspection, they discovered the pilot that had flown the aircraft before me thought he might have hit a bird but failed to write it up. Apparently, the bird had been ingested on landing and got stuck somewhere on the center shaft of the engine likely damaging some blades. As I lifted off, the engine shed all but seven of its compressor blades, shrapnel throughout the aircraft systems. Essentially, I had no engine. I just had a lot of fuel exploding forwards and backwards and through the plane's various plenum chambers. I was a flying furnace. By the way, I did fly another mission later in the day. Real fighter pilots do that!

In 1967 at the end of my Vietnam tour, I was assigned to Nellis AFB, NV as an instructor to train F-100 Weasels. They rightfully canceled the F-100 Weasel program just as I arrived at Nellis. They did not know what to do with me because technically I did not yet have enough time in the F-100 to be retrained in another aircraft. After a couple of months as

Assistant Editor of the Fighter Weapons Newsletter, the Wing Commander wrangled me an F-111 assignment. Accepting that assignment would have precluded my getting a PhD in Astrophysics, my lifetime goal. I resigned within the hour. Having a Regular Commission, I was involuntarily extended for a year. I enjoyed and did very well that extra year serving in the Command Post at Nellis. I took college courses in Astrophysics. I handled eight bailouts/crashes, secret stuff about secret planes (SR71) and multiple times documented UFO reports. I separated from the USAF in 1969 to get my MS degree in '72 and my PhD in Optics in '79.

I applied for and was accepted by a new program at the University of Arizona; the Optical Science Center (OSC). I was accepted based on my course work in Astrophysics at the University of Nevada, Las Vegas. Two years later the Center realized they needed to straighten out my paperwork, and I had to take a written qualifying exam. I failed. I was allowed to take it again; I failed again. I became the first PhD student to be washed out. They let me stay for a MS in Optics, but I did so well they re-admitted me into the PhD Program in 1972. Two years later, I took the Written Prelims, almost the last hurdle for the PhD. I was the first student *below* the pass level. Not again! They winced again. They "conditionally" passed me, but I was told that everything now hinged on the Oral Prelim Exam. Under a doctor's advice I was hypnotized to lower my anxiety syndrome. It worked marvelously well. I passed. They even hired me as a Research Assistant. In my work I pioneered the concepts of stray light analysis and design. I improved the performance of the Hubble Telescope by a factor of 100,000. Years later, when I graduated with my PhD, my dissertation won the Dissertation of the Year Award for Applied Engineering at the University level. For me it was one last time from the bottom to the top. Lesson: PERSISTENCE PAYS OFF AND HUMILITY IS LEARNED IN SMALL DOSES.

Upon graduating with my PhD in 1979, I founded the Breault Research Organization, Inc. (BRO), because by then I was internationally recognized as one of the world's leading experts in optics in the area of stray light analysis and suppression. In my career, I have been involved in over 275 stray light analyses: IRAS, DIRBE, Hubble, Galileo, Cassini, LBT, VLT, LIGO. I have worked with six Nobel Laureates on various projects.

In 1992, I went on to pioneer global economic development in terms of Clusters, groups of regional like-type business competitors that worked together for a common cause. I have helped in some way 54 other structured Optics Clusters around the world. I worked at the Presidential level in two countries, two at the Prime Minister level, and 15 at their Cabinet level. It is a lot like piloting a single seat plane. There is a lot of parallel processing – albeit at a slower pace.

One might ask, so what? What did I learn from my life journey? I think about "the four Ps" - planning, preparation, persistence and patience. If you don't have a plan, if you don't know where you are going, you'll get there - nowhere. If you are not "prepared" by education, training and study, you won't survive, whether it is in a malfunctioning airplane or as a car mechanic. If you aren't "persistent," you'll be able to handle success but not failure and life is likely to bring you some of both. Finally, if you aren't "patient," you'll be passed over for others who may have waited their time, studied and gained experience.

I didn't become a recognized scientist and optics expert because I was smarter than everyone else, but I had a plan, was prepared, persistent and patient through success and failure, and I've had lots of both. Faith in God also helps. I desperately needed that when I lost my son in a tragic automobile accident. Lesson: LUCK ALSO PLAYS A PART IN LIFE - THE CABLE HELD!"

CHAPTER THREE

A SALTY TALE: LESSONS LEARNED IN AND OUT OF THE COCKPIT

by Frank Brown

Born in Kodiak, Alaska in 1950, I was a Navy brat and moved 12 times while growing up. We always had kids to play with and spent most of our time outdoors; played Little League; no video games; rotary dial phones, no smart ones; ate TV dinners; watched Roy Rogers, Sky King, Disney and Ed Sullivan on Sunday nights. Flying was not even in my sights.

My high school freshman year, Dad asked me what I wanted to do when I grew up and I said, with no real clue, "An engineer." Halfway through my freshman year I was not doing very well in Algebra I, sort of a core course for engineers. With no progress in raising the grade, Dad pulled me from the freshman swim team. I finally got my grade up to a passable "C" but missed swimming in the league championship. I quickly got my act together, graduating near the top of my high school class. A couple of lessons were dearly learned. First, I academically was not destined to be an engineer, and BE CAREFUL WHAT YOU ASK FOR, THERE MAY BE SOME UNINTENDED CONSEQUENCES.

Senior year came with college application time. Being in competitive swimming, I applied to schools with strong water polo and swimming programs. Scholarships were key to my being able to attend college. I had a couple of swimming scholarships, applied to the Naval Academy (selected as first alternate), and got an NROTC scholarship. I ultimately chose NROTC at UCLA.

College went okay despite my discovering beer. I struggled through the physical science classes (engineering?), but I had a bent for history, especially Far Eastern/Asian history, which saved my GPA. I went the political science route with a dream of someday becoming a naval attaché.

During my second summer of midshipman training, I was introduced to aviation. My flight in a TA-4F at NAS Corpus Christi, TX hooked me. I didn't have pilot eyes, but I qualified for the Naval Flight Officer school at NAS Pensacola, FL, the "Cradle of Naval Aviation." While there, I had no clue what type plane/mission I wanted to fly. I initially flew in the T-34 to check my "air adaptability." (I did clean-up a couple of cockpits before I got used to the various maneuvers.) During this time, I also lost a friend in a T-34 crash. I learned early the meaning of: "THE BREAKS OF NAVAL AIR."

I started navigation training in the T-29. At the end of nav course, I got a low-level flight in the F-9F. I was briefed on all the pre-flight checklist items including an "alternate ICS check." When the check was called for, I was to speak into the alternate ICS device with, "Roger, alt-ICS check." Great flight. Later, I learned the alternate ICS was the piss tube. I performed my part well.

I decided to go for fighters and with my nose to the grindstone, placed very high in my class and was able to select the Radar Intercept Officer course. At NAS Glynco, I also kept my nose to the grindstone and was doing well in a really tough fast-moving syllabus. About halfway through training, I eased up, thinking, "I got this." Bam! Two "downs" and a visit to the long green table in front of Major Sweeney, USMC. It was very humbling, but I got a second chance and did not squander it, subsequently earning my wings. This NAS Glynco experience stayed with me for the rest of my career/life. LESSON: ALWAYS DO YOUR BEST. LOTS OF COMPETITION OUT THERE.

In May 1973, I reported to VF-121, the F-4 replacement training squadron (FRS) at NAS Miramar in San Diego. On my first F-4 flight, I was introduced to high "G" air combat. Postflight, I was seriously questioning whether I was cut out for this business. That was never again an issue, and I graduated top in my class. GLYNCO LESSON WAS NOT FORGOTTEN. Next came orders to VF-114 Fighting Aardvarks deployed aboard the USS Kitty Hawk currently in the South China Sea. I went through jungle survival, "Snake School", and a couple other courses. We got underway and continued patrolling operations in the East and

South China Seas and the Sea of Japan with port visits to Hong Kong and Yokosuka.

Flying the F-4J was a dream come true. I loved the fighter missions. Flying off the carrier was also a blast. The catapult shots are something you never get tired of even though it is 2-plus seconds where you have no control. Night cat shots on moonless nights are like being shot into a dark closet with no outside visual reference. Night carrier landings with rolling seas and weather were a real challenge. And those night noises! At sea, we were flying almost every day, sometimes twice. The Vietnam war was over, but the Cold War was still in play. Depending on where we were at sea, we stood the Alert 5, meaning we sat in the cockpit on the catapult, strapped in with an air huffer and electric cart attached, ready to be launched within five minutes against any foreign aircraft. I stood many alerts. Learned early that it was not out of kindness when the Skipper or the Ops officer would come out to "relieve" us from the Alert, then see them launch 15-20 minutes later. LESSON: "RHIP," RANK HATH ITS PRIVILEGES. And KNOWLEDGE IS POWER.

Intercepting a Russian TU-95 Beaor IL-38 May is a very common event on Western Pacific cruises. Their mission is to collect electronic intel and photo recce the carrier and its battle group. When they came, we were launched to intercept them around 180-200 miles out from the carrier. Inbound, we flew loose cruise until they started a descent to pass near the carrier. It would get dicey when we got down to around 100-200 ft. while approaching the ship and maneuvering to stay in between the Russian photographers and the ship in order to block their view of the carrier. They would occasionally make a turn/jink into us, trying to drag us into the water. Fun sport. LESSON: ROUTINE PEACETIME INTERCEPTS CAN INADVERTENTLY CAUSE AN INTERNATIONAL INCIDENT.

Another lesson learned happened while in port at Subic Bay. As a junior officer, I pulled Shore Patrol duty. I had a few of these during some of our port calls, like Olongapo in the Philippines. This town is infamous in Naval history, a place where sailors get to let off steam after long periods at sea. We were assigned a couple of Petty Officers to accompany us as we patrolled. One difficult place was called, "Soul Town," because it was where a lot of the African Americans hung out. It was a time of high racial tension. Being a white guy, in a white Navy officer's uniform I was not a welcome sight to these kids fueled with liquid courage. We were there to "take care of our own" and to deter them from doing harm to themselves and others. Our caring attitude was not always appreciated. I got some great advice from an ordnance chief. "Go early to the SP Office and pick the two biggest Petty Officers you see and place them on either side of you to protect you." LESSON LEARNED: "SIZE MATTERS."

My second Kitty Hawk cruise was interesting. For instance, it's a moonless night recovery in the South China Sea, we are about 1 1/4 miles from the ship, doing a self-contained approach due to our getting minimal calls from the ship's controllers. At about 1 mile aft of the ship, we finally called the LSO telling him no one is talking to us, and he quickly responded with "Start it down, you are high." Simultaneously, he waves off an EA-6B in front of us. Continuing our approach, we hit the climbing EA-6's jet wash causing our plane to rapidly roll 60 degrees right in a stalled condition and losing about 200 ft. My pilot quickly lit the burners and got the plane wings level. Now, we are below the flight deck level inside 1/2 mile with our afterburner plumes deflecting off the water and we're pointed right at the ship's island. All this time, my hand is gripping the lower ejection handle. Slowly, we began climbing and saw that we would miss hitting the ship - barely. Things happened extremely fast. Ejecting would have been a disastrous decision. Now, well below bingo fuel, we find the tanker, get some gas and bingo to Cubi Point. Great airmanship and our being crewed together for most of the cruise saved us as crew coordination/trust was key. LESSON: THERE ARE TIMES WHEN IT'S BETTER TO BE GOOD THAN LUCKY.

Home from deployment, time to rotate to shore duty. I wanted to fly the F-14, but the detailer gave me orders to be an instructor in the East Coast's F-4 FRS. I was courting a young lady and the idea of moving cross-country was not in her plans. So, the detailer said if I would extend my sea duty for another cruise with a Miramar squadron transitioning from the F-8 Crusader to the F-4J, he would get me orders to the F-14 fleet. It was still flying so I took the deal.

In April '76, I joined the VF-191 Satan's Kittens and newly married. I was the first pure back-seater the squadron ever had in its long history. We deployed on the USS Coral Sea, operating primarily in the East/South China Sea and Sea of Japan. Early on in the cruise, we managed to get banned from Yokosuka's O-club FOR LIFE. Our F4s had new J79 smokeless engines. It was strange to see these F-4s flying without its usual smoke trail. Unfortunately, we lost a couple F-4s during the cruise due to an afterburner blowout anomaly. One instance was at night. The CO was flying when both his burners snuffed out during the cat stroke. The crew ejected immediately and were quickly recovered. Another was during a day launch when the starboard burner snuffed out right at the cat stroke. The plane, now underpowered, struggled to stay airborne with the crew having to eject. The RIO made it, but the pilot was struck unconscious by debris from the F-4 when it hit the water and subsequently dragged down by his chute. Despite the above, it was a great deployment. LESSON: YOU JUST DO NOT KNOW WHEN IT'S YOUR TIME. "BREAKS OF NAVAL AIR" STRIKE AGAIN.

We flew-in off the ship in October 1977 back to NAS Miramar. I was eager to see my new bride but also to call my detailer to see if he came through on his F-14 promise. He did with orders to VF-124, F-14 FRS, as an instructor. The Tomcat had been in the fleet about seven years. It was built with the RIO in mind as a fleet defense interceptor with a weapons system that was the best in the world. We had the state-of-the-art AWG-9 radar/AIM-54 Phoenix missiles where we could engage six separate targets over 100 miles away in a jamming environment. And the plane could turn and burn. It was a joy to come out of the F-4 rear seat "cave" to the F-14's open cockpit visibility. The F-14 was still dealing with engine and control problems, and we lost a number of fellow Tomcatters due to them. There was even a spot across the Miramar airfield on the downwind leg where, over time, three F-14s had augured into the ground due to a split spoiler problem during the break with no time to safely eject.

My first ground school assignment was teaching radar theory, not a pilot favorite. My first flight qual as an instructor was taking nuggets to get carrier qualified in the F-14. Interesting that I had about the same F-14 hours as the guys going to the boat! (The F-14's nickname around the ship was "Turkey" because of how the plane looked with its stabilizer and spoilers flapping while coming aboard the carrier.) I moved quickly through the instructor syllabus becoming a tactics instructor in record time for a transition RIO. I was often flying two hops a day against the local adversary squadrons and TOPGUN. I was in the top tier of the instructor cadre and teaching how to fly/fight the F-14. Life is good!!

One day, my XO, CDR Jack "Fingers" Ensch, calls me to his office. "The Wing Commander fired his flag lieutenant/aide and needs a new one. I want you to go over and interview for the job." I emphatically said I was not interested. "I have just gotten tactics qualled and been here only six months!" He cut me short. "Shut up and go to the interview." I said "Yes, sir, but I plan to tank it." Five other great guys went over to interview, and I wound up being selected. It turned out to be a great experience, working closely with RADM Paul "Gator" Gillcrist. He was a tremendous mentor. He taught me to understand the bigger picture of naval warfare and the role of all the various elements. We flew together in the F-4, F-14 and the F-5. One day, I was strongly upbraided after he overheard me make the comment in his outer office that I would quit the Navy the day a woman lands a tactical fighter on the carrier. In his office, he made it <u>very clear</u> why my thinking was wrong. LESSON: RECOGNIZE SEXISM AND THE IMPORTANCE OF INCLUSIVITY. Gator and I later became very good friends. RIP, Admiral.

My aide tour went surprisingly fast, and I was now a father to a handsome boy. Orders came sending me to VF-114, again, for a department head tour, now flying F-14s (with "Fingers" Ensch as CO!). A quick refresh at the FRS, and I was off to Singapore to meet the Varks aboard the USS America (CV-66). The performance capabilities of the Tomcat were huge compared to the F-4J. The minute the F-4 got off the cat, we were worried about gas. The Tomcat with its turbofan engines almost made gas while airborne. Our CAP missions were routinely pushed out to 300-400 miles from the ship to provide an extended shield against Soviet bomber and anti-ship missiles. Besides the Western Pacific, we operated in the Indian Ocean and the Arabian Sea, closely watching Iran and protecting the Strait of Hormuz while positioned in the Gulf of Oman. We returned home via the Red Sea, the Mediterranean and the Atlantic Ocean.

After the end of the USS America cruise, we were cross-decked to the USS Enterprise for our next deployment. After getting underway, we were briefed that we were going to do something to "thump the Russians' chests." President Reagan wanted to show our Navy's might and demonstrate the "Freedom of the Seas." The plan was for the USS

Enterprise to steam covertly from San Diego to the Kamchatka peninsula north of Petropavlovsk, skipping our usual stop in Hawaii, and rendezvous with the USS Coral Sea, also sailing covertly, and the USS Midway that was overtly emitting/operating as usual. When a Russian recce bomber was "surprisingly" intercepted by an F-14 from the Enterprise, a ship supposedly making its way to Hawaii for pre-cruise provisioning, and then discovering the Coral Sea, the "stuff" really hit the fan when the Russians figured out there were not just two but three carrier battle groups. Initially, a few Russian recce planes and bombers came out to surveil the area. As the three battle groups started a slow southernly transit out of the Bering Sea, the number of overflights dramatically increased. They were now carrying anti-ship weapons, ASN-4s/6s, and employing intermittent jamming, which per our ROE, was considered a hostile act. Very tense times. There were so many planes coming our way, the A-7s were loaded with Sidewinders to help with escorting the Russian planes. The new Russian Backfire bombers were practicing targeting runs toward the carriers. Intercepting the Backfire became a real game as they avoided the F-14s when we got within 25 miles of them. It was an intense five-six days. As we sailed into the Sea of Japan, some North Korean MiGs ventured out but quickly turned away when we went to intercept them. This event shook up the Kremlin and helped strengthen President Reagan's stature in the world order. LESSON: WALK SOFTLY AND CARRY A REALLY BIG STICK. While we were in the Indian Ocean, my beautiful daughter was born.

It's January '84, and I got orders to the VX-4 "Evaluators" at NAS Pt Mugu. Another flying tour! VX-4 was the operational testing squadron for new fighter weapons, testing software/hardware in threat realistic conditions and developing tactics against the evolving threats. I became the Chief Operations Test Director overseeing over 50 CNO projects led by 28 great officers of whom 85% were TOPGUN/WTI graduates. Additionally, I was getting involved in a number of classified programs. Unfortunately, the five cruises plus the time I spent away from home on detachments and travel proved too much for our marriage. We separated and eventually were divorced. It was the lowest period of my life. LESSON: TOO MUCH TIME AWAY DOES NOT THE HEART FONDER MAKE.

During my tour at VX-4, we had four different commanding officers. My last CO became one of my heroes, Capt. Larry "Hoss" Pearson. Hoss probably had more influence than anyone in what I would be doing for the next 25 years.

In June '87, I was ordered back to San Diego to a staff/flying job at Commander Air Forces Pacific, as the F-14 Class Desk Officer in charge of the material readiness/support of all West Coast F-14s. In April '89, I got a call from Hoss Pearson wanting me to come to the Pentagon to help stand-up a new requirements office. Hmmmm, depart San Diego a year early, no more flying, move cross country away from my kids and leave a new girlfriend for a desk job in the reviled Pentagon - let me think. Well, similar to my aide interview experience, in August, I left for D.C. It proved to be an important move for me in the long run. We successfully stood up the Special Programs Requirements shop for the Deputy for Air Warfare, OP-05. Interestingly, I learned duty in the Pentagon is mainly about money. The cutthroat nature of that environment was intriguing. LESSON: DON'T TAKE ANY BUDGET BATTLES PERSONALLY.

From 1991-1996, I had a number of Naval Air Systems Command assignments including Chief Engineer for future weapons programs such as the Advanced Anti Air Missile, AAAM, the AIM-9 Sidewinder, where I was involved with drafting the requirements for the new AIM-9X and the deputy PM for the new Joint Stand Off Weapon (JSOW). Four months into my last NAVAIR job, I got an offer from Hughes Aircraft Company that I just couldn't refuse. In March 1996, I retired as a Captain, O-6, with just under 24 years in the Navy, flying jets for 17 of them, all stationed in Southern California. What a ride.

I also had a great 19 year run with Hughes Aircraft Company/ Raytheon working in the world of advanced programs in various senior positions eventually rising to a VP position. THE GLYNCO LESSON WAS NEVER FORGOTTEN.

Summary - For a guy who started college not sure what he wanted to do, then decided after one tactical jet flight what he wanted to do, a lot of lessons were learned, and some career decisions were made for me in the course of my time in the Navy and industry. LESSON: SENIOR FOLKS SEE THINGS IN YOU THAT YOU DON'T AND TRUST YOUR ABILITY TO RISE UP TO THE TASK.

Ironically, for a guy who in high school nonchalantly thought he might want to be an engineer, my last 26 years, between the Navy and industry, were spent in engineering leadership positions. So, go figure. And that girlfriend I left in San Diego when I took those Pentagon orders - well, we just celebrated our 30th wedding anniversary.

Now retired, I humbly get to rub elbows with some of America's finest warriors/patriots…. these glorious Friday Pilots. LESSON: YOU KNOW YOU HAVE LIVED A GOOD LIFE WHEN YOUR HEROES LATER BECOME YOUR FRIENDS.

CHAPTER FOUR

LOOKING BACK
by Pete Carpenter

It was the same location, but this time the sound was different. My mind flooded back to 1952 from the ramp at Suwon, K-13 airfield during the Korean War and the run-up of the old J-33 GE engine in my F-80 Shooting Star. It was a great aircraft for its time, the first combat ready jet after WWII; 3,850 lbs. of thrust and a max gross takeoff weight of 14,000 lbs. Overhead was a new F-16, 27,000 lbs. of thrust, max takeoff weight of 37,500 lbs. - more engine thrust than my fully-armed F-80 weighed. Lesson: THE FIGHTER AIRCRAFT WORLD HAS CHANGED.

It was September of 2007, and I was part of a group of eight Korean War veterans visiting Korea on behalf of the Air Force's 60th birthday celebration. Our group included Korean fighter aces, Lt. Gen. (Ret.) Chick Cleveland and Hoot Gibson, and astronaut Buzz Aldrin, who had two MiG kills. The country and Air Force we visited was far different than what we left 55 years before. When I left the Suwon K-13 ramp 55 years ago, the country was in ruble and the base was a ramp and runway, a rapidly kludged together collection of temporary buildings and early Air Force fighter jets. Today, Korea it is a vibrant democracy and a technological marvel, one of the leading counties in Asia. The Air Force is likewise a modern marvel of people and equipment of which we only dreamed. Lesson: WE VISITORS HAD A PROUD PART IN THE TRANSFORMATION OF BOTH KOREA AND OUR AIR FORCE.

I am 91 years old, born in 1929. I was a farm kid from a subsistence farm near the small village of Chatham, Louisiana. I spent a lot of time behind the back end of a mule and it didn't take me long to figure out there must be a better life out there somewhere. WW II provided early motivation. Fighter airplanes, P-40s, were in abundance, lots of them, flying over daily from hastily constructed training bases. I was hooked on aviation early in my life. Lesson: EVEN BEING BEHIND A MULE CAN BE MOTIVATIONAL.

On the farm, we had what all farmers at the time had, land and our own labor that produced enough to eat. Kerosene lanterns provided light. We didn't get electricity until the mid 1930s. An ice truck delivered ice twice a week for our "ice box," and indoor plumbing came about the same time as electricity. I have read novels and articles about the serene and simple life with animals on a farm. These are written by people who never grew up on a farm. I had "kid hand calluses" and longed for airplanes. Lesson: RETIRING ON A FARM SOUNDS ROMANTIC, BUT TRY GROWING UP ON ONE.

WW II and the attack on Pearl Harbor changed everyone's life. My three older brothers joined the Navy. One was on the USS Tennessee in Pearl Harbor anchored near the USS Arizona. We heard the news on the radio and sweated until two weeks later, when a card came saying simply, "I'm OK." I also wanted to join the Navy, get two years of college and go to pilot training, but since I was under the age of 21, I required parental permission. Mother said, "NO! Three is enough!" and that was that. Lesson: IN THE OLD DAYS WHEN MOTHER SAID - NO! - THERE WAS NO ARGUING.

After high school graduation, I attended a local college with many WW II vets. Then, the Korean War came, and it was finally my turn! I no longer required permission and was off to Randolph AFB, TX and Aviation Cadets en route to pilot training with class 51E. My first airplane ride was in the front seat of a T-6. What a thrill! I was almost a pilot. After six months of primary pilot training, I was off to Williams AFB in AZ and the brand new T-28, a dream to fly, much easier than the T-6. Three months later, I got a backseat and frontseat ride in a T-33 and then started training in the F-80 A and B.

The early jets were good airplanes, but nowhere near as reliable or capable as today's fighters. By comparison to today the washout rate in training was very high. Simulators were rudimentary and in some ways counter-productive training. There were many accidents. One had to grow up fast in early jet aviation. My first close call came during a flight out of Williams. Over Phoenix, I had an oil system failure. I declared an emergency and retuned to Willy for a precautionary landing. By the time I arrived, I had 10% engine RPM. I touched down normally but as I passed Mobile the controller yelled, "YOU ARE ON FIRE, PULL THE BATTERY DISCONNECT!" I did, and that killed my radio. I rolled to the turnoff, and my canopy would not open. I couldn't call for help with a dead radio. I finally pried the canopy open with a screwdriver that I carried.

After basic training at Willy in the T-28 and F-80, it was off to Nellis AFB, NV for advanced tactics and gunnery training. War was on the horizon and Nellis was great training with lots of activity on every mission - bombing, strafing and attacking targets in the mountains. There were also lots of opportunities to practice air-to-air and dogfighting with sometimes as many as 20 aircraft involved in a swirling fight. I was in heaven.

After Nellis, I was sent to Korea via ship with a one day stop in Honolulu, then another stop for two months in Okinawa with the 26th Fighter Squadron. In Oki, the flying was fun and honed my F-80 skills, but I was eager to get to the war. I was soon on my way with a brief stopover in Tokyo, a slow train ride to the south of Japan and finally a C-47 Gooneybird ride to K-13 at Suwon. When I exited the aircraft, an old friend pulled up in a weapons carrier, grabbed my bag, and we left my buddies wondering if I was some type of celebrity as we proceeded to the 36th Fighter Bomber Squadron.

By the time I arrived in January, 1952, the ground war was in a back and forth, semi-stalemate phase, but in the air, we were still in daily combat. Early in 1950, the North Koreans had pushed the combined South Korean and U.S. forces into the Pusan Perimeter, almost into the sea. Gen. Douglas MacArthur was sent by President Truman and conducted the famous "Inchon Landing," threatening to encircle and cutoff the North Korean forces, causing their rapid retreat from Pusan to the Yalu River. As U.S. forces reached the Yalu, it appeared the war was won, and I would not be needed; however, the Chinese got a vote. They invaded south across the Yalu, drove a wedge between the 8th Army in the west and the 10th Marine Corps in the east and by Christmas of 1950, over 200,000 American Marines were being withdrawn in full retreat from the port of Hungnam in eastern Korea under heavy Chinese artillery barrages. 1951 saw more back and forth ground combat. I was sent as a trained killer, a full-up 2 Lt. in the F-80, to personally bring the war to a close.

The K-13 base was typical of a hastily constructed functional base in a war zone. We had a single north-south, bumpy, partial asphalt, partial perforated steel planking (PSP), 5-6000 ft. runway and a large PSP ramp that could accommodate about 150 aircraft, a combination of F-80s and F-86s. Our sleeping quarters were open-bay temporary Quonset huts with cots separated by about 4 ft. We had oil-fired potbellied stoves for the winters and mosquito nets for summer. We were just inland of the Yellow Sea on the west coast of Korea. Winter was bitterly cold from the Siberian winds out of China. Summer was warm but not blazing hot, with very high humidity. Toilet facilities were very basic, group showers in a tent and non-flush toilets. They worked to steadily improve facilities, and we finally got showers and hot water. Our quarters were maintained by young, 13-14 year-old Korean boys, good kids. The Mess Hall was run by Korean cooks and we had very good food. The O-Club was simply a bar in a Quonset hut where we could BS and listen to the stories from WW II Aces.

We were protected by ROK Army ground forces. Unlike Vietnam, we were never attacked from the ground, but the North Koreans employed a few ancient biplanes to harass our bases at night. With the moniker, "Bedcheck Charlie," they appeared about midnight, dropping a few small weapons, hand grenade-like. I remember we once sent an F-94 to shoot down "Charlie." He didn't, but he did run into him. Lesson: A KILL'S A KILL. We had bunkers that were sand-bagged trenches with no cover. I ran to them a couple of times at night. The main intruders from outside the base were poor, starving Korean children who learned if they could get on base, we would feed them. I cannot describe how utterly devastated was Korea during the war with North Korean, Chinese and U.N. forces shooting their way back and forth through every town and village from north to south.

Our F-80s had six .50 cal. guns and were armed with bombs and rockets. In 1952, all our missions were interdiction or close air support against North Korean or Chinese forces. Our flight gear and personal equipment was pretty basic. We wore flight suits (fire-retardant NOMEX had not been invented) and long underwear in the winter. We also wore a scarf to prevent neck chaffing and had underarm inflatable life preservers.

We sat on a seat pack that contained survival equipment. We carried an extra battery for our radio in a survival vest, but the radios seldom worked well. By Vietnam everything had been improved.

In 1950 and '51, the F-86s had really hammered the Chinese MiGs and by 1952 they provided air cover for our F-80 operations. I saw some MiGs but never had to tangle with them. Surface-to-air missiles had not been invented. Our main threat was from AAA, automatic weapons or small arms fire. I got stitched from nose to tail with 15 holes from .50 cal. on one low level mission over Inchon, when I was number 12 in a formation drop and on the inside of the turn forcing me low as the leader banked, not the smartest of tactics. It was not unusual to see a Lt. leading a 60 aircraft strike. When you saw 150 F-80 and F-86 aircraft launch, it was a sight to behold, but when they tried to all come back and land, many minimum or emergency fuel, some with battle damage, on a single, short runway, it was an adventure.

About a month into my tour, I landed from my 12th mission and received a message my father had passed away. I was given 30 days leave to assist my family. I returned to Korea, and my commander wanted me to become Squadron Ops Officer. I was given a spot promotion to 1 Lt. and was only one year out of pilot training. I completed my 100-mission tour and it is a little-known fact that I won the Korean War. After I completed my tour, the North Koreans and Chinese agreed to the Korean War Armistice. Lesson: IT WAS OBVIOUS I SCARED THE CHINESE TO DEATH.

I went to a stateside assignment that turned out to be more dangerous than combat, the 1739th Ferry Squadron at Amarillo, TX. Our mission was to ferry aircraft all over the world. One of my first missions was to deliver a P-47. I had never flown a P-47 and in fact had not flown a taildragger since primary flight school. I had to get three "backseat" T-6 rides to requalify. I did that and was given a Dash-1 and a test with the answers already marked to complete my P-47 "qualification." I was to be wingman on a two-ship delivery, so my leader showed me how to start the aircraft. As I took the runway, ran up the power and released brakes, the aircraft began to drift left. When I applied rudder, the pedals were locked. Unfortunately, the P-47 test that I took did not include answers on how to unlock the rudder controls. The aircraft became airborne for about 20 seconds, departed the runway and cartwheeled. The engine went one way, me and the cockpit went another. I was a P-47 pilot for less than a minute. I scrambled out of the burning pieces and took off my parachute and helmet. Civilians from the terminal ran to the crash site. One asked me, "Where is the pilot?" I said, "I don't know, I just got here myself."

Despite my less than elegant entry into the world of ferrying aircraft, some of my subsequent flights were no less dangerous. I began to ferry F-84s and F-86s from the factories to U.S. and overseas bases. I made numerous "High Flights" delivering aircraft to Europe along the northern route - Bangor, Maine, Goose Bay, Labrador, Narsaruaq, Greenland, Keflavik, Iceland, Prestwick, Scotland. It is difficult to describe the danger involved in these flights in the days of lousy weather forecasts, roiling seas with freezing water, unreliable navigation aids, defective survival equipment, lack of air-sea rescue, depending on a single aircraft UHF radio with no long range capability, few if any alternates. Lesson: HOW I SURVIVED ALL THOSE DELIVERIES, I DO NOT KNOW.

I subsequently went to an unexciting Communication Officers School in Illinois, but met a beautiful professional model, the love of my life and subsequent wife, Honeyjean Roos. We were married, and she moved to Cannon AFB with me as I transitioned into the F-86. We later converted to the F-100. Those were the TDY days in TAC. We lived out of a suitcase/duffel bag with numerous three and six-month deployments on short notice to hotspots around the globe, mostly in Europe. The deployments with tankers were no less dangerous than island-hopping. Flying in multi-ship formations, meeting tankers in weather and at night, rejoining with UHF/ADF steers to KB-50s, slowing without any flaps to 190 kts., hooking up with short, straight refueling probes, destination weather going below minimums, and there was always the new kid in the formation making his first crossing. I cannot think of one crossing that was just "routine."

In 1961, Honeyjean and I finally got our "dream" assignment, an "accompanied" tour with the 417th Tactical Fighter Squadron at Ramstein Airbase, Germany in the F-100. Almost immediately, I was selected as the aide and T-39 pilot for the Commander 17th Air Force at Ramstein but continued to maintain combat ready status and fly F-100s with the 417th. I traveled all over Europe visiting units and staffs. It was a GREAT experience.

At the end of a three-year tour, we returned to the states, and I went to Air Command and Staff School (ACSC) in Montgomery, AL. After ACSC, I went to the 19th Air Force staff, then was sent on a four-month "tour with industry" to act as Air Force representative to a highly classified program being developed for use in Vietnam. The program was subsequently cancelled, but as I would later learn, I should have paid more attention. I left 19th AF for F-4 training at Davis Monthan AFB and was on my way to my second war.

My Vietnam F-4 tour started in Da Nang where an old friend, Lt. Col. Robert "Earthquake" Titus offered me a job as Squadron Operations Officer. The offer lasted two days before I was summoned to 7th AF Headquarters in Saigon to head up the old program for which I represented the Air Force on my previous tour with industry. The program was now called "Igloo White" and would deploy sensors along the Ho Chi Minh Trail. I was "promised" I would be released for my Da Nang Ops Officer tour in three months; however, my boss departed unexpectedly, and the promise to return me to Da Nang was forgotten, plus a gall bladder operation put me off flying status for three months, and I was trapped at 7th AF HQ.

But, my gall bladder wasn't the only thing that trapped me. I lived downtown in a Saigon hotel, and on the early morning of 30 January, 1968, I was awakened by loud gunfire and the sound of a Puff the Magic Dragon, C-47 "Spooky" aircraft dropping flares, and a helicopter overhead shooting down while groundfire was shooting up at him. I quickly dressed and stepped out of the room to go downstairs and get my motor scooter. A hotel maid yelled, "YOU NO GO, VC ALL AROUND!" I went up on the roof and viewed what we have now all read about - TET 1968 was at my doorstep! - utter chaos - the VC attacking government facilities all through the city, rockets, grenades, automatic weapons fire. Who is shooting who? Who are the bad guys? And, me with no gun - we weren't allowed to carry them off base. I found another officer who had a jeep and convinced him we should try to make a run for the Tan Son Nhut airbase. He agreed, and we headed out hoping to dodge bullets. I slept on my desk for several days and learned one of my junior captains and a couple of others were trapped off base in town. Me and a friend borrowed a jeep, gathered up some guns and made a run for town. We drove fast through a really hot area of gunfire. We figured if we didn't know who to shoot, maybe they didn't either. I also stopped at my hotel to pick up some clean clothes. It was dumb, but I was beginning to stink. Lesson: RISKING YOUR LIFE FOR CLEAN UNDERWEAR IS PROBABLY NOT SMART.

As Tet began to wind down across the country Khe Sanh was gearing up. I was tasked with drawing up the air plan for defense of Khe Sanh, which Gen. Westmoreland said must be "defended at all costs." We employed all sorts of airplanes, B-52s, fighters from all services, FACs, transports and helicopters as two regiments of Marines battled two-three division-sized formations of North Vietnamese forces in Quang Tri province near the DMZ. The battle of Khe Sanh lasted six months before the base was eventually abandoned.

I was promised to return to Davis Monthan after my Vietnam tour, but no such luck. We were PCSed (Permanent Change of Station) to HQ Pacific Air Forces (PACAF), not where we wanted to be, but not a hardship tour. From PACAF, we PCSed back to Shaw AFB, SC and my war was not yet over. In 1972, I was sent back from Shaw to Tan Son Nhut as the Tactical Air Command Liaison Officer. President Nixon was determined to end the war and force the North Vietnamese to peace talks. We launched Linebacker II, the "Christmas bombings," in the Hanoi and Haiphong area from 18-29 December 1972. With 792 B-52 sorties, it was the largest heavy bomber raids since WW II. Ten B-52s were shot down over North Vietnam and five others were damaged and crashed in Laos or Thailand. The Air Force flew an additional 769 support sorties and the Navy and Marines 505. 12 support aircraft were also lost. I worked the plans along with many others as more rockets rained down on our 7th Air Force headquarters in Saigon. The plan worked. The U.S. signed the Paris Peace Accords in January 1973 and our POWs came home. The Vietnam War was over for the United States.

I retired as a Colonel in 1979 with 29 years military service, and Honeyjean and I moved to Merrit Island, FL. By that time, our family numbered three. Our daughter, Cricket, just a few hours old, had been adopted in Tucson in 1968. Cricket added immensely to the joy in our life, and she and husband Raymond later gave us our grandson, Sebastian. He and I are buddies.

After considering establishing a fixed base aircraft operation and rejecting the idea, Honeyjean and I moved back to Tucson. We made some real estate investments with our old friend Hoot Gibson and even dabbled in the deli and catering business. Sadly, Honeyjean, the only love of my life, good sport, good wife, good mother, beautiful woman, passed away of a brain tumor in 2002. Lesson: PICKING A GOOD SPOUSE IS ONE OF LIFE'S MOST IMPORTANT DECISIONS.

My life has been unbelievably fulfilling. The wars in which I fought made a difference to the country we served, to the allies we supported and to our Air Force. The kids we visited on the 60th Air Force anniversary in Korea in 2007 will never see a Lt. recently out of pilot training, leading a 60 aircraft package in combat. They will never have to go to war without standoff and precision weapons, without stealth and electronic countermeasures, without good radar warning receivers, without chaff and flares, without redundant and long-distance radios. They will never have to say, they have no night attack capability. They have these capabilities because we did not. I was one of the many who helped get these for them.

Yes, I am 91 years old, but have many pleasant memories to keep me occupied as I take my afternoon nap. And, I have my Friday Pilot buddies to make me laugh at our Friday lunch.

CHAPTER FIVE

IN GOD I TRUST

by Kenneth S. "Ken" Collins

I was born in Leavenworth, Kansas, the home of Fort Leavenworth, the oldest army post of the newest western frontier. It was from there that my grandfather, Sergeant Edward E. Collins of the 10th U.S. Cavalry, rode out with the troopers to fight in the battle of Wounded Knee.

Across the Missouri River from Fort Leavenworth, is Park University, where I attended for two years and joined the Naval Air Reserves. During the summer of 1950, I applied for Air Force pilot training. I was sent to Goodfellow AFB, TX for basic flight training in January 1951. I completed advanced pilot training and was commissioned at Vance AFB, OK on 9 February, 1952. In late May 1952, I completed F-80 jet transition at Moody AFB, GA. I volunteered for Korea and was transferred to Shaw AFB, SC in the 18th Tactical Reconnaissance Squadron (TRS) photo jet for combat crew training in the RF-80A.

I arrived at K-14, Kimpo Air Base, Korea in mid-August 1952. I checked out and flew combat missions in the RF-80A, F-80C and the RF-86A. By March 1953, I had flown 117 combat missions while in the 15th TRS (the Cotton Pickers).

My 88th mission was highly classified. I flew an RF-80 over North Korea to Mukden, Manchuria, China. On 18 January I was briefed on a classified combat mission to take place on 19 January. I would rendezvous with four F-86s from K-13, Suwon, over K-14, Kimpo, at 0800 hours.

The 19 January classified mission was an exciting day:

0630 – mission briefing
0730 – preflight RF-80 #362

34

0745 – taxied to departure runway

0750 – takeoff

0800 – made visual/radio contact with the F-86 escort lead and headed into North Korea.

0830 – crossed the Yalu river into Manchuria, China

0840 – cameras "ON," first Chinese Mukden MiG airfield photoed.

0845 – second Chinese Mukden airfield photoed (MiG training base) many MiGs in the air below me. I was flying at 24,000 ft.

0850 – made 180 degree right turn overflying and photo-ing the third Chinese Mukden airfield. More MiGs at my flight level. My F-86 escort engages with the MiGs.

0855 – heading south with MiGs close behind. F-86s are keeping the MiGs off my tail. Full power (the RF-80 is a SLOW jet) descending. Crossing over the Yalu river into North Korea, I jettisoned my external fuel tank to reduce drag. I needed all the speed I could get. The external fuel tanks landed in North Korea, so the Chinese had no evidence that I had violated their airspace. Continuing my descent down to 5,000 ft., I now need the fuel that was still in those external fuel tanks, but I needed the extra airspeed more. I reduced power since I was now approaching the South Korean border.

0915 – called the Kimpo tower requesting immediate landing - minimum fuel, straight in landing. I made it, taxied in, shut down and the camera crew was waiting for the hot target film. The squadron commander, Lt. Col. Wilson, met me as I climbed out of the cockpit. He shook my hand and said that I would receive the silver star for this critical mission. Lesson: BEING ON A COMBAT MISSION IN AN RF-80 OVER CHINA, IT IS GOOD TO HAVE FOUR F-86s AS ESCORT.

Had I been shot down on the 19 January mission, I would have been a prisoner of the Chinese and charged with illegal entry and spying. Two CIA pilots were caught earlier, after landing in China, and were sentenced to execution, but instead got 20 years in a Chinese prison.

I got 100% photo coverage of the three Mukden airfields with great weather and they were in order: a North Korean training base, an operational combat wing manned by "Russians" and a Chinese combat operational airbase. Because of the high classification of this mission (we were not supposed to violate Chinese airspace), it was not critiqued or debriefed with the F-86 pilots. I was informed that one of the F-86 pilots had been shot down but was unable to confirm.

My 104th mission was an RF-86A combat mission into North Korea to "mark the target." The RF-86A was a good flying aircraft. It was one of the reconnaissance aircraft inventory of the 15th TRS at Kimpo. When I arrived at K-14, there were 15 RF-80As, 4 F-80Cs and 2 RF-86As. The RF-80 was a fully equipped, photo capable reconnaissance aircraft, the backbone of the squadron. The F-80C was fully armed with machine guns and carried rockets. The machine guns had tracers and the smoke rockets were also for marking valuable ground targets for fighter-bombers strikes. The RF-86A had been modified by removing the top two guns and installing a nose oblique camera. The remaining four guns, two on each side, were loaded with tracers. I was current in all three aircraft and I was only a Lt.

The 5th Air Force operations order called for the 15th TRS to support this recon mission. The squadron was to provide an aircraft and pilot to execute the mission as directed. The ops order directed that the specified North Korean radar site be "marked" and the four fighter-bomber F-80s were to "take it out" by bombing the site.

Our squadron executive officer, a captain, decided that this was a "good" combat mission for him. It was not too far above the demilitarized zone (DMZ); however, he wanted an experienced RF-86 pilot to be on his wing. I was selected. Our briefing was that I would locate the target then fly his wing as we strafed and marked the target for the fighter bombers. I guess the captain's theory was, a good "recce" pilot could find any coordinates and the target. I had been an Air Force combat pilot for six months and a pilot for one year. Lesson: IT WAS A DIFFERENT AIR FORCE FROM TODAY, BACK WHEN A LT. WAS CONSIDERED AN EXPERIENCED PILOT AND AN "OLD HEAD."

We took off in formation and headed north of the DMZ about 200 miles to locate the radar site. I identified the site and took lead's wing. He contacted the four F-80s, notifying them that we were going in to mark their target. They acknowledged that they had us in sight. We armed our guns and lead rolled into the target. I was behind and below him. Both of us began firing into the target. As we passed over the target, I was in trail and getting some small arms fire. We pulled up and out of the way of the fighter bombers. The fighter bomber lead said that he did not see our marking of the target. Lead said we would go back in and mark it again. Lesson: A SECOND PASS OVER AN ALERTED TARGET IS NOT THE BEST OF IDEAS! On the second pass, lead was lower and started firing sooner. Tracers are easy to see. I was firing, but had to stop, because he was so low that he was in my gun sight.

As we pulled off the target, it felt like I had hit a telephone pole with my left wing. Checking the left wing, I could see that the external fuel tank had exploded and wrapped up and over the wing giving me a tremendous yaw to the left. I called lead telling him I had been hit. No response. I fought to get control of the aircraft. I was losing altitude because of the drag. I hit the left external tank jettison switch. Nothing! I then hit the combined tank ejection switch. The right tank jettisoned, but the left was still hanging on. Heading back to South Korea, I saw that I was losing lots of fuel. The left internal wing tank had been shot up and was leaking badly. The sun was going down, and I was running out of fuel fast. My next move was to severely yaw the RF-86, but the tank was stuck on the wing slat. I kicked the rudder hard and rapidly almost losing aircraft control. As I continued the hard rudder yawing, the damaged tank began to slide. Finally, it came off. I climbed a couple thousand ft. checking the flight controls and the aircraft stability to assure it wouldn't stall on final approach.

Crossing the DMZ, I called Kimpo tower for a straight in emergency landing. Minimum fuel! I touched down a little fast to insure flight control. As I was taxiing into the squadron revetment area, I flamed out, no more fuel! The squadron commander, Major Houser Wilson, was there to meet me. He was very pleased to see that I made it back. The captain, lead, said that I had been shot down. He didn't come back around to look for me, nor respond to my radio call. The RF-86 wing and body was too damaged to repair. Lesson: IT OCCURRED TO ME I WAS EXHAUSTING MY QUOTA OF CLOSE CALLS.

After Korea, I returned to Shaw AFB, SC as an instructor in the RF-80A and the RF-89F in the 18th TRS. In 1955, I volunteered for an assignment to the 10th Tac Reconnaissance Wing (TRW), 38th TRS, at Spangdahlem Air Base, Germany as an RF-84F Instructor Pilot and Flight Commander. After two years at Spang, in 1957, I had the opportunity to go to Erding Air Base in Bavaria as a Military Advisory Group Instructor Pilot in the RF-84F with the German Air Force, Waffenschule 50, (Weapons School 50). I again returned to Shaw AFB, SC in 1959, to the 20th TRS in the RF-101 as Flight Commander and Ops Officer.

In late 1960, I was contacted by the Pentagon Special Projects Office asking if I would be interested in volunteering for a special classified space program. This evolved into a totally thorough physical examination at the Lovelace Clinic in New Mexico. It included many

psychological evaluations for me and my wife and lie detector tests in Washington D.C. Lesson: WHEN YOU TAKE A DOD LIE DETECTOR TEST, YOU'LL BE GLAD YOU LED A CLEAN LIFE. This selection process lasted through mid 1962. When I was approved for the program, I was sent to the David Clark Company, a company in Worcester, MA, that manufactured high technology pressure suits. I was fitted and familiarized with my new "uniform." In October 1962, I went to the Pentagon, resigned my Air Force commission and was hired by the CIA. I still had not been told what my job would be, only that I would be only that I would be flying a totally new aircraft, no pictures or drawings. Then, I was told to go find a house in Los Angeles, CA. I moved my wife and four kids into a house in Northridge in the San Fernando Valley. I was called by "Seth" and told to be at Lockheed, Burbank on Monday morning. At Lockheed, I boarded a Lockheed Connie with a full load of people and flew to area 51. Lesson: IT IS GOOD TO HAVE AN UNDERSTANDING WIFE WHEN YOU MOVE HER TO A NEW HOUSE AND CAN'T TELL HER WHY OR WHAT YOU ARE DOING AND YOUR NAME IS NOW "SETH."

Colonel Doug Nelson (later Major General) walked me over to a hangar. Inside, was this long, black, beautiful A-12. It was named "Oxcart." It had first been flown in April 1962 by Lou Shaulk, Lockheed's chief test pilot. The J58 engine was not ready. We had the A-12 airframe with two J75 engines. At first, all we could do was takeoff, air refuel, get out to

Mach 1.6 and make landings. We had F-101s for chase and proficiency. I would arrive at Area 51 on Monday and take the Connie back to Burbank Friday or Saturday evening, depending if I had a flight. My first flight was on 6 February, 1963.

On 24 May, 1963, I had an A-12 test flight, a subsonic J58 engine test. My F-101 chase was Jack Weeks, another CIA test pilot. I flew north and west of the Salt Lake. On my return route we ran into some heavy clouds and rain at 25,000 ft. I climbed to 30,000 but was still in the weather. My chase said that we were getting slow. All my instruments looked OK. The F-101 has a pitch up problem and Jack indicated he was pulling away. The A-12 felt stable, but I was in heavy weather. Shortly, all the instruments began to wind down. I saw the airspeed hit 102 knots. The A-12 pitched up into a flat inverted spin. The flight controls were ineffective. Not knowing my true altitude, I ejected upside down. I guessed that I broke out of the clouds around 20,000 ft. The seat had separated, and my parachute had opened. After looking up to check the chute, I looked down to see where I was going to land. At that time the chute separated. I was free falling. I said, "S- - t, I'm dead! In God I trust." That was the high-altitude drogue chute, not my parachute. At 15,000 ft., the main parachute opened. I hit the ground, collapsed the chute and started collecting my scattered checklist. I was west of the Salt Lake.

A pickup truck with three guys in the cab came bouncing across the desert. They had my canopy in the back. They said, "Get in, we'll take you to your aircraft." We did not want "gawkers" around a new super-secret aircraft, even one in a smoking pile of rubble. I had to create a quick "cover story." I said, "No, no, it's a F-105 out of Nellis AFB with a nuclear weapon on board!" They said, "Get in, we' re leaving." They dropped me off at a Windover Highway Patrol office. I made a phone call to Area 51. Within an hour, the Connie, Kelly Johnson's jet, loaded with security and recovery crew, picked me up and flew me to Kirkland AFB where I got a physical at the Lovelace Clinic. Cause: an off the shelf pitot tube froze and the air data computer (ADC) failed. The ADC was replaced and a new pitot tube, "the Rosemont redundant pitot probe," was installed on other A-12s.

The Oxcart experimental flight tests continued from 1962 to 1967. There were some critical moments. Mel Vojvodich, CIA test pilot, retired as a USAF MGen, was on takeoff roll at Area 51. What the engineers said could not happen, did. He had a nanosecond to make a decision. When he pulled the stick back, the nose went "down," pushed forward, the nose went "up." Then, he lost all control and ejected. As the chute opened, his feet hit the ground. Lesson: TIMING IS EVERYTHING IN AVIATION.

In January 1967, Walt Ray, was testing the A-12. The route took him out to the four corners area and back. He was returning to Area 51 because he was having electrical problems that affected the fuel cell sequencing. About 60 miles out, he said that his right engine had flamed out. Shortly after that, at 15,000 ft., the left engine failed. He ejected and never separated from the seat.

In 1967, the agency declared the A-12 operational and DoD agreed to deploy it to operate out of Kadena Air Base, Okinawa. We began flying "Black Shield" combat missions over North Vietnam. Two operational combat missions were flown over North Korea. Jack Weeks' mission found the USS Pueblo in Wonsan Bay harbor. His flight was at 83,000. Ft. Mach 3.12. Historically speaking, the Black Shield combat missions were aviation's first Mach 3+ above 80,000 ft. missions.

By 1968, the Air Force decided that they were operationally ready to take over the North Vietnam missions with the SR-71 replacing the A-12. The A-12 was a single-cockpit aircraft with a good center of gravity (CG). Kelly Johnson called it his "perfect airplane." The SR-71 added a second cockpit with a Reconnaissance System Officer and moved the CG further back. The A-12 flew higher and faster than the SR-71.

I was at Area 51 from Oct 1962 to 1968. 1962 to 1967 was experimental flight tests of the A-12 Oxcart. 1967 to 1968 was Black Shield out of Okinawa. These flights over North Vietnam and North Korea were aviation's first Mach 3+ 85,000 ft. combat missions. We had no mission losses after 29 combat missions. The only loss was Jack Weeks during an engine test flight out of Kadena. I went to the SR-71. Three of the other CIA A-12 pilots went to Peterson AFB thinking they would fly ADC's YF-12 which was terminated. The fifth went back into the Air Force. Without the extensive flight testing we, the six CIA test pilots, did in Area 51, there would not have been an SR-71. The J58 engine was the critical link to the success of that aircraft. The spike, the engine and the afterburner had to be perfectly matched or you would have a severe "unstart"...it would "pop" the shock out of the inlet, compressor stall the engine and blow out the afterburner, causing one hell of a yaw. If you didn't catch it soon enough, the other engine would do the same thing, usually at 60,000 to 70,000 ft. at Mach 2.4 to Mach 2.8. The unstarts were initially routine until they went digital on the inlet controls. One unstart was so severe that the shoulder level camera lenses were broken out of their mounts by my shoulders.

The CIA pilots began flying the A-12 Black Shield aircraft back to the States. Before one A-12 could fly back across the Pacific, it required an engine change and test flight. The A-12 had the "birdwatcher" installed. It was a high frequency (HF) transmitting system with internal connections to the hydraulic gauges, canopy, throttles, altimeter, etc. If a system was failing, the "birdwatcher" chirped. A signal was sent back to operations indicating that systems condition. It worked well.

Jack Weeks, my very good friend, was scheduled for that test flight out of Kadena air base. His test flight route took him north of the Philippines at 80,000 ft. with a 180 degree turn returning back to Okinawa. Takeoff was routine. The birdwatcher was normal. The birdwatcher chirped climbing through 75,000 ft. The next chirp was unexpected! The right throttle was instantly retarded out of afterburner back to idle. This was followed with a chirp of the A-12 descending down through 75,000 ft. That was the last that we heard or saw of the A-12 and Jack Weeks. Search and rescue aircraft and ships covered many miles north of the Philippines. The A-12 pilots believe that the right engine being tested, exceeded the compressor engine temperature rapidly before the throttle could be retarded fast enough to prevent a catastrophic engine explosion. Jack Weeks is the only fatality that can be directly attributed to the failure of the A-12 or the SR-71. God bless Jack.

Unscheduled mission - Area 51

I was having breakfast in the mess hall around 0830. Shortly after I sat down to eat, Major Roger Anderson, from the ops staff, ran in saying that I had to go to ops immediately, like, RIGHT NOW! When I walked into the door at ops, Lt. Col. Burt Barrett told me to go to the physiological support division (PSD) and get suited up. He would brief me as I was getting into my pressure suit. I was to takeoff in the A-12 within 30 minutes.

Normally, prior to an A-12 flight, we had breakfast, went to our mission briefing, then to PSD for our leisurely suiting and 30 minutes of 100% oxygen pre-breathing. Thirty five minutes prior to scheduled takeoff time, we would get into the PSD van and drive us out to the A-12. But, not today! The suiting was rushed. The faceplate was closed and pressure checked. Into the van I went and out to the A-12.

My briefing consisted of, "There is a low flying Russian satellite coming across the Pacific coast and the Agency wants an A-12 up there to confirm. You will be given instructions after takeoff. Get going."

I climbed into the cockpit and the crew chief strapped me in and closed the canopy. As the canopy was closing, I heard the Buick wildcat engine start cart rev up. At 3200 rpm on the left engine, throttle to idle, the Triethyl Borane (TEB) fired the engine. After both engines were started, the chocks were pulled. The tower cleared me for immediate takeoff. After power checked 100% on both engines, I advanced the afterburners and took off.

I received further headings as I passed through 50,000 ft. at Mach 2. Heading in the direction of the "alleged" Russian satellite, I went through 60,000 ft. at Mach 2.5 and climbing. Leveling at 70,000 ft. at 2.6 Mach, I still had no sighting. New directions, "Turn hard right!" To my right, I saw a slow drifting container at the end of a very large balloon. My guess was that the balloon was at 60,000 ft. moving to the east at 10 miles per hour.

Here I am at 60,000 ft. at Mach 2 chasing a slow-moving balloon. To make a 180 degree turn at Mach 2 at 60,000 ft., it took me 80 miles to come back around to even see the balloon. After reporting the sighting, I came out of afterburner and descended down to traffic pattern altitude for landing at Area 51. I debriefed and went to House 6, our "pilot's lounge," and had a beer. I never heard any more about the "Russian satellite."

I flew the last A-12 Black Shield aircraft back to Palmdale, California, thus terminating the A-12's operational life. Lesson: IT WAS AN EXCITING AND REWARDING LIFE ABOVE 80,000 FT. AND MACH 3. I was given a choice of going with Lockheed or returning to the Air Force. I volunteered to go to Beale AFB, CA to fly the SR-71. In

1968, we moved to Beale, and I became the Operations Officer of the 99th Strategic Reconnaissance Squadron (SRS), advanced to commander of the 1st SRS and in 1972, I was promoted to Colonel as the 9th Strategic Reconnaissance Wing Director of Operations position where I worked for the Wing Commander, Col. Pat Halloran. In 1974 we moved to March AFB, CA where I became the head of 15th Air Force Intelligence. I retired as a Colonel in 1980.

Throughout my Air Force career, I have been awarded the Silver Star, the CIA Intelligence Star for Valor, three Distinguished Flying Crosses, the Legion of Merit, several Air Medals and the service medals for United Nations, Korea and Vietnam.

I am life member of the Society of Experimental Test Pilots, the Distinguished Flying Cross Society and have been inducted into the Kansas Aviation Hall of Fame and the Nevada Aerospace Hall of Fame.

In God I trust.

CHAPTER SIX

WE WON THE SECOND TET OFFENSIVE BITTER END TO THE WAR IN VIETNAM

by Peter Collins

A sign on the wall of Base Operations at Davis-Monthan Air Force Base in Tucson reads, "There is no peacetime mission that justifies penetrating a thunderstorm." I wish I had learned that lesson early in my career. My life apparently revolves around thunderstorms.

I grew up in and around New York City, where we regularly saw thunderstorms in late summer. They didn't bother me much, as I worked 8-10 hours a day, working in big box stores as an inventory clerk (shelf stuffer) and teaching children to play my favorite sport, tennis.

The day I graduated from Georgetown University in D.C. with a celebration on Healey lawn, we had a huge thunderstorm. Whew! I was free to start law school at the University of Connecticut. Two days later, another thunderstorm struck: I got DRAFTED. Law school was down the drain.

I always wanted to fly jet fighters. My uncle was an Army Air Corp accountant during WWII. Later, he was an aviation analyst on Wall Street. He went on junkets to McDonnell, Boeing, Douglas, Vought, Fairchild, and other aircraft companies, each of whom hoped to impress him and other Wall Street types with their latest and greatest jet fighters. My uncle sent me these terrific brochures. I was fascinated by the speed, power, fire, glory personified and the afterburning power of these fabulous machines. By fate, I got my chance.

I elected to go into the Air Force. Before leaving, I played in the 1969 US Tennis Open at Forest Hills. Great moments. Two weeks later, my head got shaved, and I became an Airman Basic. After an extended stay at Lackland AFB in Basic Training (where I taught 17 of my fellow classmates to read), then OTS, I landed at Laughlin AFB, in beautiful Del Rio, Texas. A long way from Brooklyn, but I was in Air Force Pilot training!

The T-41 was bad, the T-37 endurable, but the reward was getting six months in the supersonic "Air Force Sportscar," the T-38 Talon, the "White Rocket." At the end of the program, we were allowed eight solo sorties to gain "confidence." Not one of us needed much - we couldn't wait to take that white rocket up to 50,000 feet, and dance around the thunderstorms of west Texas. And as John Gillespie Magee wrote we "... danced the skies on laughter-silvered wings...and joined the tumbling mirth of sun-split clouds," chancing a flameout of our J-85 engines. We paid zero attention to those smart people who taught us that there was hail in those high cumulonimbus clouds, but we survived.

I did well in basic pilot training, graduating near the top of my class, and qualified for jet fighters. Much to my dismay, our class was assigned just one F-4, and zero F-105s. I stood under the wing of the mighty F-105 at Lackland and dreamed of firing up that huge motor and heading into North Vietnam. Not so fast! Instead, I got the first jet fighter to go supersonic in level flight: The F-100 Super Sabre. It was tricky and blew up on occasion, but was a marvelous combination of guts, power and speed. The "Hun" felt like riding a bucking bronco at times, especially when you got too slow, and tried to recover speed by stroking the burner – flames out of the nose and the tail simultaneously as the J-57 stalled due to lack of airflow; feet blown off the rudder pedals; and all of a sudden, you lost 100 knots! But, under better conditions, with low-G and good airspeed, you stroked the burner at 400 knots and suddenly reached 550 knots. It felt like a rocket!

Six months at Luke AFB in Phoenix, training with German F-104 pilots and various other various ne'er do 'alls. We gathered at the legendary Luke Officers Club on Friday nights. Pilots from all over the country and multiple services gathered to tell lies and stories. Lesson: IN AVIATION HALF OF WHAT YOU LEARN COMES FROM "BAR TALK" AT THE O-CLUB (hardly PC and now much of it expressly forbidden in the USAF).

Luke was terrific. We were the last F-100 class, so the instructors basically let us do what we wanted and as much as we dared. On my last flight, we went deep into the Grand Canyon, rolled upside down, and took photos through the top of the canopy! (Uh, not today). Since we were the last class, Barry Goldwater came and gave a commencement speech, and gave us awards. We were headed to Phan Rang to be real fighter pilots and win the war! Next thunderstorm: on the following morning, our orders changed to a small propeller "spotter" plane in Vietnam. We learned to be Forward Air Controllers (FACs) in the O-2A aircraft, a specially-modified Cessna 337, push-pull engines without turbochargers, plus two rocket pods and plus 1,000 pounds of radios.

Survival School in the snow of Fairchild AFB in March (yes, we killed and ate "Fluffy," our assigned rabbit), and then Snake School in the Philippines prepared us to survive alone in the jungles of Vietnam (sure).

I arrived in Nha Trang, Tan Son Nhut and Bien Hoa, just in time for an entirely different sort of thunderstorm, not the monsoon storms which shut us down for days at a time, but the Second Tet Offensive of 1972 (aka The Easter Offensive). North Vietnam attacked Saigon with 300,000 regulars, 700 Soviet tanks, thousands of anti-aircraft guns and the first combat use of shoulder-fired heat-seeking missiles.

I was overhead when the provincial capital, Loc Ninh, was overrun by NVA regulars. There was nothing we could do. Late one afternoon, I told Sgt. Mark Smith (Callsign "Zippo") that we would talk to him in the morning. He responded: "No you won't. They are coming through the wire, and I am escaping out the back." He was captured and spent a year in a Cambodian prison.

The NVA moved south to the town of An Loc, 50 miles north of Saigon, surrounding it on three sides. Three NVA Divisions pounded An Loc with 25,000 artillery rounds and rockets during the first three days of the attack. Two weeks later, at 0500 on May 11, 1972, An Loc was struck by 10,000 rounds of artillery fire. Resupply was forbidden due to unrelenting anti-aircraft gunfire and missiles.

To be clear, we faced nothing like the anti-aircraft and SAM fury faced by Russ Violett, Bill Hosmer, Bob Barnett, GAR Rose, et. all. up north in RPs 5 and 6, but we were sitting ducks for the North Vietnamese. Lesson: THE SAM-7 "STRELA" HEAT-SEEKING MISSILES WERE

LETHAL TO SMALL PROPELLER AIRCRAFT AND THEY CHANGED EVERYTHING. WE LOST DOZENS OF MEN AND AIRCRAFT, INCLUDING SEVEN AIRCRAFT ON THE FIRST DAY. With superior grit from South Vietnamese Rangers, and thousands of round-the-clock airstrikes from TAC Air and B-52s, we stopped the NVA at An Loc.

Lesson: DESPITE OVERWHELMING GROUND SUPERIORITY, AIR POWER PROPERLY APPLIED CAN MAKE THE DIFFERENCE. During the battle, 297 sorties were flown on May 11, followed by more than 250 on each of the next four days. We talked on three radios, sometimes simultaneously: FM radio to the commanders on the ground; VHF to the "superiors" at Bien Hoa and Saigon; and UHF to the incoming fighters. We put in three airstrikes simultaneously on the sides of that three-quarter mile wide city, sometimes with 20 sets of fighters waiting overhead - chaos!

Once fighters arrived on station, we "talked their eyes" onto the targets, briefed them on threats in the area, location of friendly troops, direction of the attack, run-in headings, pull-off headings, minimum distance from the friendlies, and safe areas for emergency bailouts. Each time a fighter was ready to attack, we rolled-in first to launch a 2.75 inch rocket armed with a white phosphorous explosive charge (affectionately called "Willie Pete"), which blossomed into a small white cloud on the ground, visible to the fighters. We then gave corrections (e.g. hit "ten meters south" of my smoke) to the pilots. We routinely directed strikes within twenty-five meters of friendly forces because NVA fighters were "in the wire," trying to breech their defenses. These encounters were known as Troops in Contact (TICs) which required exacting care to avoid friendly casualties. It was my job to ensure the fighters were lined-up exactly on the target and abort them if it appeared that they may hit the friendlies. It was a daunting life and death responsibility to safeguard our ground forces while stopping the enemy assault.

We directed airstrikes by Air Force A-1s, F-4s, A-37s, AC-119s and AC-130s, Navy A-7s, A-6s, A-4s, F-4s, F-8s, and even an RF-5A Vigilante, against Soviet T-54 and PT-76 tanks, armored personnel carriers and anti-aircraft guns. After about one month, two squadrons of Marine A-4 "Hellbornes" arrived from Iwakuni, Japan. This little attack jet performed the close-in close air support that the Air Force previously supplied with

F-100s, dropping up to six 500 lb. Mark-82 bombs each. They were fearless, attacking through fire from twin ZPU-14.5 mm, 23mm, 37mm, 57 mm AAA guns and Strela anti-aircraft missiles to protect American advisors, helping the South Vietnamese Rangers defending An Loc.

We also worked with the AC-130 Spectre gunships, who were most effective, especially at night. Due to sapper attacks stopping all radio communications to HQ in Saigon, we placed one FAC high (11,000') to coordinate incoming fighters and placed them in non-conflicting orbits above the battlefield. Three FACs below directed simultaneous attacks on three sides of An Loc. Lesson: WAR WAS ORGANIZED CHAOS, BUT WE WERE ALL ON OUR OWN AND FIGURED OUT HOW TO MAKE IT WORK.

One of my most memorable missions was with two Hellbornes, defending an encampment of 62 South Vietnamese Rangers and one American, about four miles south of An Loc. They were surrounded, with NVA troops attacking, primarily on the north side of their camp. They had been eating roots and sucking water from the ground, having been surrounded and isolated for over 50 days. Big problem: they were under attack from the NVA, but also from a huge thunderstorm. The bottom of the thunderstorm was about 2,500 feet above ground level, tough weather under which to work airstrikes. We placed 500 lb. bombs on their northern perimeter within 20 meters of friendlies. The A-4s made multiple attacks with one bomb on each delivery. The ground was so saturated that the A-4s could not see the white phosphorous smoke – it was not blossoming in the mud. So, as I turned final approach at 200 knots, each A-4 turned in behind me, and positioned himself so he could follow the red fire from my rocket motor onto the perimeter, and the targets - NOT FUN - lots of ZPU 14.5 mm anti-aircraft fire. After delivering all their bombs, the A-4s fired their 20mm cannons until the NVA withdrew. It seemed like an hour, but it really lasted just about 20 minutes - my most satisfying sortie of the war.

Big Lesson: DON'T BELIEVE WHAT DAN RATHER SAID AND DON'T BELIEVE ANY MEDIA REPORT THAT DOES NOT TALK TO SOMEONE WHO WAS THERE! AMERICAN AIRPOWER AND SOUTH VIETNAMESE RANGERS WON THE SECOND TET OFFENSIVE. THE NORTH LOST <u>EVERY</u> TANK

AND ANTI-AIRCRAFT GUN AND MOST OF ITS MEN IN AND AROUND AN LOC. Later figures from the NVA showed losses of all their tanks and over 150,000 men (probably a low number).

About a month later, in July 1972, another thunderstorm: I was directing an airstrike in Cambodia near the Parrot's Beak at the southern end of the Ho Chi Minh Trail. As we finished the strike, the two A-4s pushed up and climbed to 20,000' for their return to Bien Hoa. Unfortunately, I had no such power. As I turned toward Saigon, I saw two tall thunderstorms. I was certain that (with my F-100 experience), I could make it between the two and return "home" to our "hooch" bar (sure wish I had an afterburner at that moment). Unfortunately, as I neared the two storms, they merged. I was trapped.

I hoped to penetrate the outer edge of each storm and emerge from the other side. NOT SO FAST! As I hit the clouds, I was engulfed with massive up drafts followed by massive downdrafts. The instruments in an O-2 are pneumatic, which means they display altitude and airspeed based on air pressure entering the "pitot tube" at the front of the aircraft. But the inside of a thunderstorm is a violent maelstrom of conflicting and interacting up-and-down drafts, pressures, and turbulence. My instruments spun wildly first in one direction and then the other, completely unreliable. My aircraft tumbled, turned, and spun in completely random sequences, bouncing with such violent force in one direction and another that it made me wonder if it would hold together. For some unknown reason, I felt it might be better to bail out of the O-2A in the middle of this, because I expected to meet the Cambodian countryside face-to-face any second.

Bailing out of an O-2A is a dodgy event. There is a twin boom and a second engine behind the cockpit. You must unbuckle, move to the right seat, manually open the right door, force yourself into the airstream, bailout and hope you "clear" the twin boom, to say nothing of the rear engine! Once out of the aircraft into the thunderstorm, I would be at the mercy of the up and down drafts, and probably would have been torn to bits; however, that prospect seemed better than a full speed crash into the ground.

Fortunately, after I unbuckled my seatbelt, moved to the right seat and was about to open the right side door, I broke out at the bottom of the storm, going straight down from 2,900' above the ground. I promptly grabbed the controls and started a recovery. What was that? Some Ass... was shooting at me with a twin ZPU 14.5 mm AAA gun! First, God tried to kill me, then this fool was trying to finish me off! As little good as it might do, I turned, fired off my remaining rockets in his direction, got below the storm, and returned to Saigon. After the boss saw the many popped rivets on my aircraft, I "earned" a few days off. I was happy to have them.

Over 12 months, I flew 896 combat hours, and was awarded the Distinguished Flying Cross three times, plus ten Air Medals. Most important: On 1 November 1972, I was awarded the Army Commendation Medal and the "Super FAC Medal" from the ARVN Rangers who defended An Loc. That medal is scratched out on the top of a ration can, attached with a piece of green webbing. Lesson: I AM PROUD OF THAT SERVICE: WE SAVED LIVES AND PROTECTED FELLOW WARRIORS FROM VICIOUS ATTACK.

The bitter end of the Vietnam war came in December 1972 when President Nixon finally took off the politically driven gloves and allowed the military to end the war with the massive bombing of North Vietnam. A ceasefire was announced for January 27, 1973.

My partner, John Chambers (Rash 15), and I were tasked to fly the last combat sorties from in-country South Vietnam. It was not exactly an honor. We flew in separate O-2As, with no rockets, no guns, no fighters on call, no Cobra helicopters, no available artillery and no ability to change anything. We hopelessly flew around Saigon, watching NVA and Viet Cong fighters shooting Chinese rockets into downtown Saigon, and occasionally shooting small arms at us.

North Vietnamese and VC were all around the city, having moved south as soon as President Nixon proclaimed the cease fire. CIA estimated there were over 145,000 NVA in South Vietnam that day. We did not want to be the last pilots shot down in Vietnam. We finally touched down and our war was over. Unfortunately for our South Vietnam partners, theirs was not. The South fell completely two years later.

I came home, joined the Air National Guard, and attended The Ohio State University College of Law. I joined the Franklin County Prosecutor's Office, where I tried over 50 felony jury trials in just over two years.

Next thunderstorm: this time, a GREAT one. I met Deborah Munger, a brilliant Columbus teacher. We have two great kids, Courtney and Melinda, and four great grandkids. We all now live in Arizona.

I needed to make a living, not just a career, so off to private practice. I learned the art of civil litigation and tried dozens of lawsuits to verdicts in Columbus. I continued to fly at night and on the weekends in the 166 Tactical Fighter Squadron of the Ohio ANG. It was a great squadron, a terrific group which was totally dedicated to the mission. We were assigned to lead flights of 225 fighters to deliver Mk-82 bombs into a secret Middle East location. The formations included RF-4s, F-15s, and Navy A-6s to provide electronic countermeasures. ANG pilots were the leaders and organizers of an important Air Force mission. This was a clear sign that the active Air Force recognized the experience and skill of ANG pilots, who averaged over 1,500 hours of fighter time, while our USAF friends at the time averaged between 500-750.

Another thunderstorm struck: I gave up the law practice and the comfort of the 166 TFS. We moved our family to Tucson, where I became the chief Night Attack Manager and night test pilot for the Air National Guard/Air Force Reserve Test Center. I completed the Air Force Fighter Weapons School and pioneered the use of night vision goggles in Air Force and Air National Guard fighter aircraft. I was program manager for the A-7 Low Altitude Night Attack (LANA) program, where the ANG outfitted 90 A-7 aircraft and trained over 200 pilots to fly and attack at night using forward-looking infrared devices and NVGs. I completed my 21-year career as a Lieutenant Colonel with over 3,700 hours of flight time, and a final checkout in the fabulous F-16A "Viper" jet.

I later returned to the law at Slutes Sakrison, a great civil trial law firm (lots of trials and arbitrations). In 1993, I joined Gust Rosenfeld, P.L.C., an aviation-oriented law firm, where I have practiced for 27 years. I have now tried over 100 jury trials and have been the Chair of the Arizona State Bar Associations College of Trial Advocacy. I handled one of the country's largest aviation insurance coverage cases. I have led the Tucson office of Gust since 1993. Gust is one of the best law firms in the country. We have a terrific mix of "young" and "experienced" lawyers. I still love trying jury trials and love being a husband, parent and grandparent. Life is great.

I am proud of each step along the way - a great ride. But, thunderstorms have been the cornerstone of every significant development in my life. Looking back, I see the pure wisdom of that sign on the wall of Base Operations at Davis-Monthan Air Force Base in Tucson: "There is no peacetime mission which justifies penetration of a thunderstorm." But, I would add: Lesson: SOMETIMES THUNDERSTORMS ARE UNAVOIDABLE, SO IF CAUGHT IN ONE, DO THE BEST YOU CAN!

CHAPTER SEVEN

HOW DID I EVER ACHIEVE GEEZERNESS???

by John Dale

I had soloed and was ready to dogfight in my PA-18 Cub. So, I saw this dust devil and thought I'd cut it in two. I dove to gain speed and split that devil in the middle! The extreme violence and deafening noise that accompanied my foolish action will always be in my memory as will be the tongue-lashing I received when the Cub was taken out of service for an inspection.

As I went on to solo the T-6 with my same instructor, a WWII P-51 pilot, he made sure I knew that I should "lock my rudder and use both hands to hold the stick in the center if I ever found myself vertical with no airspeed." He had not cleared me for solo acrobatics, but as I deemed myself perfectly capable of doing anything with an airplane...what could possibly go wrong? My barrel roll went perfectly and I started a loop. I had never looked at the airspeed DURING a loop before and saw it slowing through 40 kts. When I saw the low airspeed, I instinctively pushed the nose forward which killed the engine and I was vertical with no airspeed or power. I locked the controls in panic, remembering my instructor's words! The very loud head-snapping "whump" that accompanies a violent whip stall after sliding backwards led me to terminate my flight early and anxiously inspect my bird for bent tail feathers. I explained my actions to my instructor, and he told me he expected me to push my limits and was pleased I had remembered his instructions if I found myself in trouble!!! Lesson: LISTEN TO YOUR INSTRUCTOR, BUT "PUSHING THE LIMIT" IS BEST RESERVED FOR AFTER YOU HAVE SOME EXPERIENCE.

Our graduation speaker from Primary Training at Malden AB, MO was none other than the famous, Col. Roscoe Turner, a good friend of the civilian contract flight school owner. The first words Roscoe spoke as he looked at the hungover cadets in the seats of that WWII theater seemed to apply directly to me. He said, "I've forgotten more about flying than any of you bastards will ever know." He was a dashing man, wearing a splendid uniform, had won major races in his "Turner Special" aircraft and was famous for carrying his pet lion cub named, "Gilmore," with him in his aircraft. After listening spellbound to stories of his daring air escapades, I walked to the stage and my new idol shook my hand and handed me my certificate of completion! I couldn't wait to get my hands on a jet!

My next assignment took me to Greenville AFB, MS for training in the T-28 and T-33. We now had all military instructors and my instructor was a captain who had flown P-47s in WWII. Our flight leader was a major who had four German aircraft kills to his credit, including a Luftwaffe ME-262 jet fighter.

Upon arrival, all new cadets were assembled in the base theater and the Wing Commander gave us our first briefing. It was not good. He showed us pictures of the wreckage of a T-33 enmeshed in the structure of the Greenville bridge crossing the Mississippi, caused by a cadet who had recently tried to fly under the bridge, but who kept "chickening out" and misjudged his speed and position over the bridge on his last attempt. Chains were hung from the bridge deck to discourage future cadets from succumbing to such a tempting challenge!!

Basic training consisted of formation and instruments with "rat-racing" in between. I found that flying aircraft with a nose wheel was a lot easier than a taildragger, especially with cross winds! My wannabe fighter pilot desire was enhanced, when Major Chuck Yeager briefed us on what we should do if we got in a dog fight with a MiG 15. I just knew I would kick my adversaries butt!

It was winter in Greenville, and I had an early morning solo T-33 flight. My preflight went well, and I didn't think much about the thin coat of frost on the aircraft; after all, this was a jet and a new one at that! I was cleared for takeoff and it felt good to accelerate rapidly in the cooler morning air. I reached my takeoff speed and raised the nose to leave the runway, suck the gear and flaps up and climb away into the blue. The aircraft didn't leave the runway! I checked my airspeed and had way more than needed to get airborne, so I increased my attitude, still on the runway! I knew something was wrong but now I was going too fast to stop and the runway end was fast approaching. In desperation, I pulled the nose way up and the plane came off the ground, barely flying with little runway left, and feeling like it was going to wobble its way back to the surface. And, my airspeed was high! Gear and flaps up, and LOTS of airspeed and I was finally climbing. As my heart rate lowered, Lesson: I REALIZED THE THIN LAYER OF FROST ON THE WINGS CAUSED A LOSS OF LIFT THAT ALMOST CAUSED ME TO CRASH; A LESSON I NEVER FORGOT. I left Greenville with gold bars and silver wings and a great appreciation for thin coats of frost. Fighters next!!

After the first phase of fighter training in AT-33s at Laughlin AFB, TX, I transferred to Luke AFB, AZ to fly the F-84. As Oscar Brand sang in his "Give Me Operations" song: "Don't give me an F-84, she's just a ground loving whore..." It was the truth, especially with the hot Phoenix temps in the summer and the loads we carried for training. I had hurt my back playing pool polo at the O-club on Saturday but felt I could still fly a high angle bomb training sortie on Monday because I didn't want to wash back a class by missing training with a medical condition. I released my bomb and started my pull out and the G-force caused a sharp stabbing pain in my lower back. I released some stick pressure to ease off the G and immediately realized if I didn't pull harder, I would make a large hole in the desert. I clenched my teeth and tried to lessen the pull, but the pain was excruciating. I raised dust on the ground at the bottom and was immediately kicked off the range. However, my sortie counted and my next one was air-to-air with lots of aspirin. Lesson: ANYTHING THAT HURTS ON THE GROUND CAN HURT A LOT MORE IN THE AIR, ESPECIALLY PULLING Gs!

The Korean Armistice stopped my fighter dreams, and I was sent to troop carriers where I flew the C-119, C-123, and later the new C-130. I was stationed at Misawa AB, Japan and was pilot in a C-119 that was climbing through 32,000 ft. attempting to get above cirrus to catch a balloon-borne camera that had overflown Russia. I needed to relieve myself and plugged my oxygen mask hose into a yellow oxygen bottle. As I descended the stairs from the cockpit, I felt funny and fell. My winch operator from the crew in back saw me and plugged my bottle back in because I had accidentally pulled it out descending the stairs. Lesson: OXYGEN HELPS WITH HANGOVERS BUT IS ESSENTIAL AT ALTITUDE. WHEN THE AIRCRAFT IS NOT PRESSURIZED, WALKING AROUND REQUIRES PORTABLE OXYGEN - OXYGEN THAT IS PLUGGED-IN!

I was showing the short field abilities of the new Assault C-123 to a congressional committee and had a very light aircraft with little fuel taking off from the dirt surface on a drop zone. Both engines quit simultaneously on my steep initial climb. I made a very abrupt push on the yolk to get the nose down and within seconds, before hitting trees, both engines roared to life. The fuel in the nacelles uncovered the drain to the engines with my rapid acceleration and steep climb. That was the flight that put the warning in the Dash One about minimum fuel for takeoff and climb. Lesson: THERE IS ALWAYS MORE TESTING TO BE COMPLETED WITH NEW AIRCRAFT. WARNINGS ARE ISSUED FOR THINGS THE TEST FORCE MISSED.

I flew the C-130 in various configurations to include the drone carrying DC-130. The drones were Ryan Firebee jets modified for reconnaissance missions over denied territory. On one of my stateside training sorties the drone was launched off the left near pylon, and after dropping, it climbed right back up and my #2 prop hit the drone's vertical stabilizer. It happened right next to my cockpit window, and I broke hard right to get distance because my prop had chewed the drone beacon off and its 100-foot parachute would open without signal in 30 seconds. It did, but I was out of the way! Lesson: IN AVIATION IF IT CAN HAPPEN, IT PROBABLY WILL, USUALLY AT THE WORST POSSIBLE TIME.

A very close call occurred while we operated out of Bien Hoa AB, RVN. I was returning at night from a drone mission, and we routinely turned our lights off on final approach due to enemy ground fire in the area. Tower had cleared me to land, and I was about two miles on final, when one of the local B-57s called-in about the same distance. We both put on our landing lights and he peeled away to the right. He had been within probably 20 feet of my DC-130. After that, I kept my formation lights on (on top of the fuselage). Lesson: EVIL LURKS IN DARKNESS AND ONLY THE SHADOW KNOWS WHERE!

There was considerable effort to take out a bridge near Than Hoa, NVN and there had been heavy AAA. I was flying a DC-130 over the Gulf of Tonkin to launch a low altitude drone to cover the bridge for BDA. Both the primary and backup drones checked good via remotes with the recovery unit at Da Nang, so I was on my way north toward my launch point, when my #3 engine hydraulic light came on. I shut #3 engine down as well as #1 to prevent damage to my flight control booster hydraulic system. I fired-up both drones and left them wide open to assist with thrust keeping speed up for my assigned launch time. The primary was launched, and I turned south towards Da Nang keeping the backup drone operating. I declared an emergency with Da Nang tower and was told to hold over the water as I was number seven in the emergency pattern! There was an AD-1 with a blind pilot whose wingman was trying to get him set down in the area between the runways. He was successful and eventually I was cleared to land behind a DC-8 and an 0-1. I was directed to turn at the second turnoff as there was another emergency close behind me. I made one of the best short field landings ever with just two engines and didn't overrun that 0-1! Lesson: EMERGENCY MEANS DIFFERENT THINGS TO OTHERS! WHEN YOU ARE NUMBER SEVEN IN THE EMERGENCY PATTERN IT'S TIME FOR YOUR BROW TO FURROW.

It was nice to have "the system" watching us to keep us from getting in too deep at times. I was on another trip up the Gulf of Tonkin at low level and happy to see the weather over NVN looking good for a low drone mission over the Haiphong port facility and naval yard. We were about to start checklists for drone start, when we received a "Sky King" message via HF radio. We authenticated and it said to abort the launch and return to Bien Hoa. I answered with an ETA for Bien Hoa. I noted during mission debrief that the weather was much better than normal and asked my Ops Officer why we had been recalled. He told us we intercepted information the NVN had found out our launch point and had sampans with AAA waiting for us. Our launch criteria for low altitude drones was 200 kts. at 2,000 ft. over the water, so we would have been very vulnerable sitting ducks had we not aborted our launch. Lesson: YOU ARE NEVER REALLY ALONE ON A MISSION, AND ALL SAMPANS ARE NOT FISHERMEN.

I returned to Davis-Monthan AFB from overseas and was given command of the U-2 squadron. I trained in the U-2C, because the new and larger U-2R was taxed to the max training pilots for the many missions being flown around the world. Both versions had the same J-75 engine, but the "R" model was almost twice as heavy as the older "C" in which the pilot used a partial pressure suit instead of the full pressure "astronaut" suit. On my first high flight, the throttle friction wouldn't hold and the engine EGT over temp light kept coming on requiring me to finally hold the throttle with my left hand. I kept thinking I'd be able to fix it when I reached cruise altitude and could use the autopilot, but trying to hand fly and navigate, it became obvious I was in danger of overtasking. The next thing that occurred was the sudden loss of heat to my face piece. The facemask immediately frosted over, and I couldn't see! Things were going really well. I felt blindly for the circuit breaker and reset it, no help. It was time to descend to an altitude where I could remove the face piece and go home. I called center and informed them I was on a westerly heading, descending but didn't know my altitude and was using the horizon to hold attitude (light is up, dark is down). I felt for the switch to open engine bleeds and knew that worked because the cabin altitude went up fast! I put down the gear, opened the speed brakes and nudged the throttle back a bit hoping my engine would keep running. I was happy I wasn't getting any buffeting that indicated I was reaching airspeed limits (slow or fast) and just concentrated on holding my attitude. I had been flying for quite a while and decided to open my face piece and found I was at just over 20,000 feet! I pushed the nose down while turning east and leveled at 13,000. I informed center that I would be returning to Davis-Monthan, and they gave me a vector toward home. Lesson: TRYING TO FIX THINGS WHILE STILL FLYING A MISSION IN A U-2 IS DUMB, ESPECIALLY WHEN YOU HAVE LOW EXPERIENCE IN THE AIRCRAFT AND WINDOW SCRAPPERS ARE NOT ISSUED FOR FACEPLATES.

Flying the U-2C was a blast due to its thrust being greater than its weight at other than near maximum gross weight. I fell victim to this seductive capability early one calm morning, when on a local currency flight. As you might imagine, acceleration was awesome, and after a short takeoff roll of perhaps 300 feet, I pulled the nose up to vertical and held a 120 kt. climb airspeed. Normally, 160 kts. was used for climb and the sensation of climbing vertically felt different because I was no longer "sitting" on the seat cushion and my feet felt like they wanted to leave the rudder pedals. I noticed a light come on near the only fuel quantity gauge on the instrument panel which indicated I had less that 90 gallons in the sump tank that fed the engine. I then realized I had a dilemma! Fuel from the wings would not transfer fast enough in this attitude to keep the sump tank full at the rate the engine was emptying it. I didn't dare push the yoke forward for fear of negative "Gs" causing the engine to quit. I didn't dare pull back and roll out as that might cause structural failure of the lightly built aircraft and the roll rate was very slow. So, I looked straight ahead (which at the time was straight up) and said, "Lord I need help!" He answered, "Use rudder, dummy," and so I ruddered the nose to the right until I was only at about a 75 deg. climb, gently rolled to center the yaw string and continued climb. As I was complementing myself on what was obviously a very good "show climb," I got a call from my mobile control stating that "Alpha" (my wing commander) wanted to see me when I landed. This was usually not good news. I entered his office and saluted, and he motioned to me to accompany him to his car. We went outside and he didn't even start the car before letting me know that he was not pleased with my steep climb. He had never flown the U-2 because he was too tall to fit in the cockpit and had no idea of its performance; however, he did understand someone "shining their ass." We drove around for an hour, and I was not sure I was going to remain in command of the U-2 squadron, or anything else. As far as he was concerned, I was not leading the squadron toward the safety award he wanted for the wing. I did keep my squadron. Lesson: YOU NEVER KNOW WHO MIGHT BE WATCHING, BUT YOU CAN BET IT WILL BE SOMEONE IF YOU DECIDE TO "SHINE YOUR ASS."

After looking at just a small review of things that happened during my 32 years in the Air Force, I feel the Good Lord wanted to keep me around so he could impress on me how much I needed Him. He's still helping, and I won't make another vertical takeoff climb until I'm on my way to Heaven.

CHAPTER EIGHT

A LIFE CHANGING CHOICE

by Pat Halloran

As a starter, I was raised on a farm in Minnesota and after high school went to Minneapolis where I was a music major in college. In 1949, I joined the Air Force and graduated with cadet class 50-E. My first assignment was the 31st Fighter Wing at Turner AFB, GA flying SAC F-84s. We didn't go to any gunnery training in those days, you just went to your new unit and they trained you. After 18 months with the 31st, including five months TDY in the UK, a large group of us pilots were transferred to Korea to backfill units.

God, I hate to get up this early in the morning, but the mission should be an exciting one, and it will be number 42 for me en route to 100. I remember when I first got to Taegu, (K-2) in December of 1951, our crew hut had about 12 pilots, sleeping on canvas camping cots, with sleeping bags and one pot-bellied oil stove in the middle to fight the bitter Korean winters. In my first month, four bunks went empty so fast I couldn't believe it. I had only flown three missions at that time, and that number 100 looked like a long reach.

Today is a "tunnel busting" mission, and they could be really rewarding if everything worked out as planned. The eastern part of North Korea is a mountainous country and the Commies have devised a plan to do all their rail activity at night and hide their trains in mountain tunnels during the day. Our missions in the F-84 were all air-to-mud, but trains had eluded us because of their hiding them during the day. If we got in the area early enough and scouted around those tunnels, you might still see a bit of steam coming out one end of the tunnel as the trains went "cold iron" and bedded down for the day. We had devised a technique of using skip bombing by approaching the tunnel entrance, right on the deck, and with practice, you could eyeball a release point and that 500 pounder might skip right down the track and into the tunnel.

We took off at about 0500 and headed north. Wally Garrick, an old timer about ready to go home, was flight lead, and I led the element as #3. As we crossed into North Korea, dawn was breaking over the horizon, so we headed for our assigned areas and started to scout for rail tracks that would eventually lead us to tunnels. Wally spotted a candidate, and we descended to a lower altitude to check out the tunnel. Sure enough, there was still a bit of smoke rolling out one end. We executed the plan of Wally and his wingman taking one entrance and I, with my wingman, would take the other on the opposite side. We separated and each element headed away to get in position to descend and head down the narrow mountain valley with a track leading to our targets. In my case, the valley made a turn to the right as it reached the mountain face, and the track continued directly into the tunnel. It provided a short but straight run over the track to get set up for the drop. Our wingmen were spaced well behind so as to observe the first drop and then go in for their run, if required.

I turned down my valley and it looked like a perfect run. As I got to the release point, I dropped a 500 pounder and made a hard right break to follow the valley. What we didn't know, was that the Koreans had seen this tactic a couple of times by now and had decided to install a AAA battery on the side of the hill right above the tunnels. Just as I released my bomb, they opened up. I was a sitting duck at ground level and looking right into the guns. I felt a number of hits as I started my break. One of the shots hit my right wingtip fuel tank, and it exploded leaving the tank opened-out like a blooming flower. The drag immediately overpowered my controls and the plane continued an uncontrolled hard right roll beyond 90 degrees. For a moment I thought I had it, as I couldn't stop the roll, and I was probably 50 feet above the valley floor. I reached for the emergency jettison handle and pulled it. The wings went clean including the tip tank remnants. I immediately regained aileron control and rolled wings level a couple of feet above the ground and headed for the sky. I called that there was a battery over the tunnel and that I had been hit. As I cleared the mountain, Wally slid in on my wing and checked me over. By this time I was getting a lot of smoke in the cockpit coming from down by my feet. I switched to 100% oxygen but had difficulty seeing the instruments. Wally said, "Let's head for the beach," and sent the two wingmen home. As the smoke continued, it was increasingly difficult to see, but Wally couldn't see any sign of fire. The smell and eye burning was extremely acrid and indicated an electrical or possible hydraulic fire of some kind. As we headed east for the coast, the condition worsened, and I considered a bailout as I was almost blind. An alternate idea flashed in my mind, and I reached up and hit the "canopy open" switch. It opened about three inches and jammed because I was still going about 350 knots. Immediately, the draft cleared the cockpit of smoke and in about another five minutes the fire also extinguished as no more smoke was coming up from the floor. I breathed a sigh of relief and proceeded to close the canopy, but it wouldn't budge. We slowed down to accommodate the open canopy and headed south down the coastline. It soon became obvious that I didn't have enough fuel to make it back home since my tips were gone and our consumption was high at this lower altitude and slow speed. Wally found an alternate field about 50 miles ahead. It was a South Korean base and they were flying P-51s from there. At least it had an adequate runway for us to use, so that's where we landed. An interesting experience followed.

On a later mission, I encountered the worst gunner in the North Korean Air Force. We were heading north to bomb a supply depot, and I filled in #4 as a spare. We had just descended through an overcast, when I suddenly had canon fire zipping right by my canopy. I glanced back and there was a MiG on my tail at about 50 yards shooting like crazy. We were right below the overcast, so I called him out and pulled up into the clouds. I held it level for a few seconds and then dropped back down hoping that he would be right in front of me. He was, but by quite a distance and pulling away. I fired at him anyway because that's what fighter pilots do, but to no avail. We didn't see many MiGs in our ground role, but I wound up getting nailed on 10 of my missions by AAA. That iron Republic product would just take it in stride. From Korea, I went to Dow AFB, Maine to another SAC F-84 outfit. In due course, our wing moved from Dow to Tinker AFB and SAC bombers took over Dow.

Most pilots didn't realize that SAC had fighter wings, but Curtis LeMay had six wings of F-84s doing the same mission as TAC. They were all led by WWII fighter aces. I had wing commanders like Dave Schilling, Jerry Johnson and Hub Zemke.

It was getting downright boring doing nothing but the same training, day-after-day on the same ranges. War is exciting, and post war is the pits. One day, my commander called me in for a special chat. He said there was a new Top Secret volunteer program about to open. He said it would be a small outfit, and the vehicle we would fly, was single engine, single seat and would fly so high that we would be wearing space suits. Now, that got my attention! I still loved flying fighters and being with some really great pilots, but the immediate future looked like a lot of "sameness." It turned out to be the major turning point of my military career and the hardest decision I had to make since entering the Air Force. I said, "I'll take it," and never looked back as I headed for the U-2 program at Laughlin AFB, TX.

The planes hadn't been delivered yet from Area 51, so the day the planes came in was exciting, as none of us had ever seen the machine, only some fuzzy pictures. We were dumbfounded at what we saw . . .a jet powered glider instead of the sleek supersonic bird that would take us to the edge of space that we had imagined! That was painful enough, but when I took a look in the cockpit, I was further dismayed to find a control wheel instead of a stick!

No simulator, no two-seat trainer, only two Instructor Pilots with about 10 hours each. It would mark the end of my boredom. A cockpit check, and away you went to figure it out yourself. The landings were the worst. It wouldn't quit flying with those long wings unless you were in a full shuddering stall. Once on the ground, it was difficult to keep directional control with that single gear in the middle and just that tiny tail wheel for steering . . .yes, the only jet in the inventory that had a tail wheel. When you finally lost aileron effectiveness, the wing with the most fuel would fall to the ground and drag you to a stop; no differential braking as both brake pedals actuated on the same center wheel.

Three days before my first flight, Fred Lowcock took off at 0800 on his first flight. An hour and ten minutes later, he crashed and was killed. Four hours later, Leo Smith, on his third flight, crashed from high altitude and was killed - maybe this self-training program wasn't quite up to speed yet.

It was a real thrill as you quickly passed 40,000 feet, probably as high as you had ever been in a fighter, and continued passing 50K, then 60K and making your initial level off as you reached 70K. You felt like you were detached from the world as you silently soared along your flight path above

95% of the atmosphere, with a nearly black sky and a thin blue line on the horizon, which was the atmosphere through which you had already passed. You were very conscious of the life-saving purpose of your partial pressure space suit as you looked at the cockpit altimeter reading 29,000 feet (hmm, that's Mt. Everest) and the aircraft altimeter reading 72,000 feet; never been here before! The only sound you heard was your own breathing of the 100% oxygen which you had started using two hours before takeoff to rid your body of nitrogen.

Flameouts were frequent in the original engines and fuel controls were constantly being tweaked to accommodate the very thin air. Air starts seemed to always work at about 30,000 feet, **b**ut there were also quite a few dead stick landings from various malfunctions; I had two of them... one was when I was returning from a Cuba mission. I was way out in the middle of the Gulf of Mexico on a direct line to New Orleans, my coast in point, when the engine suddenly quit for no apparent reason. My cockpit pressurization was lost, so my cockpit pressure slowly climbed to 70,000 feet and my space suit activated in a full squeeze. That probably saved my life. I headed for Eglin AFB, FL 200 miles away, and did a very long glide at 100 kts, making it to the field at 1,200 feet, and circled for a landing. I had attempted several air starts during the descent, but the engine wouldn't start.

We had detachments all over the world from which we flew our missions. A couple of our missions out of Alaska went all the way to the North Pole using celestial navigation. We found the missiles in Cuba in 1962 and continued that coverage until they were removed. One pilot, Rudy Anderson, was shot down by a SAM. We moved into Bien Hoa, Vietnam in February of '64 and spent the next year photographing almost all of the North. On one later mission, we photographed the first SAM site that we found in the North. It was the same day Friday Pilot, Russ Violett's flight, was attacked by a different SAM. We stayed in theater until the end of the war.

I had one major incident happen in the U-2 that was the closest I ever came to getting killed flying airplanes. I was at altitude on a training flight, when I felt a hot flush in my face followed by some hyperventilation. Suddenly the oxygen breathing bladder inside my pressure helmet collapsed, and I realized I was out of oxygen. I was at 72,000 feet, but 29,000 in the cockpit, with no oxygen. Useful consciousness at that altitude can be about a minute. I quickly went through a dozen options on how to get down, but there is no rapid descent in the U-2. You can't just pull the throttle to idle, roll over and head down. It'll tear apart. Any abrupt throttle movement would flame out the engine and you would lose pressurization immediately and then be at 72,000 feet in the cockpit. I was trapped at altitude! In one more frantic sweep of the cockpit, through rapidly narrowing gun barrel vision, I happened to look at the rearview mirror on the right windshield frame. In the mirror, I saw a flash of polished aluminum swinging back and forth. It was my oxygen hose connection between the aircraft system and my suit. On the very last edge of consciousness, I managed to twist, grope behind me, find the hose and hook it up; a very, very close call. Since I was on autopilot, heading west, I would have wound up somewhere in the middle of the Pacific Ocean as I had almost 10 hours of fuel! Lesson: OXYGEN, NOT LIQUOR, IS THE AQUA VITAE OF LIFE.

After nine years of exciting flying in the U-2, eight of us were selected to join five crews from the B-58 Hustler and go to Beale AFB to start the SR-71 program. Lesson: THE SR-71 IS THE FASTEST AND HIGHEST FLYING JET AIRPLANE ANYWHERE IN THE WORLD. AS WE REACHED MACH 3, WE THROTTLED BACK TO CRUISE; A LOT OF POWER LEFT. At normal cruising speed, we went coast-to-coast in about an hour, Yew York to London in an hour and 55 minutes and flights to the Middle East, and back, in a little over 10 hours. Our cameras could photograph 100,000 square miles in one hour. Like all of Kelly Johnson's Lockheed airplanes, it was a dream to fly…impossible to make a bad landing and smooth as glass at over 2,000 mph. In 600 hours of flying the plane, I never had a major problem or malfunction. Our two primary detachments were at Kadena, Okinawa and Mildenhall, U.K. From those two locations, plus home base at Beale AFB, CA, we could cover the world.

My mind goes back to that difficult decision I made back in Oklahoma to leave my comfortable career in fighters and take on something new and unknown. It was the decision that changed my life. I can only say, Lesson: DON'T BE AFRAID TO LOOK AT OPTIONS. OUR LIVES ARE A RESULT OF CHOICE. I had 34 years of service and retired with over 8,000 hours of flying time - what a ride!

CHAPTER NINE

SO, YOU WANT TO BE A THUNDERBIRD?

by Bill Hosmer

I flew on the U.S. Air Force Thunderbird team in F-100s for two and one-half years in 1961-1963. I flew left wing and could still do it today, but I am 90-years old, and I can't find anyone dumb enough to let me try.

Growing up in Dunseith, North Dakota, 13 miles south of the Canadian border was a cold and isolating experience, at least in the winter. My dad was a mailman and my mother a nurse. It was a town of about 500 people, a farming community with limited opportunities. My first seven grades were in a small schoolhouse, two grades to a room. My uncle graduated from West Point in 1936 and entered the Infantry. He later transferred to the Army Air Corps, became a pilot and on a couple of occasions buzzed our town and landed in a nearby pasture in pre-WW II trainers. My interest in aviation began in that pasture south of Dunseith. My interest in the Thunderbirds would come much later.

To my family's eternal credit, they realized I had a serious interest in pursuing West Point and a flying career as had my uncle. They also realized the academic level of our small Dunseith high school with its limited curriculum would not prepare me for the journey to which I aspired. I moved to Seattle to live with my grandparents and pursue a better education. I stayed in Seattle for two years, then moved to Minnesota to live with my pilot uncle who was getting a masters degree at the University of Minnesota. One of my "chores" was to babysit my younger cousin, Bradley Hosmer. I think I did a good job. Brad was a cadet in the first class at the Air Force Academy, graduated first in his class, became a Rhodes

Scholar and retired as a three-star general and Superintendent of the Air Force Academy.

My family did not "farm me out." It was out of love, realizing my limited educational opportunities in Dunseith, that they decided to let me go to better schools starting in eighth grade. I know it was sad for my mother, when she dropped me off with my grandparents, but their investment in my education paid off. Lesson: THERE IS NO GREATER LOVE THAN A PARENT'S SACRIFICE FOR THEIR CHILD'S EDUCATION.

I received an appointment and started West Point in 1949, graduating with the class of 1953. I was not first in my class, nor a Rhodes scholar like my cousin, Brad, but I was tan, fit and ready to take my commission in the United States Air Force and become a pilot.

Pilot training in T-6s, T-28s and T-33s followed West Point, and I received an assignment to F-86s at Nellis AFB, NV, my first step towards "Thunderbirdism." The F-86 was "the" fighter of the Korean war but was soon to be replaced by the F-100. I was really excited by becoming a fighter pilot in the airplane that swept Korean MiGs from the skies, but I had an auspicious beginning. On my "first" solo flight in the F-86, I crashed on landing, a serious, no-fooling crash that knocked me unconscious, beat me up and bloodied me badly. My carpool mate crashed on the same day and another classmate was killed a week later. I was down for six weeks before resuming training. It was a rough introduction to fighter aviation. After Nellis, I spent a one-year unaccompanied F-86 tour in Korea. My wife, Pat, a patient and dedicated mother, and our growing family, stayed in Montana. After Korea, I returned to Nellis to be an Instructor Pilot (IP) in the F-100A.

The F-100A was the first of the Century Series fighters and the first jet capable of supersonic speed in level flight. It also had a small tail and could be a wild ride at high angles of attack. The accident rate was very high. Also, it required good briefings and "quick" instruction because it had "short legs," only 45 minutes of fuel, with its internal tank and hard wings. The closest I came to losing an A-model was not me, but a student. We went up on an instrument ride. We did not have any two-place aircraft, the two-seat F-model came later. So, I told the student to lower his seat, stay on instruments, don't cheat and don't look outside, and hold the heading I gave him. He was compliant, STRICTLY compliant, and at the same time I realized he had a radio failure. I came up on his left wing. I came up on his right wing. I came from high and I came from low to get his attention, but he kept his head down as instructed and held his heading as we were approaching "Bingo" fuel with our 45 minute endurance. Finally, I cut right in front of him, shaking his airplane and got his attention. I patted my shoulder as a signal for, "get on my wing," and we returned to the Nellis pattern well below minimum fuel. Lesson: STRICT ADHERENCE TO ORDERS IS AN ADMIRABLE QUALITY BUT HAS ITS LIMITATIONS.

Having returned from my remote in Korea and now well into an F-100 IP tour at Nellis, and assignment to the Fighter Weapons School, Pat and I were prepared for an overseas "accompanied" tour in Europe. We didn't care whether we went to Italy, Germany, France or the U.K., but we were excited we would be together as a family on a foreign adventure. Not so fast, Capt. Hosmer. The country was in recession and the Berlin Crisis was simmering. President Eisenhower cancelled all European overseas accompanied tours as a budget saving measure and a message of resolution to Nikita Khrushchev over Berlin. Our hopes for family foreign adventure were down the drain, and I talked to Pat about volunteering for the Thunderbirds. She agreed it was our next best option for some semblance of family life. As we joined the team in 1961, President Kennedy reversed Eisenhower's decision and permitted accompanied travel once again. Lesson: TIMING IS EVERYTHING IN LIFE.

The process of Thunderbird application was well-defined in Air Force regulations: letter of interest, paperwork including flying time and education, interviews with the team, flying tryouts with the lead, selection and approval by headquarters and notification. Five of us applied. I did not emphasize the crash on my first F-86 solo as a qualifier, but they all knew about it. I flew once with the team leader, Maj. Bob Fitzgerald, just basic formation, stuff, nothing exotic. I only knew one team member, Bob Janca. The interviews with the team were friendly, non-threatening. They were all looking for chemistry, image and would a selectee fit well with the team. I guess I was OK, because I was selected. I wasn't too fat, nor too skinny, and I didn't have any ugly facial scars from my crash that detracted from team PR photos, no limp, could climb the cockpit ladder with vigor, owned a big watch and could hold my beer. I was assigned to train for the "left wing," #2 position, to replace Bob Janca.

My training for the team started in February 1961. We flew the F-100C and practiced northwest of Nellis and north of the Indian Springs airfield in the wide valley south of the super-secret Area 51. The Indian Springs runway gave us a good target to train over for our airshow season tour. By mid-March, I was a full-up round and ready for my first season, wet behind the ears, but ready. The train-up flights were intense, two-a-day with briefings and debriefings. We started simple and then introduced more complicated maneuvers. Hoot Gibson came on the team as the new leader after I joined. Hoot was one of the nicest fighter pilots I ever met, a true gentleman and a good leader. We finally got an F-100F two-seat model, and Bob Fitzgerald whom Hoot was replacing, took Capt. George Nial, our advance pilot and team narrator, in the backseat to watch Hoot's leadership techniques, offer suggestions and checkout the recovery altitude from over-the-top maneuvers. As we were practicing, out of my peripheral vision on the left wing, I caught sight of our chase F and saw a huge fireball. The old team leader and narrator had crashed while observing us. Lesson: THERE IS NO SIMPLE MISSION WHILE FLYING FIGHTERS. EVERY TASK DEMANDS YOUR FULL ATTENTION.

This was a rude introduction to the team and a sad start to the season, but we headed for our first show at Seymour Johnson AFB, NC attended by many of the head Air Force brass. It was my first big event and I was naturally nervous, but after our arrival show and a couple of beers, I settled-in for the season. Signing autographs for the crowd was always enjoyable, moms, dads, kids thinking you were some kind of god to be able to perform such daring and dangerous feats. Little did they know the practice and planning that went into each event to prevent it from being daring and dangerous.

The season itself was a brutal schedule, two-three shows a week, back home for five or six days, two practices a day while home, time to wash your flying suits, relearn your kids' names and back on the road again. We started the season with one solo pilot and integrated another. That required additional practice with new maneuvers. It was hard on families. Pat and I had a "Thunderbird baby," now a family of three kids, and it all fell on her. Lesson: GOD BLESS WOMEN!

Pilots have heard that Thunderbirds flew with "full nose-down trim." Is it true, and if so, why would anyone do that? The answer is, yes, but let me explain. We all started out as "trim wimps," trimming the stick for neutral as we had always done in formation. As we progressed into difficult maneuvers, you realized you did not want a neutral stick force. You wanted to always know where your aircraft was headed in any maneuver and with full nose-down trim, it was always nose down and you held stick force against it and learned it gave you better and more predictable stability in formation. Also, full nose down trim was a natural enabler for inverted flight. Lesson: WHEN YOUR RIGHT ARM BICEP IS AS BIG AS YOUR LEG, YOU ARE A REAL THUNDERBIRD. We even had pictures taken showing our large right biceps.

One of my most enjoyable trip was our South America tour. It was enjoyable with huge and enthusiastic crowds, but also some of it, very tough flying with high altitude shows. The things that make a show difficult are weather, winds, terrain and altitude. Weather goes without saying and the very lowest we could do a "low show" was 1,500 ft. overcast with 2,500 ft. preferred. Bright and sunny days did not always mean a good show as they could bring strong winds. Strong winds meant heavy turbulence and heavy turbulence meant very difficult formation flying. As a general rule, we flew with "three feet wingtip overlap." There were stripes painted on the Thunderbird aircraft wings, one red, one white, one blue separated by one foot each, and the lead could tell us to move it out a foot or two or three feet. Terrain was always a factor to consider in preflight briefings. When you came out of an over-the-top maneuver, you did not want to bottom out pointing into rapidly rising terrain. Locations such as the Air Force Academy with its nearby steep mountains provided particular challenges. In South America we did an airshow in Ecuador at 9,600 ft. field elevation and another in Bolivia at 13,485 ft. The aircraft does not perform at high altitude in less dense air like it does at sea-level. The controls feel mushy and engine thrust is less. The South America shows required great care and planning.

People ask if I was ever "scared," during my Thunderbird shows. No, but I was certainly "concerned" when my engine quit going into Rhode Island for an arrival show. I could not get an airstart and was too far out to attempt a flameout landing, so I ejected. My concern came when

I came down in trees near a public highway with significant spectator presence. I badly needed to relieve myself, and I could just see my picture in the morning papers. Lesson: ALWAYS EMPTY YOUR BLADDER COMPLETELY BEFORE EVERY FLIGHT.

Is the team a real tight "Band of Brothers?" Honestly, yes and no. There is a rumor that most fighter pilots are fiercely competitive, strong-willed, independent, risk takers and resistant to authority. It's a good guess. Given that, it should be no secret a team carefully assembled for compatibility can occasionally breakout into petty squabbles. In 1962, we were scheduled to perform at the United States Air Force Academy for the graduation flyover. '62 was the fourth class to graduate from USAFA and Vice President Lyndon Johnson was attending as was Gen. Curtis LeMay the Air Force Chief of Staff. Rejoins after a flight breakup maneuver are always dicey. Judging high speed closure rates for a rapid join up requires practice, skill, timing and some say, luck. On a rejoin, #3 on the right wing and #4, slot, clipped wingtips and an outer panel of one wingtip departed. It was not noticed by the crowd, but #3 said to #4, "Did you hit me?" The replay was, "No, you hit me." One can imagine such an unusual occurrence stresses team camaraderie. The debriefing was lively. Our ground crew did a miraculous quick fix for the next day departure, and I doubt the incident was ever reported up the chain. If anyone at USAFA ever finds a piece of Thunderbird wingtip on the Academy grounds, we can put it in the Thunderbird Museum at Nellis. When the class of '62 heard about the incident, they were sworn to a "code of silence." Lesson: SOMETIMES THE PRICE OF FREEDOM IS SILENCE.

A Thunderbird tour was normally 18 months, but at the completion of my tour, I was asked to extend a few months due to pilot rotation. I did and became the maintenance officer for our next European tour and flew the spare airplane on the rotation over and back. It was a great experience with days even longer than my flying days and included the Paris airshow and meeting and flying with demonstration teams from other countries. It was exciting and an honor to meet and associate with professional airmen from allied countries, a fantastic end to a Thunderbird career.

At the end of my tour, we were sent to Okinawa, a final opportunity for the family to be together, we thought. The Vietnam war intervened. I flew an F-105 tour in Vietnam followed by a return to Tactical Air

Command HQ for a staff job, then a second Vietnam tour as a squadron commander in F-100s at Tuy Hoa. After my second tour, we finally got our shot at a European assignment at Lakenheath AB, U.K. It was a great time. After Lakenheath, I attended Air War College in Montgomery, AL followed by a move to Vice Commander of the 355th TFW at Davis-Monthan AFB in Tucson. I later became Wing Commander. I was not on the promotion list to Brigadier General, so I decided to retire after 24 years of service with a smile on my face.

I had a subsequent career of 12 years flying as a Cessna Citation demonstration pilot all over the world. I flew to ever continent except Antarctica. I had my third, and hopefully final, crash during my years as a demo pilot. On takeoff in Wichita, I had a copilot in the right seat and two newsmen in the back. Takeoff was normal, but as I rotated and retracted the gear, both engine thrust reversers deployed. Whoa! When such happens, there is only one way - DOWN! I did not have time to put the gear back down and bellied the aircraft in on the infield grass. We all got out of the aircraft exit, no casualties, no injuries, no fire, lucky. Lesson: WHEN THE UNEXPECTED HAPPENS, YOUR INSTINCTS AND TRAINING TAKE OVER. I remembered the legendary Bob Hoover's great advice, "Fly the aircraft as far into the crash as possible."

I finished my flying life as a pilot in a Challenger for a Japanese businessman until the Japanese stock market crashed. I lived a dream flying life. Pat and I started "Snowbirding" to Tucson, and we spent time with my old Thunderbird lead, Hoot Gibson, who had become a real estate broker and also lived in Tucson. Tragically, Hoot was surveying a property, fell backwards off a rock and was killed, a tragic end for a wonderful man. Lesson: LIFE IS NOT FAIR EVEN TO THE BEST.

Pat passed away in 2010. She was a wonderful woman, wife and mother jerked through a rapid-fire military life in places she didn't want to be at times she didn't want to be there. It was a privilege to love her.

Since Pat's death, I have established a relationship with another wonderful woman in San Antonio, Elizabeth Russell Smith. Liz is the sister of one of my West Point classmates. Her older brother was killed in Vietnam. Lesson: HE WHO HAS TWO WONDERFUL WOMEN IN HIS LIFE IS INDEED BLESSED.

I am most often asked two questions about flying with the Thunderbirds: First, is what the Thunderbirds do dangerous? Second, are the Thunderbirds the best pilots in the Air Force?

On the first question, we report, you decide: The Thunderbird mission is to plan and present precision aerial maneuvers to exhibit the capabilities of modern, high-performance aircraft and the high degree of professional skill required to operate those aircraft. Flying high performance aircraft is inherently hazardous, especially when combined with close formation. The Thunderbirds were officially formed 67 years ago in 1953. They are the third oldest military aerobatic demonstration team continuously flying under the original name. The Patrouille de France is the oldest formed in 1931, followed by the Navy Blue Angels in 1946. In the Thunderbird team history of over 4,000 airshows, 21 pilots have been killed, three during airshows. So, you decide. Lesson: TRAINING AND PRACTICE CAN BE AS DANGEROUS AS THE REAL THING. Same goes for war.

On the second question: Surprisingly, any competent fighter pilot possesses the skills to be a Thunderbird. It takes desire, training and perseverance to put up with a rugged schedule, and it helps to have an understanding spouse. It also takes patience and a dose of humility. The skills required to safely fly tight formation under all kinds of circumstances do not come overnight. It requires practice and the ability to admit and handle criticism and mistakes from people who have already made them.

Lesson: SO, YOU WANT TO BE A THUNDERBIRD? - YOU CAN.

CHAPTER TEN

AS THE ROTORS TURNED
by Bruce Huffman

On the evening of November 3rd 1948, the headline of the Fairmont Times read "Dewey Defeats Truman" as Carl watched the youngest of his four sons, John Bruce, scoot across the linoleum floor of their Benton's Ferry home under the ever watchful eye of the family's collie mix, Butch. Bruce had come as somewhat of a surprise to the Huffman household being the youngest of four boys born into the family of Carl and Louise. His next oldest brother, Bob, was 15 years his senior. Brother, Ben, 18 years senior, was overseas with the 11th Airborne Division, while the oldest, Bill, 20 years his senior, was finishing his undergraduate degree at Fairmont State College.

The Huffman Family was blessed to be middle class, have two working parents with college educations, and a family home free of a mortgage in West Virginia. Good fortune brought many things, but the money never seemed to go far enough to support more than one college education which was granted to the oldest. The next son in line was left to make his way as a paratrooper in Japan. Having a new baby in the household gave Louise a new love in her life to dote after and shower with affection. I enjoyed my life as a toddler, but the shadow of cancer came over the family and cast a deep pall. This horrible disease claimed Louise a month before my fifth birthday. I remember my last moments with my mother as all said their goodbyes. I stood on my brother's shoulders and touched my mother's hands for the last time as she leaned from a lower window of the Fairmont General Hospital. Medical protocols of the period prohibited children under the age of 12 from entering the ICU.

Dad earned a promotion to Division Manager for a public utility that involved a relocation to the town of Mannington. He and I settled into a huge home at 23 Center Street, just behind the Methodist Church. I enrolled in the second grade and instantly made friends with other children whose parents shared similar education and backgrounds. Growing up in Mannington, a town of 2,762 total population, the son of a single parent, gave me endless opportunities for mischief. Dad tried to give me opportunities that his other sons had missed.

School and learning came easily to me and I was an above average student but was drawn to adventure. Along with a huge collection of DC Comics featuring Sgt. Rock of Easy Company, I built every model that Revell produced of the great military airplanes of the era. There was always something to do, and I relished it all. From Cub Scouting, Boy Scouts, 4-H, square dance lessons, nature camp, swimming, pony racing, skating, camping, biking, hiking, go-kart racing and, of all things, German lessons, I tried to see and do it all before the teenage years vanished.

Dad gave me many gift. Among them was Sunday following church. Dad and I would load up our 1950 Buick Roadmaster with the destination being my choice. Among those most favored, was the Greater Pittsburg International Airport. From the observation deck, one could watch and listen as those round motored TWA Constellations, Martins, and Allegheny DC-3s belched flame, made loud noises, and filled the air with blue smoke. Stories of West Virginia's two aviation heroes stimulated my interest. Pete Everest and Chuck Yeager were local heroes. Yeager hailed from the town of Nitro while Everest was from Fairmont. Finally, after failed attempts to go aloft in a secretly purchased helium filled Navy surplus weather balloon, I took my first flight at 13 on a Sunday afternoon in a V-tailed Beechcraft Bonanza from Clarksburg's Benedum Airport. My dream of becoming a military aviator gained traction.

Life had yet another sad hand to deal me. In October of 1962, Dad died unexpectedly of a heart attack sending me on an odyssey of growing up quickly and discovering the world beyond West Virginia. For the next three and a half years, my oldest brother, Robert, and his wife, Adrienne, graciously opened their home and became my legal guardians. Bob was a Master Sergeant in the U.S. Air Force living in Plattsmouth, Nebraska, while stationed with the Strategic Air Command at Offutt AFB. I adapted quickly to my new environment and got a job in produce at a local supermarket, thenmoved up to be a cashier. I also worked as a hired hand at a nearby farm. Times were good. Minimum wage plus .25 cents an hour seemed to be adequate compensation and met all the needs of cheerleaders, football games, learner's permit, and summers at the beach. Just when things had settled down to a comfortable routine, Bob walked into the apartment in the fall of 1964 with a set of orders in his hand assigning him to Chateauroux, France. FRANCE? How in the hell could this happen and where is France?

To say I was reluctant to leave the cheerleader behind and give up a job for a place where people barely showered on a regular basis and didn't even speak English, would be an understatement. How could life be any better than Plattsmouth, Nebraska? Within a week of arrival at Chateauroux, I was invited to Sunday dinner with a nice girl who lived in a chateaux with a French movie following desert. From that moment forward, Nebraska was in the rear-view mirror, and I never looked back.

As a military dependent, I participated in student government and high school varsity athletics. I traveled extensively with my brother and wife, with friends, and by myself throughout Europe. At the Châteauroux-Déols Air Depot (CHAD), I developed a deep and lasting love for things that flew. Many of my heroic role models included the parents of friends who had served in the Office of Strategic Services (OSS), Army Air Corps, Army and Air Force and were decorated veterans of WW II, Korea and the burgeoning conflict in Southeast Asia.

Following graduation from Chateauroux American High School, I bid adieu to the blond cheerleader in France, returned to West Virginia, and enrolled at West Virginia University as a pre-med student. Brother Bob gave me three career choices: engineer, lawyer, or doctor. "Aviator" was not in the mix. Academics became an afterthought to 3.2% beer, Paul Revere and the Raiders, employment as a carpenter to a local florist and other distractions. The semester ended, and I finished the semester with a C+ average for my non-efforts.

The call of the open road beckoned, and it was off to Nicholls State College, Thibodaux, LA to become a pre-med transfer student. The allure of the coon ass French culture, the promise of a job in a dairy, and no restrictions on alcohol consumption (the age of majority being 18 in Louisiana) beckoned. Academic mediocrity persisted as distractions consumed time I should have devoted to education.

Salvation came from the sky, as a UH-1D circled the campus and landed in the quad. Out popped a resplendent Army Major in an orange flight suit, a white helmet and a big handlebar moustache, sporting the shiniest Cochran jump boots in the world. I hung back until the crowd thinned and I approached the cockpit and looked in. I asked the Major, "How do you get to fly one of these?" The Major answered, "Son take this form to your local Army Recruiter, and he will schedule you to take the Flight Aptitude Scoring Test (FAST). If you qualify, you too can fly above the rest!" Boom! In a flash all problems were solved and my path to the future was clear. I took the tests, was poked and prodded by the medics, and an oath was administered. I boarded the "Grey Dog" for a six-hour ride from New Orleans to Ft. Polk, LA to complete Basic Combat Training as a precursor to entry into the Warrant Officer Flight Training Course. Lesson: WHO AMONGST US WOULD NOT TRADE MEDICAL SCHOOL FOR A LIFE IN HELICOPTERS? I HAD NO IDEA WHAT I WAS GETTING INTO.

The bus stopped, next to a partially lit parking lot, at 01:15 AM. The meanest, biggest, and angriest black guy in the world immediately began shouting obscenities as the new "meat" filed out of the bus and double-timed over to a painted number where we stood shivering, at parade rest for the next hour and a half, until bunks were assigned. I began to question my sanity. For the next eight weeks, I would share a latrine and shower and shave with 49 other new friends as we chanted, "More PT Drill Sergeant, More PT!" We ran to classes, learned to be expert marksmen and other tasks essential to the U.S. Army. Lesson: LITTLE DID I APPRECIATE HOW IMPORTANT SUCH SKILLS WOULD BECOME.

The anguish finally ended. I finished the course, surprisingly, as the distinguished graduate of the BCT Platoon with a perfect score on my PT test. The big benefit was I didn't appear on the kitchen police (KP) roster and was awarded a temporary set of corporal's stripes.

It was now off to Ft. Wolters, TX for the Primary Helicopter School as an E-5 - no more Drill Sergeants. As I descended the stairs of the bus in the Warrant Officer Candidate pre-flight area, familiar shouting began. This time it was a CW2 TAC Officer calling the cadence and the bullshit began anew with a vengeance. For the next 30 days, the TAC Officer gave the "Candidates" more floors to shine, more toilets to clean, more boots to polish, more PT to perform all while shouting, At least this time, the classes were ones that interested us: Rotary Wing Aerodynamics FM-1-51, meteorology, dead reckoning navigation, map reading, more assorted military field manuals, and technical manuals along with weapons qualification course on the M-16A rifle.

Finally, the effort paid a dividend. I found myself at the Downey Heliport where I was alphabetically assigned to a civilian instructor from Doss Aviation. Mac LeDoux was a Baptist pastor in Ft. Worth, with a large congregation, but had a passion for helicopter flying and teaching. Eight- and one-half hours of instruction later, I soloed in the TH-55 Osage. Initially a danger to myself and others, I gained experience in night flying, cross country navigation, formation flying, pinnacle and slope operations, all of which resulted in a graduation certificate. I was then off to Ft. Rucker, AL for tactical instrument training in the OH-13S, transition to the UH-1A, and finally into the UH-1D/B for tactics and gunnery. Providence was following me, and I survived a crash at Tactical Field X-Ray. It was a Class A (aircraft destroyed) on the last half of my final check ride. The UH-1A had a low side governor failure while the 21-year-old IP used all the rotor energy to clear a power line. The aircraft settled into the Alabama pine trees. I remember counting the rotations of the rotors as they chopped through the foliage. The only thought in my mind was, "This is really going to hurt!" and I wasn't disappointed. We survived with minor injuries. I had a slight spinal compression, but the graduation flight formation and pass in review were already completed. I had finally earned the wings of an Army Aviator.

Following graduation, I was assigned to the 1st Squadron 9th Cavalry, 1st Cavalry Division as a Huey pilot but soon transferred to the Hughes OH-6A LOH, attending the New Equipment Training Team aerial reconnaissance scouting team.

I joined the Cav, in the Vietnam post-Tet period, on the tail end of Operation Jeb Stuart at Camp Evans in the I Corps Tactical Zone. The Troop was withdrawing its forward deployed elements to Evans from Dong Ha, chased out of that position by 122 mm NVA artillery fire. Camp Evans was a big, dusty, dirty place with a runway, a fuel dump, an ammo dump and a helicopter maintenance battalion surrounded by nearly two hundred parked helicopters. I spent my first night in a bunker as the NVA 122 mm rockets slammed into the base camp. Our unit was made up of six UH-1H helicopters that supported the Blue infantry platoon, Long Range Reconnaissance Patrols 1/9th Delta Troop infantry, and an occasional mission to Forward Operating Base 1. The "short-timer" platoon leader assigned me to fly as the new guy for CW2 Gary Hoffman. I think that was done so he could just shout one name, "Hoffman!" and someone would answer.

Operation Pegasus kicked off along with snatch missions, resupply, Blue insertions and a big push to open Route 9, into the Marine Combat Base at Khe Sanh. I put my "new guy" tag behind me and was placed on Aircraft Commander orders within sixty days after stepping off the C-7A at Evans. The flying was fantastic, the camaraderie bordering on close family, and the food was acceptable (if one could just get through the chow line before the dark flakes of recently burned crap settled into your reconstituted potatoes) washed down with either bad coffee or warm orange Kool Aid. War became an exhilarating experience and the learning of life's lessons never stopped. One quickly adapted and learned to stay alive. Lesson: ONE LEARNED TO AVOID THOSE WHO WOULD MOST PROBABLY GET YOU KILLED; THAT GUY COULD BE A GUNNER, A GRUNT, A FELLOW PILOT, A PLATOON LEADER OR EVEN THE TROOP COMMANDER.

Operation Pegasus was deemed a great success. Route 9 was opened and secure, so the "thinkers" above Corps level, dreamed up the next adventure which turned out to be the 325th NVA Division and the logistical elements occupying the A Shau Valley. Operation Delaware was born. Charlie Troop was given the mission to neutralize an air corridor from Camp Evans across the mountains to the airfield at A Loui. The mission was to draw out the anti-aircraft artillery (AAA) assets by allowing them to shoot at us, marking their location, and then bringing in an airstrike to send them to "gomer heaven." The Troop did a good job. Unfortunately as those things go, the location of that corridor was never passed on to the division assault pilots. They lost 19 aircraft on the first day of the campaign. The "thinkers" failed to calculate the affect that low clouds and poor weather could have on success. Two full brigades were on the ground running short of nearly everything as huge pallets of badly needed supplies would fall from out of the clouds into the center of the valley floor. I went out on day one, inserting my Blues into what was known as Signal Hill. We from Lift, Scouts, and the Guns spent eleven nights before the clouds lifted enough to permit our return to Camp Evans. A few days later. the weather broke, and it was time to withdraw, declare a victory, and haul back the new NVA Russian truck and a 37mm AAA gun as prizes.

May 19th, 1968 was a day at Camp Evans like any other, filled with bad smells, noise, oppressive humidity and more orange Kool Aid; however, to the North Vietnamese it was a special day. It was Ho Chi Minh's Birthday! Late in the afternoon, four 122 mm rockets, were fired from the ridgeline south of the base. Their launch warning was relayed to the tower by a Bravo Troop Scout returning from a mission. The first round was long, the second round was short, but the next two landed in the POL storage area and the ammo dump igniting fires and explosions that would rock the night for the next twelve hours destroying 124 aircraft parked in revetments. Charlie Troop was three-fourths of a mile from the explosive epicenter, but the next day only seven of thirty-six aircraft were flyable. The "thinkers" should have been court-martialed, but it is uncertain if punishments were ever meted out. I spent a very restless night at the bottom of a bunker and hope never to hear noises as loud, nor see fireballs as big, ever again.

It was about this time in the twelve-month tour that my Troop Commander, Major John M. Toolson, became my mentor and lifetime career counselor. John saw character and other traits and encouraged me to develop my potential by pursuing continued military and civilian education. I took his advice to heart and did both before the end of my career. Major Toolson submitted me for a MACV commission and it was awarded, launching what would become a 31-year military career with 25 years of continuous aviation service. Lesson: MENTORS ARE PEOPLE WHO SEE THINGS IN YOU THAT YOU CANNOT SEE IN YOURSELF.

I completed transition to the Scout Platoon and learning began anew: I learned how to read signs of enemy movement; how to track them into their base camps; finally, how to attack them. Among arrows in my new quiver were how to employ organic fires, artillery, a quick reaction force and tactical air strikes.

The 1st Cavalry Division was ordered into III Corps Tactical Zone to relieve the 1st Infantry Division and sit astride the traditional invasion route from Cambodia pointed toward Saigon. Charlie Troop was to screen the operation between Song Be and Tay Ninh mountain along the Cambodian border and neutralize the NVA. From their base Camp in Phuoc Vinh, Charlie Troop launched multiple daily forays into the assigned areas. The Scout teams quickly learned the local NVA were a mean bunch having survived their journey down the Ho Chi Minh Trail. When we opened fire on them, every single one would fire back with deadly fire. Fate brought the loss of the beloved Scout Platoon leader callsign, "White," on New Year's Eve during a holiday truce and I made a personal decision to return to Lift and haul LRPs out of hot LZs until my tour finished and I had a confirmed seat on a Freedom Bird.

I finished my Vietnam tour, returned to the U.S. as a 2nd Lieutenant, became an Instructor Pilot and decided to leave active duty after nearly four and one-half years of devotion to my missions, my comrades and the country I love. My life continued an incredible journey of flying offshore in the Gulf and then becoming a factory instructor for Bell Helicopter in Iran. Upon returning to the United States, my wife, Beverly and I, raised our two sons in New York while I rose through the ranks of the IBM Flight Department, eventually retiring after 20 years. I finally caught the academic bug and completed my BS degree, cum laude, and earned my MS with a 4.0 GPA. I then went on to lead the Seagram Flight Department flying Gulfstream aircraft around the world before taking a role as the Managing Director of NetJets Europe based in Portugal. I held several leadership roles in the business aviation community developing a reputation for expertise in "regulatory compliance, aircraft completions, and avionics specifications." I started my own business, Flight Assurance LLC in 2009 and continue flying all models of the Global Express aircraft around the globe while assisting others with their regulatory needs from our home in Tucson, AZ.

Thinking over my life and career, I offer a few of my LIFE LESSONS FOR OTHERS.

1. Life may deal you a bad hand at the beginning as it did me, but the way you play the cards, determines how many chips you will cash in at the end of the game.

2. Combat is one of life's most exhilarating experiences. To be good at it, you must practice it daily. You will never be closer to death nor more alive. If you survive, you will always be grateful to providence.

3. A mentor is a gift of an opportunity you would not have otherwise had. Make the best of it and reward your mentor with your own success.

4. Education is the key to your journey along the pathway of life. Never reject a chance to embrace a new idea, a new concept, nor should you ever discard history. A dedication to the continuum of learning will give you comfort and make your journey through life much easier.

5. Family is a gift from God. Embrace and hold those you love closely while you can, because you don't get to choose the time nor the place where it ends.

CHAPTER ELEVEN

THE ART OF CRASHING (OR NOT)
by Terry Johnson

The last chapter I wrote for The Friday Pilots book took me by complete surprise. Writing a second chapter for this book, even more so. On both occasions, I've faced a formidable adversary - PROCRASTINATION. He dims your memory and convinces you that your experience won't be of much value to the reader.

Potential Crash Number One:

One nice sunny spring day, I was flying an airliner from Georgetown, Grand Cayman Islands to Memphis with a stop in Miami to clear customs and refuel. The trip from the Caribbean over Cuba and on to Miami was uneventful. We cleared customs along with the passengers. After refueling, reloading the baggage and catering, we were off to Memphis.

The takeoff and climb were all normal except for what I thought at the time was a small detail. The fuel flow to the engines was normal, but one of the main fuel tanks was decreasing a bit faster than normal. I wasn't overly concerned because a gauge can sometimes be off just a bit. I planned to keep an eye on the indicator.

We had just been given clearance from Jacksonville Center, the air traffic control agency for the area we were in, to climb to our cruising altitude, when the cockpit door flew open. The lead Flight Attendant rushed in to inform us that a deadheading pilot in the cabin saw fuel pouring out over the wing. Because this aircraft had fuselage mounted engines, this fuel was pouring directly into one of our engines.

By now, I realized what I was seeing on the fuel quantity gauge, was not a mistake but a real problem. A fuel line had broken between the left wing and center tank that fed the engines. I asked the First Officer to go back and have a look. He returned to the flight deck very alarmed. We could deal with the fuel loss and if necessary, shut down one engine; however, we were concerned about all the raw fuel being ignited by the operating engine into which it was pouring. Fire in the air is not a good thing.

We declared an emergency and returned to Miami for an uneventful landing. We minimized the amount of fuel being ingested by using only idle thrust on one engine. We gave the airport firefighters a little excitement. Lesson: YOU CAN TRAIN FOR EVERY IMAGINABLE PROBLEM, BUT YOU CAN'T BE PREPARED FOR EVERYTHING THAT CAN GO WRONG. Our training and aircraft manuals address most everything, but to this day, I've never heard of a fuel line breaking. Fortunately, it happened over the mainland. If it had happened between Grand Cayman and Miami, we would have for sure made the six o'clock national news, because Havana would have been our only landing option.

KNOWLEDGE OF YOUR SITUATION: In this case the aircraft you are dealing with and thinking on your feet. Doctors deal with this in the OR when surgery does not go as planned, trial lawyers in the courtroom and pilots of aircraft. Lesson: YOU CAN'T GO BACK TO THE LIBRARY AND LOOK SOMETHING UP FOR EVERY CONTINGENCY. SOME THINGS, YOU JUST HAVE TO KNOW.

Potential Crash Number Two:

Here is another incident, this time involving subtle incapacitation. This can be a problem in an aircraft even with two pilots. It can be a fatal situation in a single pilot aircraft. I was the First Officer on a flight between Phoenix and Omaha. I was flying with a Captain with whom I had not previously flown. After a brief introduction, we discussed the destination weather - 800' overcast, 1 1/2 miles visibility with light snow. Not bad, but cloudy enough to require an instrument approach.

The flight was routine en route; however, I did notice the Captain miss a few directions from the air traffic controllers. It was at this time I noticed he was wearing a hearing aid. Our descent into Omaha was started a bit late, and we were a little high on the profile. As we approached the field from the SW to eventually turn around and land to the NW, the Captain extended flaps 10 degrees followed by 20 degrees and then lowered the landing gear to hasten our descent. We entered the overcast at approximately 17,000 feet. I noticed the aircraft was getting 5 to 8 knots slow on the flap 20-degree airspeed, but we were descending, and I didn't worry about it.

We were being radar vectored to a downwind leg all this time. When we were turned back to a heading to intercept the final approach course, things began to change rapidly. On intercepting the final approach, I noticed our airspeed dropped to 130K with 20-degree flaps and the gear down. I asked the Captain if he knew what the airspeed was for 20-degree flaps. He did not reply. With the combination of leveling off with 20-degree flaps, landing gear extended, already 20K slow and with the power back, the airspeed fell almost instantly to the stall speed. We immediately got the stick shaker and audible warning. I pushed the throttles to maximum power, but the airspeed was dropping so rapidly, we actually stalled. One wing dropped followed by the other in a series of dutch rolls. The instrument panel was shaking badly, and it was difficult to read the horizon indicator with the dark overcast and the dark ground only 1,000 feet below us. I'm quite sure we were in at least 60 degrees of bank on either side. I believe it is an absolute credit to the DC-9's stability that with minimum input from the pilots, it actually flew out of the situation on its own. We had maximum power, flaps at 20 degrees, landing gear out (I couldn't reach the handle to retract the gear due to the buffeting) and the aircraft recovered on its own. It is remarkable, that we only lost about 200 feet in the entire maneuver. With the aircraft recovered and the airspeed about 15K below flap 20 airspeed, the Captain started to reduce the power. I pushed it back up and reminded him again of the flap 20 airspeed.

The remainder of the approach and landing were uneventful. The Flight Attendants reported being flung to the floor or landing in passengers' laps with passengers panicking. One Flight Attendant was so traumatized she asked to be relieved and did not return to work for several months.

Back in Phoenix, I discussed the incident with the Captain. He felt that possibly because of a recurring blood pressure problem, he really was unaware of the seriousness of our situation. He subsequently dropped the remainder of the trip. It turned out to be his last flight. He died a couple of years later of a brain issue.

In this incident the questions was, how far do you let things go before doing something about it? Whether it is a ship at sea or an aircraft, the Captain is the one in command and responsible for the safety of everyone on board. Lesson: IN RARE CIRCUMSTANCES, ALTHOUGH THE CAPTAIN IS IN COMMAND, YOU HAVE TO USURP THAT COMMAND AND DEAL WITH THE CONSEQUENCES LATER.

I have not discussed this incident with anyone over the years. What I did do after moving to the Captain position was to let my First Officers know that I was very capable of making a mistake and to not be afraid to speak up if something doesn't look right. I flew commercially over 30 years, and no one ever made a comment. Operating a flight is a team effort involving the entire crew. I always wanted everyone to feel free to have an input into making a trip better and safer. Airlines now teach this concept. It was formerly called, Cockpit Resource Management (CRM). A new term for it is Risk Resource Management (RRM). The program is the equivalent of the Department of Homeland Security warning: See Something, Say Something. It just makes sense.

Actual Crash Number Three:

My next story is a non-flying incident. I competed in Sports Car Club of America (SCCA) sports car racing for a number of years. One of the lessons learned from those experiences was to not let the circumstances you are in distract you. Having been fortunate enough to fly fighters in the USAF, ride motorcycles and race cars, I often get tagged with the idea that you have to be some sort of daredevil to do those things. That is not the case at all. Lesson: TRAINING AND TECHNIQUE ARE THE RELIGION OF ALL POTENTIALLY DANGEROUS ENDEAVORS. IT IS RISK MANAGEMENT. You don't stick your neck out any further than necessary.

I was lucky enough to be part of Nissan's SCCA teams back in the 1990s. Nissan supported three of us in the 300ZX. During a race weekend in Oklahoma, I had a suspension problem during the morning warm-up prior to the afternoon race. We scrambled around getting parts and doing repairs to get ready. This process took us right up to the five-minute warning to be on the grid for the start of the race. I was literally getting strapped in the car while the last pieces were being put into place and tightened down. I wasn't totally focused on racing. The track in Oklahoma was a fairly tight, not too fast, circuit. During the race, I managed to lose control of the car's rear end on the track's quickest corner, slid off the track and rolled the car. I was hanging upside down in the safety harness with the roof collapsed in such a way I couldn't get out. I was watching fuel pour out onto the hot engine. Fortunately, there was no fire and safety crews were there quickly. The only damage was to the car and my ego for allowing something to distract me from being totally focused on the job at hand. Lesson: WHEN YOU SELECT A DANGEROUS TASK, STAY FOCUSED. Every weekend the ERs are full of people who fall off ladders, misuse power equipment or drive with less than their full attention.

Actual Crash Number Four:

I remember almost none of it. One minute I was playing tennis with my friends and the next minute I was sprawled on the court with my heart stopped. This was the BIG ONE, a REAL 911. The main left descending artery, the Widow Maker, was totally blocked. I went down and had no heartbeat for five minutes. Because it was a Saturday morning, two doctor friends were playing tennis on an adjacent court. They immediately started CPR (breaking ribs) and kept me alive for the EMT's arrival.

Divine Providence: the tennis pro caught me as I was falling preventing any head trauma. I usually play tennis four times a week. If it had been any other day of the week, there would have been no doctors playing, and I would have died before an ambulance arrived.

I wasn't a complete health nut; but I always believed in exercise, eating properly and getting sleep. I got regular medical checkups. As far as I knew, other than the aches and pains of old age, I was a healthy person -yet I almost died. For those who have had a serious heart attack, it is no small matter, either the attack itself or the slow recovery. I am back playing tennis, slower than before. I learned one very important lesson: IF YOU ARE GOING TO HAVE A HEART ATTACK WHILE PLAYING TENNIS, PICK A COURT NEXT TO A DOCTOR.

I've had a number of things happen in my life which could have had very different outcomes. You could attribute that to good luck, but I choose to thank God for His grace and hope that my identity in Christ will serve Him well in the future. Hopefully, the nearest I get to crashing will be an afternoon nap.

CHAPTER TWELVE

FROM MACH 0.3 TO MACH 3+
by Tom Keck

The B-52D with a big belly mod could carry 108 500 pounders. That's 324 MK-82s in a three-ship cell. Although they weren't considered precision weapons, the effectiveness of that many weapons impacting a target almost simultaneously had a quality all its own. Today, with precision long range strike weapons, targeting pods, and plans to re-engine, the B-52 could be in the inventory until around 2050.

The highlight of my aviation career was flying the SR-71, a strategic reconnaissance jet, at 2,200 mph, above 85,000 feet with my Reconnaissance Systems Officer, Tim Shaw. That's 15 miles high, looking at contrails 50,000 feet below while moving 35 miles a minute. At those speeds, with a 90-mile turn radius, the Blackbird took 180 miles to turn around. In the daytime, the sky was a dark blue, and you could just barely see curvature of the earth. Without getting younger, you could make the sun come up in the West. Heat at that speed is the challenge that Kelly Johnson of the Lockheed Martin Skunk Works solved with a slide rule. Collecting photo, radar and electronic data in a denied area, the SR was an exciter. Air defenses would strain to find the first-generation stealth Blackbird, and signals collectors like the RC-135 and Navy EP-3 would scoop up all the electronics data for analysis. Of note, my Dad, Lt. Gen. Jim Keck, flew the SR on an orientation flight in the mid 70s. The Guinness Book of Records lists us as the only father/son combo to fly above Mach 3+ in an air breathing aircraft. The jets are in museums now, but still hold the world's speed and altitude records. When matched with elite crews, it was an extremely potent reconnaissance resource that owned the high threat environment throughout its lifespan.

Other experiences in the A-10, U-2, RC-135, and Tu-22M3 Russian Backfire with instructors and fellow crew members provided valuable leadership perspective and character lessons…some good, some not so good. From the beginning, pilots are trained to "maintain aircraft control, analyze the situation and take the proper action;" or basically, fix or work around the problem. As we get more senior, we may spend more or less time on parts of the mantra, but it's a framework, gateway and thought process that is immediately recognizable when aviators meet for the first or the 1,000[th] time.

The Second Day of Infamy

Everyone knows where they were, who they were with, and what they were doing on 9/11, a day of national tragedy, shock and loss. I was in a position to observe high level command presence and leadership lessons under an extremely stressful environment.

Early morning 9/11: We had been exercising the strategic forces for two weeks in our annual Global Guardian training and evaluation session. As the 8th Air Force Commander, I was supervising and testing the bomber, reconnaissance and cyber elements of USSTRATCOM. The crews and aircraft were fully generated and on alert. We were in the Command Post waiting for a coded message that would sprint the crews to aircraft, have them report in the green ready to launch, and stand by for guidance.

0800 Barksdale AFB time, 0900 East Coast time: Coded message received, klaxon sounds and crews sprint to their 54 loaded for war B-52s.

During the response, a Command Post Captain tapped me on the shoulder, and handed me a note that said, "An aircraft has hit the World Trade Center." I decided to go into the instruct mode and addressed the young man with, "Captain, when you make an exercise input, make sure you preface it, with this is an exercise inject." He solemnly replied with a, "No Sir," and pointed to a CNN screen that showed the tower billowing with smoke. My thoughts, the same as most, were, how on a clear and a million day, could an aircraft mistakenly hit the World Trade Center? The second aircraft hit shortly thereafter. I said, "Lock it down," and we were catapulted into a real world Threatcon Delta.

The good news was that with the Guardian Exercise running we had fully manned Battle Staffs up and running with nearly instant communications. An early message was received that stated a "Code Alpha" was inbound requesting 150,000 pounds of fuel, 70 box lunches, 25 pounds of bananas, and 40 gallons of juice and coffee. What's a Code Alpha? "Big," was the response. The National Military Command Center called and said not to acknowledge Air Force One (AF1) was at Barksdale. I looked over at CNN showing AF1 in the flare with a banner at the bottom of the screen saying "Barksdale AFB Louisiana." I said I wouldn't tell anyone.

Today it's possible to transmit live from AF1 with an updated wideband system. That capability wasn't available in 2001. Why stop at Barksdale? Our guess: en route from Sarasota, Karen Hughes, the media counselor, convinced POTUS to land and tell America we're going to be alright.

With 20 minutes notice that the President will be on your base, there is no time to preplan with the Secret Service, paint the grass green or shine your boots. Just meet him, give him your best salute and say, "Welcome to Barksdale AFB Mr. President!"

Lesson No.1

A LEADER CAN SET THE TONE FOR A MEETING WITH THE FIRST WORDS HE SPEAKS. He can relay concern, panic, specific tasking, professionalism, fatigue and hundreds of other tones. After our exchange of salutes, President Bush's first words, "I guess I put you on the map!" In other words, relax. My response, "Yes Sir, you did." His second sentence, "I need to get to a secure phone and speak with the Vice President, SECDEF and Gov Pataki." My response, "Come with me, Sir."

In my office, White House Comm was making the secure calls. Karl Rove and Andrew Card were also on the phone and extremely busy. The President was reviewing the words of his press conference that would be transmitted around the world.

Lesson No.2

CONSIDER INPUTS FROM OTHERS. While reviewing and editing his press conference words, he said, "I use the word resolve twice… should I?" All others were busy, so I said, "America will want to know we have strong resolve and reinforcing it is probably a good idea." POTUS shrugged and said "OK." So, MORE OF THE LESSON WAS, ASK FOR INPUT AND BE OPEN TO INPUT. Note: I later reviewed the press conference tapes and he only used "resolve" once. That was the end of my White House speech writing career.

Lesson No.3

After completing the phone calls and seated at my desk, President Bush leaned back, put his feet on my desk (it was protected with the Shreveport Times) looked at me and said, "In a few minutes I am going to address the world…people will look at me and see if I look nervous, am perspiring or my voice cracks." I remember thinking, why is he telling me this? But it was clear, he was getting his head in the game. The lesson was to ALWAYS TAKE TIME TO BE MENTALLY READY… GET YOUR HEAD IN THE GAME (WITH GAME FACE) BEFORE ENGAGING. We proceeded to the 8th Air Force conference room where POTUS briefed the nation.

The press conference went OK. We returned to my office as the reporters ran outside with their brief cases and portable satellite dishes to send the press conference to the major networks. While there was significant confusion that day, POTUS was professional and in command. He told me he had stated his intention to return to DC ASAP three times. The Secret Service was hesitant to allow that with the unknown threats still looming. I remember thinking how personable he remained with a constantly changing scenario.

The Chief of Intel, Col. Mike Reid, knocked on the door and handed me a cryptic message saying, "Boss, you need to see this." It read, "High speed object moving toward the Texas Ranch." I handed it to the President. His focus broke lock for about 15 seconds as I could see him mentally tabulating who was at the Ranch. It fortunately turned out to be a false report, one of many that day.

Concerned with the threat to our B-52s sitting on the ramp, I called Brig. Gen. Jack Ihle, the Reserve A-10 Wing Commander. I didn't even explain the problem, I said, "Jack, what can you give me?" His response, "Cockpit alert, end of the runway?" I said, "Do it." A day later, I received a call questioning the Rules of Engagement (ROE) for the alert Hogs (A-10s) on cockpit alert. My response was, "Common sense."

Lesson No. 4

While sitting on my office sofa, POTUS saw video of the towers collapsing for the first time. He turned to me, looked me in the eye, and his verbatim words were, "I don't know who this is, but we're going to find out...and we're going to go after them...and we're not going to just slap them on the wrist, we're going after them!" That was all President Bush talking. The lesson: SAY WHAT YOU MEAN AND DO WHAT YOU SAY. That's exactly what he did when he returned to Washington seeking immediate justice. POTUS, Rove, Card and I took 10 minutes to briefly discuss initial thoughts and theories on who was behind the attacks.

Lesson No. 5

Time to go: By our timing count, AF1 was on the ground for one hour and 53 minutes. The plan was to proceed to the Command Center at USSTRATCOM at Offutt AFB, Nebraska. As we arrived downstairs to proceed to AF1, I noted the Security Forces had provided a Humvee with a 50cal. gun on top. You have to love the Security Forces...their intent to protect POTUS was pure. President Bush looked at the Humvee and pointed to a white minivan and said, "We'll take that." The van belonged to the Supervisor of Flying to put eyes and communications on the flight line. Call sign on the minivan was "Soccer Mom." We later changed it to 'Air Force One.'

The Lesson: BE AWARE OF AND CONTROL APPEARANCES. If the public had seen the President in an armed camouflaged Humvee, many Americans would have panicked.

Although the thought crossed my mind that POTUS would be fun to play golf with, this visit was clearly not a normal POTUS visit with handshakes and photos, all business. As we entered the flight line, the crew chiefs were still on headsets in front of their loaded B-52s in case we needed to flush-launch the fleet. The crews were giving President Bush the thumbs up out the B-52 cockpit windows. At the base of the stairs of AF1 I asked President Bush if he saw the thumbs up. He did. I said, "Mr. President, these troops are trained, ready, and they'll do whatever you need them to do." He said, "I know," exchanged a sharp salute and bounced up the stairs.

Brig. Gen. Curt Bedke, the Wing Commander, and I saluted AF1 as it taxied out and departed. Two F-16s pulled up on its wings as it lifted off. Yes, we're starting to get our act together.

Three weeks later, Curt asked me if I remembered what I said when AF1 pulled away. I did….I said, "Do you feel like you're in a Tom Clancy novel?"

Bonus Lesson No. 6

April 15, 2002: Fast forward ahead - a small group of us flew to New York City on tax day 2002 to commemorate and celebrate the 50th Anniversary of the B-52. The day was packed: interview on Fox News, visit to the Twin Towers site, close the New York Stock Exchange, and throw out the first pitch at the Mets/Braves game. It was an honor and privilege to visit the city and help recognize the victims of 9/11. The City had pulled itself together along with the country. As the first uniformed group to visit the Stock Exchange since 9/11, we brought out an emotional response on the floor. The high pressure of the day was throwing the first pitch of the Mets/Braves after receiving advice from Braves Manager Bobby Cox. It was the best advice I ever had: MAKE SURE YOU DON'T BOUNCE THE PITCH, THEY'LL BOO YOU! I didn't.

CHAPTER THIRTEEN

PERSISTENCE PAYS AND THE THIRD TIME IS A CHARM

by Chuck Kennedy

I was born in Santa Monica, CA during WWII while my father was serving with the Navy in the Pacific, but my memories of that time are vague. Almost everyone I knew also had a father who had served in the war, and there was a huge Douglas Aircraft factory at nearby Cloverfield Airport. The television was full of shows like Victory at Sea, and I was always interested in airplanes, made plastic models with too much glue and graduated to flying free-flights and radio-controlled models. I devoured the stories of the test pilots at Edwards AFB, and when I saw a Life Magazine article on the Air Force Academy, I decided that is where I wanted to go.

For me, wanting to attend and being accepted at the Academy were two different things. I applied for an appointment through my Congressional Representative, who had one slot. After a series of tests and interviews, I was ranked second alternate. College was the obvious second choice, and off I went to New Mexico State University, determined to apply again the following year. I was ranked first alternate on my second attempt, which was certainly discouraging, so I went back to college for my sophomore year. I had joined ROTC and was prepared to get my commission through that program. Deciding to give it one final shot, I applied for a third time, and was finally accepted. First big lesson learned: PERSISTENCE PAYS OFF AND THIRD TIME'S A CHARM. Equally important: my college grades could certainly have been better, so DO NOT LET FOCUSING ON A FUTURE ASSIGNMENT LESSEN YOUR COMMITMENT TO EXCELLING AT YOUR CURRENT JOB.

My four years at the Air Force Academy were challenging but not unusual. My vision deteriorated, and I no longer met the criteria to be a pilot. The Vietnam War was ramping up, and as an Academy graduate, I was granted a waiver for my vision, so flying school was my first assignment, with hopefully a fighter airplane at completion.

I had five weeks of leave before I was to report to flight school. To pass the time, another classmate and I decided to go to London, buy 500cc Triumph motorcycles, and spend a month touring England and the continent. This was a great way to celebrate graduation, and for a month we released all the pent-up energy kept inside from the past four years. Starting in London was a bit ragged, as neither of us had ever ridden motorcycles. We had some challenging moments, but fortunately the only damage was to our pride. We drove through England, France, Spain, Switzerland, and Germany. Leather jackets, helmets, a couple of 23-year-old kids on big bikes – man, did we look good going down the highway! Lessons learned: RIDING A MOTORCYCLE IS A LOT MORE FUN WHEN IT IS NOT RAINING, AND IT REALLY HELPS TO KNOW WHAT YOU ARE DOING BEFORE HOPPING ON A BIKE IN A BIG CITY, particularly when they drive on the wrong side of the road.

Reporting to flight school at Webb AFB at Big Spring, TX, I was eager to rejoin my classmates from the Academy and start learning to fly. When I checked in, I informed the Flight Surgeon that I was not feeling well. He quickly determined that I had hepatitis, and I was placed in quarantine at the base hospital. Turns out I probably picked it up from eating seafood in Spain – there must be a lesson learned in there somewhere. I spent two weeks in the hospital (isolation) and then went home for two additional weeks on convalescent leave. I was devastated. My classmates had already started flying and I was now six weeks behind, certain that the war would end before I had a chance to go. I should not have worried. This was in 1966 and the war would grind on for nine more years. I loved flying school and was blessed with good instructors. Graduating pilots get to select the airplane for their follow-on assignment based on their class standing, and I had done well. As a class, we were fortunate because if you wanted to fly fighters there were 32 F-100s and 28 F-105s allocated, and I chose the F-105. As a side note, my original class had no single seat fighters available and a smattering of back seat F-4s. The old saying about,

A DARK CLOUD CAN HAVE A SILVER LINING, certainly applied to me.

When I started F-105 school in 1967, the war in North Vietnam was going strong. The F-105, along with the F-4, were the workhorses and the loss rates were high. All the Instructor Pilots (IPs) had completed their 100 missions over North Vietnam and were tasked with making a bunch of spanking new pilots combat ready in the biggest single seat fighter in the USAF. We were the first large group of brand-new pilots to fly the F-105 in several years. While I am sure the IPs shook their heads at times, they did a great job getting us ready to go to war.

After checking out in the F-105, I was assigned to Takhli RTAFB in Thailand. By the time I arrived in June 1968 there was a bombing pause in the area around Hanoi and Haiphong, but we were still bombing in the southern part of North Vietnam as well as in Laos. Our missions in both were the same – interdict the supply of equipment flowing from the North Vietnamese to their forces in the south. Our targets consisted of bridges, roads, vehicles, storage areas and occasionally troops. Innumerable books have been written about the futility of that effort, and the lessons learned are well documented: A ROAD CAN ONLY BE CLOSED FOR A SHORT PERIOD OF TIME, AND BRIDGES CAN BE REBUILT OR TRAFFIC MOVED TO A FORD. By the time the war was over, we had converted steep mountain passes into gently rolling terrain, and the trucks kept on coming down the Ho Chi Minh Trail. When I arrived at Takhli, a combat tour was 100 missions over North Vietnam. Before I reached that milestone, bombing was halted throughout the North, and my tour lasted for a full year (1968 – 1969).

The F-105 is a legendary airplane, and I was fortunate to have the opportunity to fly it as my first assignment out of flight school. Fast, it could carry a huge bomb load, was a stable bombing and strafing platform and could survive incredible punishment. However, there was another airplane that I wanted to fly, the A-1 Skyraider. So I volunteered for a back-to-back tour in that old venerable airplane. The A-1 was a radial engine, tail dragger which was designed at the end of WWII and first used by the Navy in the Korean War. Flying it could not have been more different from flying the F-105 – rather than approaching supersonic, we flew the A-1 below 200 knots. The engine produced so much torque it could get you in trouble on takeoff, and landing a tail dragger was always a thrill. The A-1 could carry a wide variety of ordnance and stay in the target area for an extended period of time. This made it ideal for close air support of our ground forces as well as for search and rescue operations of downed pilots.

Training for the A-1 was in Fort Walton Beach, FL and I spent the summer there in 1969. As most everyone knows, that is where Jimmy Doolittle trained for his raid on Tokyo. Just outside the base was a dive called "Bacon's by the Sea." It is now long gone but was still open in '69. Story goes that General Doolittle and others ate dinner there one evening and used the paper placemat to illustrate plans for the Tokyo raid. After the meal, they took the placemat with them because it was classified - supposedly it ended up in the Air Force Museum. I met my wife on the Officers Club beach, and we are now celebrating our 50th wedding anniversary! Lesson: PERSISTENCE ALSO PAYS IN MARRIAGE.

The year I spent flying the A-1 was the most rewarding of my Air Force career. I was stationed at Nakhon Phanom RTAFB (NKP) located on the bank of the Mekong River in northeast Thailand. Laos was right across the river. Although the Thais were very friendly, there was a statue of Ho Chi Minh in the town square. The base was the most primitive for the USAF in Thailand, although far better than the most luxurious base in Vietnam. NKP was used for special operations. We had Forward Air Controllers (FACs), HH-3E (Jolly Green) rescue helicopters, propeller driven, twin engined A-26s (flew night missions attacking trucks) and three squadrons of A-1s. There was also a US Army Special Forces unit that had missions that may still be classified. The A-1s worked closely with them, and to reach their camp we drove from a paved road to a gravel road to a muddy dirt track. The camp itself consisted of tents that sat in mud during the rainy season. To call it rustic would not do it justice. I asked their Captain why they lived like that when they could at least be comfortable when in camp. His response, "I do not want them to be comfortable. If they are, their morale will suffer when in the field." I nodded my understanding and drove back up the hill shaking my head to my air-conditioned hooch and hot shower. I think any lessons learned would be obvious.

At NKP the Skyraiders had three main missions: close air support (CAS) of General Vang Pao's Hmong troops in Northern Laos (day and night); interdicting the Ho Chi Minh Trail (night); and search and rescue

(SAR). As I mentioned, the A-1 was designed at the end of WWII and had many ways to trap an inattentive pilot. For example, the external fuel tanks were gravity fed to the engine with the fuel line at the front of the tank. If the nose was raised (as in pulling off the target) fuel would no longer flow, the engine would quit and the pilot's heart rate would rapidly increase, particularly if at night and being shot at. The engine would restart if the propeller was still turning, and if the pilot rapidly switched to internal fuel (where he should have been in the first place). Everyone made this mistake once, few repeated.

I learned a most valuable lesson on a night mission attacking vehicles on the Ho Chi Minh trail. Other than gunships, the A-1 destroyed the largest number of enemy vehicles, but we never were able to stop the traffic. A FAC would locate the target (often a single truck) mark it with a ground flare, and then the A-1s would attack using napalm and cluster bombs. We flew in two ship formations with all exterior lights out. The procedure was to fly with 500 ft. altitude separation, the lower aircraft striking first (while the higher aircraft looked out for ground fire). Once the first A-1 had expended its ammunition, we got on opposite sides of the target and switched positions. One night, as the lower aircraft pulled off the target, he started taking 37mm AAA fire. South of the target, I rolled in on the gun, thinking that the other pilot was to the north. That was not the case. We collided, and my prop cut through the aileron of the other plane. Luckily, both of us were able to recover back at home base. I do not have enough room to list all the lessons learned from this massive screw up, but Lesson: ONE GETS HIS FANGS OUT AND DISREGARDS SOUND TACTICS AT HIS PERIL.

The most rewarding mission we flew was search and rescue (SAR) of downed pilots. The A-1 (call sign Sandy) had the responsibility for controlling the rescue and would make the decision when to bring in a Jolly Green helicopter to pick up the survivor. During my year tour, I participated in many SARs, and led a few. Nothing beats the emotions after a successful rescue. By the same token, nothing can match the dismay when we failed. The one SAR that sticks vividly in my mind was for Boxer 22, an F-4 shot down in Laos on the Ho Chi Minh Trail near a pass coming out of North Vietnam. This area was frequently bombed and heavily defended. Both pilots were able to safely eject and ended up on opposite sides of a river running between two karst cliffs roughly 1,000 feet high. The front seater (Boxer 22A) was on the north side of the river, and the back seater (Boxer 22B) on the south. We immediately launched a four ship of A-1 Sandys to start a rescue attempt, along with two Jolly Green helicopters. Hoping for a quick pickup, they attempted to rescue Boxer 22A shortly after arriving in the area but were driven off by intense ground fire coming from caves in the karst cliffs. Realizing we needed to reduce the ground fire before another attempt could be made, the A-1s and a FAC started attacking the guns with jet fighters that were holding in the area. Meanwhile, more A-1s and Jolly Greens were being launched from NKP. Thinking that the guns had been silenced, the A-1s and Jolly Greens arrived in the area, and made another rescue attempt. Again, they were driven off. It became apparent that enemy gunners were holding their fire until the helicopters were hovering over the downed pilots. The rest of the day was spent finding and attacking the guns, bringing in the helicopters, being driven off, and repeating the process. We made seven attempts that day, without success.

Although the Jolly Greens have some self-defense capability, they are extremely vulnerable once in a hover. One of the jobs of the Sandy is to troll for guns and make sure they are silenced before bringing in the helicopters. Here, the enemy gunners held their fire until the helicopters were slowing down for a rescue attempt. In effect, the Jolly Greens knew they were the ones trolling for the guns.

Meanwhile, the enemy forces on the ground were trying to find the downed pilots, but they remained undiscovered throughout that day and night. Early the next morning, Boxer 22B heard screaming and shots fired across the river – the enemy had found and killed Boxer 22A. The second day consisted of finding and silencing the guns – creating a "safe" corridor for Jolly Greens to reach the pilot - bringing them in to attempt a pickup – being driven off by more ground fire – and repeating the process eight times. We were not lacking in resources to attack the guns. In fact, other than close air support of our troops in South Vietnam, most of the jet fighters in the entire theater were dedicated to this rescue. Day two of the SAR ended without success, but Boxer 22B was still alive and we remained hopeful.

On the third day, we launched almost every flyable A-1 for an early morning attempt. It was successful (third time a charm once again). There were FACs directing jet fighters blasting the karst; sixteen A-1s expending rockets, CBU, smoke and 20mm cannon creating the helicopter access corridor; four A-1 Sandys controlling the operation; and two Jolly Greens (one for the pickup and one as a spare). The rescue of Boxer 22 was the largest search and rescue mission of the Vietnam War. A total of 336 sorties were flown by aircraft that expended 1,463 smart bombs, high-explosive bombs, cluster bombs, smoke bombs, napalm bombs and rocket pods over the course of three days. Skyraiders alone flew 242 sorties; the HH-3 and HH-53 helicopters, over 40. Five Skyraiders were damaged, but the Jolly Greens got the worst of it. Five of the 10 involved never flew again. The lead Sandy for the pickup was awarded the Air Force Cross, and there were numerous other medals awarded for bravery.

It is impossible to over emphasize the raw courage of the Jolly Green crews. They knew what they were flying into and never hesitated. For the rest of us, it had been apparent for some time that the enemy forces in Laos did not take prisoners, and we knew that extraordinary effort would be taken to rescue us if we were shot down. It is difficult to explain to the uninitiated the enormous effort and risks that will be taken to rescue just one downed pilot. Lesson: IN RESCUE EFFORTS AIRCREWS EXPOSE THEMSELVES TO INCREDIBLE DANGER BECAUSE THEY KNOW THE PILOT ON THE GROUND WOULD DO IT FOR THEM. IT'S SIMPLY PART OF THE MILITARY ELAN THAT MAKES IT ALL WORK. IT'S WHAT MAKES US DIFFERENT.

Following my A-1 tour, I was assigned as part of the first combat ready A-7D squadron being formed at Myrtle Beach AFB, SC. After flying the F-105 and A-1, the A-7 was a giant technological leap forward. It had an excellent navigation system, a moving map display, a heads-up display (HUD), and, for the first time, a computerized bombing system that really worked as advertised. While in our initial stages of manning-up, the USAF Chief of Staff visited the squadron, and all the pilots lined up to be introduced. When he got to me and learned what I had flown, he asked how I felt about plans to retire the A-1. I responded something to the effect that its capabilities could not be replaced by a jet fighter. He was not pleased, and as he moved on, the Wing Commander made a comment along the lines of, "What the captain meant to say, is…" After two years at Myrtle Beach, the squadron deployed to Korat RTAFB, Thailand for a six-month TDY. Although the Navy had been flying the A-7 in combat for many years, we were the first Air Force squadron to do so. Going back for a third time was hard, as my lovely wife was pregnant (third time was not a charm in this case). Fortunately, I returned home in time for our son's birth, and then went back again for several more months. Combat in the A-7 was not much different than in my previous airplanes. We flew the same missions (interdiction and close air support) and also took over the SAR mission from the A-1. Another pilot and I were the only ones with previous A-1 Sandy experience, and we were responsible for developing the tactics and training program for that transition. The A-7 was much faster than the A-1 (which made escorting the Jolly Greens challenging), could not carry the wide variety of ordnance, or safely employ weapons as close to the survivor as could the A-1; however, the advanced avionics were a game changer. The first SAR we had after taking on the Sandy role was to rescue a pilot shot down in North Vietnam. To reach him, the rescue force needed to descend into a valley through a total overcast extending below the mountain tops. Relying on his radar and moving map, the lead Sandy descended into the clouds and broke out at less than 1,000 feet above the ground. He guided the Jolly Green in for a successful rescue and was awarded the Air Force Cross for his heroism.

After returning to Myrtle Beach, I was posted to the Pentagon in the office of Colonel's Personnel Assignments. I was responsible for all the colonels in the fighter community, along with base commanders, air attaches, and professors of air science. I was there when our POWs came home. Since most had fighter backgrounds, I had the honor of working their assignments back into the Air Force.

Returning to the cockpit after four years at the Pentagon, I was assigned to fly the A-10 at Davis Monthan AFB in Tucson and remained there as an Instructor Pilot for three years. I was then posted to England AFB in Louisiana to help the wing's transition from the A-7 to the A-10. The A-10 is a great airplane, specifically designed for close air support, which is my favorite mission. My time in the cockpit ended when I was assigned to TAC Headquarters.

Looking back, I had the privilege of flying four single seat fighters, three in combat. Lesson: THE PILOTS AND GROUND PERSONNEL WERE UNIFORMLY COMMITTED TO SERVING OUR COUNTRY WITH HONOR AND DISTINCTION, AND I WILL ALWAYS BE THANKFUL FOR THE OPPORTUNITY TO SERVE ALONGSIDE THEM.

Retired from TAC and looking for a job, I interviewed with several aerospace firms. I received several offers, including one from Northrop Grumman. They would not tell me what I would be doing but promised I would like it. Turned out that I was being hired into the B-2 stealth bomber program, which was still black at that time. I spent 18 years working on the B-2, starting out as the engineer responsible for the bomb rack and rotary launcher assembly. Over the next 18 years, I moved back and forth between engineering and the program office. When I retired, I was in charge of all engineering on the airplane except for structures and flight controls. The B-2 is an amazing airplane, and Northrop Grumman was a great place to work. The B-2 has been criticized for its cost, but severely reducing the number to be built (from 134 to 21), combined with almost constant change in requirements, were major cost drivers. Lesson: THERE IS A SAYING IN THE AEROSPACE INDUSTRY: "FAST, CHEAP, GOOD – PICK ANY TWO," and that certainly applied to us.

We moved to the Florida Panhandle after retiring from Northrop. For several years, I had volunteered for a not-for-profit which runs robotic competitions for kids. Its mission is to motivate students in grades K-12 to pursue careers in science and technology. I was hired by them as the Regional Director for the southeast U.S. responsible for fundraising, recruiting teams and volunteers, and of course, running the competitions. I was the only paid employee and relied on hundreds of volunteers to make it all happen. Having the opportunity to work with dedicated volunteers and eager, amazing kids was a perfect way to make the change into retirement.

In 2017, my wife and I returned to Tucson, and I was invited to join the Friday Pilots. We come from many backgrounds, and our weekly meetings are special. Hopefully, we can resume getting together once the covid-19 virus is defeated.

The photos in this book are the property of the individual story authors from their flying careers and family lives. In several cases the high-quality individual photos were provided courtesy of Christopher Vasquez, www. christopherfilm.com. Chris photographed and interviewed all the Friday Pilots at the Pima Air and Space Museum (PASM) in Tucson. He is a filmmaker, former Air Force F-16 pilot and aviation enthusiast whose work includes feature films, commercials and aerials for TV and advertisements.

The Friday Pilot Group lunching at Hacienda del Sol resort, Tucson, 2019

Col USAF (Ret.) Bob Barnett by F-105 from Vietnam
War at PASM, Tucson, 2020, pic. Chris Vasquez

Bob Barnett, Vietnam POW five and one-half years, 1989 long days, with
one of his POW cellmates, Dwight "Sully" Sullivan (Sully RIP 2019)

Bob Breault by Vietnam War F-100 at PASM, Tucson, 2020, pic. Chris Vasquez

1st Lt Bob Breault by fully-loaded F-100, Phan Rang AB, Vietnam 1967

Capt USN (Ret.) Frank Brown by Navy F-14 at
PASM, Tucson, 2020, pic. Chris Vasquez

CDR Frank Brown, USN and Maj. Larry Cohen,
USMC, by F-4 at NAS North Island, CA

Col USAF(Ret.) Pete Carpenter by Korean War F-86,
PASM, Tucson, 2020, pic Chris Vasquez

Pete Carpenter, 13th ferry mission over North Atlantic in single engine jets,
behind the old KB-50 and KC-97 tankers,1960, Incirlik Airbase, Turkey

Col USAF (Ret.) Ken Collins by his CIA A-12 on an Oxcart
experimental flight test, Area 51, Nevada, 1963, the first
Mach 3.2 combat missions were flown 1967-68

Ken Collins, 100th combat mission Korean War,
RF-80A, Kimpo Airbase, Korea, 1953

Pete Collins by a Vietnam War FAC O-2, PASM,
Tucson, 2020, pic. Chris Vasquez

Pete Collins by an Air National Guard A-7 at PASM,
Tucson, 2020, pic. Chris Vasquez

Col USAF (Ret.) John Dale by an F-84 at PASM, Tucson, 2020, pic. Chris Vasquez

John Dale with his 1947 Bellanca Cruisair at Ryan Field, Tucson 2021

MGen USAF (Ret.) Pat Halloran on left with his SR-71, Beale AFB, CA circa 1967

Pat Halloran and replica 1936 Schonfeldt Firecracker racer

Col USAF (Ret.) Bill Hosmer, F-105, Korat,
RTAFB, Thailand, Vietnam War, 1966

Bill Hosmer, Thunderbird #2, Left Wing, second from top on ladder

Col USA (Ret.) Bruce Huffman by an Army AH-1S
PASM, 2020, pic. Chris Vasquez

2 Lt Bruce Huffman, Phouc Vinh, Vietnam, OH-6A "Loach" and crew, 1968

Terry Johnson by a F-101 at PASM, Tucson, 2020, pic. Chris Vasquez

Terry Johnson in his Minnesota Air National Guard F-102

LtGen USAF (Ret.) Tom Keck, Commander 8th Air Force

Historic photo: LtGen Tom Keck in his office with President George W. Bush on 9-11 at Barksdale AFB, LA after the attack on World Trade Center

Chuck Kennedy by a Vietnam War F-105, PASM,
Tucson, 2020, pic. Chris Vasquez

Chuck Kennedy as a Sandy A-1 rescue pilot in the Vietnam
War, Nakhon Phanom RTAFB, Thailand,1969

LtGen USMC (Ret.) Bruce Barry "Knute" Knutson, in undergraduate
pilot training with USAF, Williams AFB, AZ, 1970

Knute Knutson, first commander of the USMC KFIR adversary
squadron, VMFT 401, MCAS, Yuma AZ, 1987

Col USMC (Ret.) Marty Lenzini by Marine A-4 from the
Vietnam War, at PASM, Tucson, 2020, pic. Chris Vasquez

2d Lt Marty Lenzini, USMC, gets his Navy wings, NAS Kingsville, TX 1963

BGen USAF (Ret.) Jim McDivitt, Gemini and Apollo Astronaut, Apollo Moon Landing Program Manager at PASM, 2020, pic. Chris Vasquez

Apollo 9 crew, Jim McDivitt, David Scott, Rusty Schweickart, March 1969

LCDR Dan Moore USN, F-18 pilot and Senior Landing Signal
Officer (LSO), Carrier Air Wing Fourteen (CVW-14) on USS
Constellation (CV-64) circa 1987, pic Ernie McLintock

CDR Dan Moore USN, his last flight as commanding officer, Strike Fighter
Squadron Eighty-One (VFA-81) "Sunliners," NAS Cecil Field, Fl 1995

Chuck Ogren by a Vietnam War F-4, PASM, Tucson, 2020, pic. Chris Vasquez

Chuck Ogren, Vietnam War, F-4, Korat RTAFB, Thailand 1969

Gen USAF (Ret.) Earl O'Loughlin, USAF bomber pilot, Korean and
Vietnam Wars, by FB-111 at PASM, Tucson, 2020, pic. Chris Vasquez

General Earl O'Loughlin, USAF, Commander, Air Force Logistics
Command, the Friday Pilots' only four-star general

Col USA (Ret.) Phil Osterli by Army Vietnam UH-1C
gunship at PASM, Tucson, 2020, pic. Chris Vasquez

Capt USA Phil Osterli with flight gear and weapon in front of his tent,
335th Assault Helicopter Co, 173rd Abn Bde, Dak To, Vietnam, 1967

Col USAF (Ret.) Bill Pitts, A-10 "Bosshawg" PASM,
Tucson, 2020, pic. Chris Vasquez

Bill Pitts with son, Andy Pitts, a high time F-35 pilot, Luke AFB, AZ

George Allan "GAR" Rose, by Vietnam War F-4, PASM, Tucson, 2020, shot down and POW 1972, pic. Chris Vasquez

GAR Rose and "Pitter" (backseater) Pete Callaghan, F-4, Vietnam War, Ubon, RTAFB Thailand, shot down in Operation Linebacker I,1972

LtGen USAF (Ret.) Gene Santarelli, by F-4 like that he flew out of Ubon, RTAFB Thailand, in the Vietnam War, PASM 2020, pic. Chris Vasquez

LtGen Gene Santarelli and wife, Kay, final flight as Vice Commander of PACAF in F-15 at Hickam AFB HI with Hawaii ANG, 1998

MGen USAF (Ret.) Don Shepperd by F-100 PASM, Tucson, 2020, 247 missions and Misty Fast FAC, Vietnam War, pic. Chris Vasquez

Capt Don Shepperd and Capt Dick Rutan ready for Misty F-100F Fast FAC mission over North Vietnam 1968

Moose Skowron by a Vietnam War F-105, PASM,
Tucson, 2020, pic. Chris Vasquez

Moose Skowron, 20 years old, by his T-6, first solo flight in pilot
training as an Aviation Cadet, Columbus AFB, MS, 1954

Jeff "Tico" Tice at PASM, Tucson, 2020, pic. Chris Vasquez

Tico Tice, Riyadh AB, Saudi Arabia, with his shootdown wingmen, Tom "TK" Moore and Emmett "ET" Tullia, after release as a POW in Iraq, 6 March 1991

Col USAF (Ret.) Rob Van Sice, by Vietnam F–4, his first
war, PASM, Tucson, 2020, pic. Chris Vasquez

Lt Col Rob Van Sice, 72nd TFTS commander, MacDill AFB, FL, 1985

MGen USAF (Ret.) Russ Violett at PASM, Tucson, 2020, by Vietnam War F-105 like that he flew out of Takhli, RTAFB Thailand, pic. Chris Vasquez

Russ Violett, F-105 Instructor, McConnell AFB, KS in a party suit, Takhli, RTAFB, Thailand, 1969

Alex Wright by ANG F-16 at PASM, Tucson, 2020, long time Viper instructor, pic. Chris Vasquez

Alex Wright, experienced A-7 Instructor Pilot

Bob Barnett and Suzanne Purcell, soulmates and world travelers

1 Lt Bob Breault, far left, the youngest F-100 Wild
Weasel pilot, Korat RTAB, Thailand, Jan 196

USN LT Frank Brown with RADM Paul Gillcrist,
F-14 debrief with Grumman engineers

Capt Pete Carpenter and Capt Paul Craw after their 1,000[th]
hr. flight in the F-100, Cannon AFB NM

Ken Collins, RF-80, Shaw AFB SC, 1954

Lt Col Pete Collins, final F-16 flight, Tucson ANG, 1991

John Dale doing what he does best - fly in his Bellanca Crusiair!

Pat Halloran and famed novelist, Ernest K. Gann, "The
High and the Mighty" (Gann RIP 1991)

Col USAF (Ret.) Bill Hosmer, former Thunderbird,
signing Friday Pilot book autographs

Bruce Huffman and wife, Beverly, at Distinguished Flying
Cross Society convention, Seattle, WA, 2012

Terry and Claudia Johnson, world travelers, Puerto Rico, Caribbean cruise

Historic photo: LtGen Tom Keck, Commander 8th Air Force, escorts
President Bush to 8AF HQ at Barksdale AFB, LA on 9-11

Chuck Kennedy flying the F-105 Thud in the Vietnam
War, Takhli, RTAB Thailand, 1968

Knute Knutson, fun deer hunting with sons in northern AZ, 2020

Col USMC (Ret.) Marty Lenzini and wife, Alice Ann, Christmas in Tucson

1st Lt Jim McDivitt in the Korean War, finished with 145
F-80 and F-86 combat missions, tour was 100

Capt Dan Moore USN (Ret.) at World Multisport Championship, Pontevedra, Spain, 2019, 2 mi. swim, 70 mi. bike. In the men's 60-64 age group, 1st of 12 for team USA, 10th of 33 for the entire age group

Chuck Ogren, staying healthy in Tucson despite the pandemic

Earl O'Loughlin, a big game hunter with a 600 lb.
black bear, Manitoba, Canada, 2010

Earl O'Loughlin and Jim McDivitt, both former enlisted, both from Michigan,
met when they were in pilot training classes, 1951 in Moultrie, GA.

Col USA (Ret.) Phil Osterli and wife, Linda, Museum of Flight
Wings of Heroes Gala for those who served in Vietnam, 2018

Bill Pitts and wife, Frieda Erickson, enjoy dinner in Napa Valley, CA

Far right, GAR Rose and wife, Becky, American Airlines Sky Ball, DFW American Airlines hangar honoring the Vietnam POWs, L-R Tom Hanton, GAR POW Vietnam cellmate, Tico Tice, Iraq POW and wife, Rose, 2018

BGen Gene Santarelli, senior Air Force officer, CENTAF with Gen. Norman Schwarzkopf, who was making his final visit to Dhahran, Saudi Arabia after Desert Strom, 1991

MGen USAF (Ret.) Don Shepperd, dedicating Vietnam
Misty F-100F at Joint Base Andrews, MD 2018

Ed "Moose" Skowron, toasts his rescuers, returning from hospital after
his shootdown over North Vietnam, Korat RTAFB, Thailand, 1966

Jeff "Tico" Tice first F-16 flight after repatriated and
medically cleared from being a POW in Iraq, 1991

Col USAF (Ret.) Rob Van Sice, official Air Force photo, 1989

Russ Violett family, 60th anniversary celebration at Hotel Coronado, San Diego, CA, 2015, 37 people, 4 kids, 14 grandkids, 4 great grandkids

Alex Wright and wife, Kathy, at first Dutch A-7 pilot training graduation, 162d TFW, Tucson ANG, 1990, Kathy, RIP 2011

CHAPTER FOURTEEN

GOOD DECISIONS
by Bruce Barry "Knute" Knutson, Jr.

My very happy and rewarding life began on 28 June 1946 in a little mining and ranching town in southeastern Arizona...Douglas. I did not grow up there, because on 7 Dec. 1941 my father, Bruce Barry Knutson, was a student at the University of Arizona 90 miles away in Tucson.

Shortly after the Japanese attacked my father, who was enrolled in the Army ROTC unit, was commissioned as a 2nd Lieutenant. My father's father had immigrated from Sweden in the 1890s. A mining engineer, he moved around America, served in the army during the War of 1898, located in Southern Arizona (Douglas), met my grandmother at a mining camp in Sonora, Mexico, married her and began a family. My father met my mother at the University of Arizona shortly before Pearl Harbor. Her parents were both of English descent. Her father was career Army, served and fought in WW I. He was retired shortly before Pearl Harbor, was reactivated, became an artillery battalion commander and was killed in action in France just after the Normandy landing.

My father went into the Army Air Corps and became a bombardier/navigator. He spent a year in the 8th Air Force flying 30 missions into Germany. A point for reference for the readers: the 8th Air Force suffered more killed in action than the Marine Corps did during the entire Pacific campaign. After the war, my father stayed in the army air corps and then the US Air Force, resulting in my being raised in various places across our United States, three different elementary schools, three different high schools.

I got lucky in July of 1963 when my father was transferred from the Naval War College in Newport, RI to Wurtsmith AFB in northern Michigan as the base commander. The base was a B-52 base next to a small town called Oscoda. I was lucky because the local high school was small, and one of its local students was a pretty, petite blond named, Cathy Rose. Her father and mother owned a trailer park right outside the back gate of the base which was occupied almost exclusively by Air Force families. On the first day of school with me knowing nobody, I was getting books out of my locker, when Cathy pulled on my elbow and said, "I heard you are the new boy in school". Good Decision: Lesson: I FELL IN LOVE WITH CATHY ROSE.

During my senior year in high school besides playing sports and dating Cathy, I was applying for various colleges. I really wanted to go the Air Force Academy and become a pilot. I had spent my life growing up in the Air Force, my Dad was not a pilot but a very successful officer. I wanted to be like him, but also be a pilot. I applied in numerous ways to get an appointment, but although accepted by the academy academically, I did not get an appointment. While trying to gain an Air Force Academy appointment, I also applied to the Navy ROTC regular program. At the time only the Navy had an ROTC program that paid selected students full tuition, books and a monthly stipend. I was granted an appointment from the Navy. As I neared high school graduation, I had a decision to make, accept the Navy scholarship or go to a college that had AFROTC. I had never previously thought about the Navy, did know they flew a lot of planes, but most importantly I knew my parents had three other children to get through college. Good Decision: Lesson: I CHOOSE THE NAVY REGULAR ROTC SCHOLARSHIP.

My next good decision was not to date any other girls while at the University of New Mexico. Cathy was putting herself through Central Michigan University and we stayed loyal to each other for four years even though we only at best saw each other two-three times a year. At the end of our college days we "decided" to get married–Good Decision. My next good decision was to go after a commission in the Marine Corps rather than the Navy. While in ROTC at UNM, I had a very impressive Marine Officer Instructor who gently persuaded me I would like the Marine Corps more than the Navy. I took the Marine Option program and gained my commission as a 2nd Lieutenant USMC. Off I went to "The Basic School" (TBS) in Quantico, Virginia. This six-month school is normally a requirement for all newly commissioned Marine Corps officers to give them a foundation in Marine Corps doctrine, things infantry and combined arms. But, during the Vietnam era, it was waived for new lieutenants who had an aviation guarantee, which I did. However, I "decided" to attend TBS anyway thinking it would help me be a better Marine Corps officer – Good Decision. Lesson: ATTENDING THE BASIC SCHOOL MADE ME A BETTER MARINE CORPS OFFICER.

There are two kinds of Naval Aviators: Navy pilots and Marine pilots. We all wear the Wings of Gold. Normally, all Navy and Marine aviation students go to Navy Flight school centered in Pensacola, Fl. Again, because of Vietnam, the Navy and Marine Corps needed more pilots than the Navy flight school could produce, so the Marine Corps made a deal with the Air Force for the USAF to train up to 100 Marines per year. I "decided" to try to go to the Air Force flight school, two reasons really, one was my family's Air Force background and two, if you successfully completed, you were guaranteed jets and didn't risk getting sent to helos. Good Decision. I did complete successfully at Williams AFB in AZ getting my Air Force wings in Sept. 1970. Not only that, Cathy and I had a ball in flight school...a really, really great year (my Air Force friends knew how to party!). After winging, I decided to go to Marine Corps Air Station MCAS) Yuma AZ. There I flew another 80 hrs. in the TA-4 winning my "Naval Wings." As I neared completion of that training, I had a decision to go single seat A-4s, or dual seat (albeit the second seat was not a pilot but a radar operator) F-4s. Good Decision. What an aircraft! It was the work horse of the Air Force, Navy and Marine Corps for most of the 60s, 70s and early 80s.

After initial training in the F-4, I transferred to MCAS El Toro in Southern California. After about two years of good flying, leaving Cathy and my new infant son, I was sent to the Western Pacific (WESTPAC). Once in Iwakuni, Japan, I was quickly assigned to VMFA 115 (Silver Eagles) and shipped to Nam Phong, Thailand where the squadron was flying combat into Cambodia. A whole Marine Corps Air Group was in Nam Phong due to President Nixon's plan to reduce the numbers of US military in Vietnam on a calendar schedule. The Marines just moved the air group from Da Nang, Vietnam to Nam Phong, Thailand. The problem was, there was nothing at Nam Phong but a 10,000 ft runway. To say it was austere, is a gross understatement. In 1973 there was a very popular song called, "I never promised you a Rose Garden." You guessed it, that was the Marines nickname for Nam Phong: the "Rose Garden." I flew 39 F-4 combat missions into Cambodia including the last Marine Corps mission in Southeast Asia on 15 August 1973. The rest of my year-long tour, although not combat, was wonderful. I spent about three months flying out of Cubi Point, Philippines, and three months flying out of Naha, Okinawa and a month or so flying out of Iwakuni, Japan. I returned to Southern California and my wife and son in the spring of '74. I was again assigned to a "gun" squadron, went on many training deployments and attended the Navy's "TopGun" school (well before the movie). I was loving life, doing well and angling for an exchange flying billet (Air Force F-4s) at Luke AFB, when one morning, I was told I had "orders." Orders said, proceed to Meridian, Mississippi and the Navy flight school as an instructor pilot. Gulp! Long story (too long), but I was also offered the choice of going back to Yuma and being an instructor in our F-4 training squadron. I "decided" to go to Yuma and stay in F-4s. Good Decision.

So, in 1976 I, my wife, and now two sons, moved back to the small Arizona town of Yuma. It was great, bought a small house with pool, great flying weather, good target ranges, and good fishing. I flew almost every day and coached baseball and soccer. Along that time, I had to make another decision, get out of the Marine Corps and become an airline pilot, or stay in the Corps and make it my career? Tough decision. Airlines were hiring big time, pay was more than the service, only had to work 15 days a month, no long separations from my family and I was promised I could join the Marine Corps Reserve and fly the F-4 on weekends. Not only that, but post-Vietnam there was a lot of unrest in Marine Aviation. Nobody knew the future of Marine Aviation, and morale was poor. It seemed at the time that at least a pilot a week in my squadron was submitting his resignation and going to the airlines. I was tempted, very tempted. I even went out and got an FAA qual as a flight engineer. After lying awake at night for a few months I "decided" if I could not make up my mind, then I probably didn't really want to get out. Good Decision. Lesson: THE OLD RULE OF WING-WALKING - DON'T LET GO OF WHAT YOU GOT UNTIL YOU HAVE A FIRM HOLD ON SOMETHING ELSE.

That decision was early in 1977. My next decision came up quickly in 1978. After studying the lessons of Marine Aviation in Vietnam, the Marine Corps made a momentous decision to stand up a graduate level training program and develop a true center of excellence for all Marine Aviation. The new unit was named Marine Aviation and Tactics Squadron 1 (MAWTS 1). It would be comprised of instructors from all the different types of Marine aircraft including ground support and command and control. I was invited to be one of the very first instructors. It was an honor to be asked to join and it was a prestigious position. The drawback being it would require quite a bit of travel away from my family. I decided to accept the job and quickly transferred to the new graduate level training squadron. Good Decision.

I spent four wonderful years in MAWTS. I got to fly with every F-4 squadron at every base in the Marine Corps. I was also up to my eyebrows developing and teaching new tactics and procedures for the F-4. Most importantly, I learned how Marine aviation as a whole should work as one team in support of all Marine operations. I also got to be the architect for a Marine operational aviation tactics test conducted at Nellis AFB. The test (Electronic Warfare Close Air Support-EWCAS) was to examine tactics vs. a Soviet ground-based air defense system. It was a large and detailed undertaking and a huge success. My role in that earned me the Marine Corps' Cunningham award as the Marine Aviator of the Year.

I was next transferred to a Marine Corps School (Command and Staff College) and then a year on a staff in Okinawa. It was an unaccompanied tour, but I "decided" to take my family at my own expense. Good Decision. Lesson: KEEPING YOUR FAMILY TOGETHER IS ALMOST ALWAYS A WISE DECISION

Despite my being off the Island of Okinawa quite a bit, the family had a great time living in the Japanese economy experiencing another culture. Towards the end of that tour, I was faced with another decision. I wanted to return to flying at El Toro and transition to the new F-18 aircraft and I had been assured I could. But, my assignment officer at HQ Marine Corps wanted me to go to a staff job at Marine HQ (Wash. D.C.) because there was a backlog at El Toro of Lt. Colonels and I may be there for three years, yes fly the F-18, but not get a chance of being a squadron commander. I pretty quickly said "no thanks" to the HQ job but did some research and asked to be assigned back to Yuma to wait in line for command of the F-4 training squadron (VMFAT 101) which only had three-four years left as the F-4 was being phased out. Good Decision.

I went from Japan to Yuma, my third tour there. While waiting to take command, I worked as the operations officer for the Marine Air Group (USAF Wing equivalent). I was working there as for a little less than a year when the Marine Corps made a big move. It acquired 13 Israeli Kfir aircraft to use as surrogate Soviet fighters. The concept was Marine Corps pilots would train/practice against this dissimilar adversary aircraft presenting Soviet Union Air Force tactics. I was offered the job of standing up a whole new squadron from absolute scratch. I decided to decline the F-4 Training squadron and accept the Kfir Adversary command (VMFT 401). Good Decision. What a blast! What a Challenge! Lesson: STANDING UP ANYTHING FROM THE GROUND FLOOR IS USUALLY SUPER SATISFYING.

My first day in the squadron, there was me. Period. I had a totally empty, beat up hangar, a metal desk and a phone. I would spend my day writing point papers trying to get money to fix the hangar, buy furniture etc. One day, I got a phone call from the base communications center. The Marine said he had Commandant of the Marine Corps (CMC) message for VMFT 401, please send a clerk over to pick it up. I told him I would be right over. It was my very first official message and it was the commissioning message for whole new and unique Marine Corps aviation unit.

It was quite an endeavor to get the squadron up and operating. I traveled to Israel twice. Once to discuss with the Israeli air force Kfir operations and flight safety and the second time to check out in the two-seat trainer version (with Israeli instructor pilots) which we would not be getting. My maintenance department would be civilian/ contracted but the leadership in the department would be all Israelis. I had 19 Israeli citizens along with their families move to Yuma, AZ. I had to ensure they could integrate into the Yuma community. I also had to ensure the American maintenance personnel would work compatibly with their Israeli supervisors. Moreover, I had to arrange for the aircraft to be shipped from Israel to Norfolk, made ready for flight, then my pilots and I had to ferry them to Yuma. As we flew across the USA, I remember an air traffic controller asking me, "What the heck is a Kfir?" I commanded this unique outfit for two years, huge challenge but great, great fun. The Kfir is a very reliable and fast aircraft.

I was transferred next to the National War College in Washington D.C. and after that year I went to Tampa, Fl to be a staff officer at US Central Command. I was in the J-5 plans shop when Saddam invaded Kuwait in 1990. Off to Saudi Arabia I went. Unfortunately, I did not stay in Saudi for all of Desert Shield and Desert Storm, because my wife, Cathy Rose Knutson, was diagnosed with liver cancer and I returned to Tampa in December '90. Cathy fought cancer with my help, and we thought she had won. In the summer of '91 I was selected to command MAWTS-1, the center of excellence I helped stand up when I was a captain 13 years earlier. I cannot say this was a hard decision. It was (is) a wonderful position and any Marine Aviator would have gleefully accepted it. We moved back for my fourth Yuma tour. I checked out in the F-18 and I flew as co-pilot in every type Marine Corps helicopter. My old squadron, VMFT 401 no longer had Kfirs but now had F-5s, and I checked out in those too. MAWTS then had 100 pilots/officers representing every type Marine Corps aircraft as well as maintenance specialists, expeditionary ground support personnel and aviation command and control experts. We put together huge six-week training events twice yearly. I learned how to run a really big integrated air operation. Tragedy struck, however.

In Sept 1993, I had in MAWTS a US Army pilot on exchange duty, an attack helicopter pilot, West Point Graduate, Desert Storm veteran. Major Phil Curtin was performing a night vision goggle check ride for three Marine pilots when their AH-1 aircraft collided, and all four pilots were killed. At two o'clock in the morning I had the very difficult and unpleasant duty of telling his wife, Elaine Curtin, that her husband had been killed. Elaine had two small daughters, more tragedy. During this time, Cathy's cancer had returned and despite a valiant fight, she passed away in January 1994, four months after Phil Curtin's death. My two sons were both in college at the University of Arizona in Tucson. It was very, very hard time for the Knutsons.

My command tour at MAWTS was about up, and being a Colonel with 25 years active service, I made a tentative decision to retire and move on to another chapter in my life. But then, the Brigadier General promotion list came out and I was of one of 12 officers selected for Brigadier General. After much thought and consideration (my sons had just lost their mother), I decided to remain in the Corps and accept the promotion to General.

Leaving my sons at the University of Arizona, I transferred to Quantico, VA and became the Director of Marine Corps Training and Education. Good Decision.

After Phil Curtin was killed, I and my squadron naturally did everything possible to ease Elaine's and her daughters' difficult time. My wife, (before she passed away) and I spent much time with Elaine as well as ensuring all Elaine's legal and financial items were dealt with. Elaine stayed in Yuma until June after Phil was killed, then moved herself and daughters to Georgia where she had family and friends. This was the same time I was transferring to Quantico. I stayed in close touch with Elaine, probably instinctively because both of us were going through the grieving process. Over time we started talking more often. Then, we started to visit each other. Then we fell in love. Then, we got married. Wonderful! Good Decision. We've been married 24 years now. I became the father to her two daughters. Lesson: WHEN NIGHTIME COMES, THERE IS ALWAYS ANOTHER DAWN.

Just after Elaine and I married, the Marine Corps gave me command of the First Marine Aircraft Wing headquartered in Okinawa, Japan. The First MAW has about 300 aircraft and 6500 personnel stationed in Okinawa, Iwakuni, Japan and Kaneohe Bay, Hawaii. To say I was busy those two years, is a large understatement. We had a wonderful time and it was good for all of us as we became a family. In the spring of 1998, the Commandant gave me command of the First Marine Expeditionary Force (I MEF) in Camp Pendleton California. This was way cool. The command is the largest fighting force in the Marine Corps. It consists of the First Marine Infantry Division, the Third Marine Aircraft Wing and the First Marine Logistics group. Altogether it had over 45,000 Marines and sailors based at Camp Pendleton, Marine Corps Air Stations Miramar and Yuma, and Marine Corp Base 29 Palms, CA. I was the first aviator ever to command I MEF. Besides overseeing daily operations, I was responsible for all of Marine operational plans for the defense of Korea, and the Persian Gulf contingencies. I traveled a lot. What a challenge! What a thrill! All went well those two years. I finished out my active duty career as the commanding general of the Marine Corps Combat Development Command in Quantico, VA. This was basically a staff job but very instrumental for Marine Corps force development.

I "decided" to retire in 2001 because I was offered the position of "Marine Corps Senior Mentor." Good Decision....but for a while, I regretted it because I retired in July 2001 and two months later 9/11 occurred. I was sick to my stomach for a long, long time in that I was not in uniform when our country went into a crisis. True story: During that period as America was gearing up for war in Iraq and Afghanistan, I had several friends and neighbors say things to me along the lines of, "Lucky you, you got out just in time." That was the exact opposite of how I felt. In senior mentoring though, I was able to contribute. I helped train every commanding general and their staffs prior to their rotation to Iraq and Afghanistan. I traveled to Iran and Afghanistan several times along with many trips to the Korean theater.

A long story, but several years (2012) after moving to Tucson, Elaine and I adopted two of our grandchildren. I am now raising my third generation of children. Good Decision. Lesson: RAISING CHILDREN IS GOOD DUTY.

Did I make mistakes? sure. Did I have regrets? A few. But, I conclude my story with my overarching lesson from all this. Simply stated: I did not make GOOD DECISIONS. I made DECISIONS GOOD! When faced with a decision affecting myself and my family, I considered, I pondered, I asked for advice, I discussed with my wife, I did an internal war game, and I "Decided." I then went forward, never looking back! It was my work, actions, efforts, attitudes, caring, and love AFTER DECIDING that turned all my decisions into GOOD DECISIONS.

Lesson: MAKE YOUR DECISION, THEN MAKE YOUR DECISION GOOD!

CHAPTER FIFTEEN

GRUNTS IN THE SKY – HOWEVER, EVERY MARINE IS A RIFLEMAN

by Marty Lenzini

I grew up in a suburb of Chicago, a hyperactive undiagnosed ADHD kid from a working family. Back in the 50s and 60s, kids like me were labeled as trouble- makers. I had lots of energy and was fearless. I had no knowledge of the military as my grandparents came from Italy and no one in my family had served in the Armed Forces.

My Dad built tanks in a factory in Chicago and was exempt from military service during WW II. I attended a Catholic grade school run by The Sisters of Loretto and a Catholic high school overseen by The Christian Brothers. The discipline at these schools kept me "in check." I received many rulers across my knuckles from the Sisters and many paddles across my posterior from the Brothers. The Catholics had a hands-on method to instill discipline. Once, in high school, I was caught fighting on the playground. I was not sent to see the Principal or suspended. Instead, I was a main feature in a boxing match. An announcement over the school public address system let all the students know that after school, in the gym, there would be a boxing match between Marty Lenzini and Joe Schmo. Joe and I put on boxing gloves and beat each other for three long rounds. My arms were so tired that by the end of the match I could hardly lift them. That was my last fight on school grounds. However, off the school campus, I still managed to stir-up trouble. During my first two years of high school I had to ride the suburban train, then transfer to the Elevated Train to get to school. There was a lot of waiting for trains, so this gave me an opportunity to explore different ways to travel. One of which was to climb to the roof of the "El Station" and then ride on the top of the train from station to station. This lasted several days until a railroad detective tried to apprehend me. He was in the train, and I was on top of the train. I lost him by jumping to a train going the other direction at the station. I learned a valuable lesson that day, ONE'S DESIRE FOR ADVENTURE CAN GET THEM INTO REAL TROUBLE. I stayed "under the radar" for many days after the incident. Years later, I looked back at this as my dormant fighter pilot gene coming to the surface.

I applied to and was accepted at the University of Notre Dame; however, my family could not afford the tuition. A high school counselor came to my rescue and gave me a NROTC scholarship application. This was my introduction to the military. Our high school senior class was over 200 students and only two of us won the prestigious NROTC scholarship. It paid for college tuition, books, lab fees and provided $50 per month for college expenses. $50 was a lot of money in 1956, my freshman year at the University of New Mexico (UNM). I chose UNM over Norte Dame because my Dad grew up in Southern Colorado and I had an uncle in Raton, NM who worked at Los Alamos Laboratory. The Marine Officer Instructor in the unit had a different mentality and focus than the Naval Officer Instructors. His was a warrior attitude vice an academic mentality. He would let us check-out an M1 rifle with 100 rounds of ammunition each weekend and go into the hills to shoot and hunt rabbits. The lesson came when we returned and learned how to clean and maintain the weapon, which was inspected in detail by the Marine Gunnery Sergeant. The unit's Marine Officer Instructor was not only a warrior, but a good leader, military teacher and mentor who was in high demand as a chaperone at our fraternity parties. Lesson: BECAUSE OF THE LEADERSHIP OF ONE MARINE OFFICER INSTRUCTOR, SIX OF THE TOP SEVEN GRADUATES OF THE NROTC UNIT CHOOSE THE MARINE OPTION AND BECAME MARINE SECOND LIEUTENANTS.

Next stop was The Basic School (TBS) at Quantico, VA. This is where I learned that the Marine Corps is a lot different than the Navy. Arriving at TBS, I brought up the fact that I was married while I was in the NROTC unit, which was strictly forbidden and which I omitted in order to keep the scholarship. I wanted to know if the Marine Corps would hold this against me. The Marine Captain checking me into TBS told me in a loud voice, "The Marine Corps doesn't give a crap if you are married or not. The Marine Corps doesn't care what color you are or where you came from. You are a Marine now and as long as you do your job and do it well you will stay a Marine." I now understand the origin of the old adage, "If the Commandant wants you to have a wife, he will issue you one." Lesson: IT WAS CLEAR THAT THE FOCUS OF THE MARINE CORPS IS ON THE RIFLEMAN. ALL JOBS IN THE CORPS SUPPORT THE MAN ON THE GROUND. YOU QUICKLY LEARN THAT ALL MARINES ARE RIFLEMEN. This focus and the bond developed between the infantrymen at the Basic School is the reason that Marines deliver the best Close Air Support (CAS) in the world. All Marine officers go through the Marine Basic School for six months to learn what Marines do. After going through the five-day war and the 600 yd. fire and maneuver at TBS, I decided that the best place for me was in the air as an aviator.

My next move was to Pensacola, FL the home of naval aviation. Navy and Marine Aviators go through the same flight training. My journey led me to flying the T-34 and T-28 for basic flight training in FL and the F-9F and F-11F for advanced flight training at Kingsville, TX. I received my Gold Wings 18 months after arriving in Pensacola in May of 1963.

My first Marine squadron was VMA-533 at Cherry Point, NC where I would be checked-out in the A-4B aircraft. A nugget (new pilot) learns a lot in his first tactical squadron. The first thing I was told when I came aboard was, Lesson: "WHATEVER YOUR JOB IS, EVEN IF IT IS THE COFFEE MESS OFFICER, TREAT IT AS THE MOST IMPORTANT JOB IN THE SQUADRON." That was good advice which I lived by throughout my career. I was blessed to have a real leader, both in the air and on the ground, as my first squadron skipper (Commanding Officer, CO). I joined the squadron a few days after he took command. One morning we were sitting in the ready room because the flight schedule was cancelled due to weather. The clouds were at 500 feet ceiling with ½ mile visibility. The skipper walked into the ready room and asked the Ops Officer why we were not flying. He said, "Because of weather, sir." The CO told the Ops Officer that you will have two flight schedules ready, so if bad weather rolls in the squadron can still fly. The Skipper turn to me and Owen Brown, (neither of us were designated section leaders) and said,

"Lenzini and Brown, get into your aircraft and do a section take-off into the GCA pattern, changing lead after each pass and fly GCAs until you run out of gas." This was a great confidence boost for two young pilots and taught me to never accept the status quo, but to be innovative.

The Skipper also had each of us fly two cross-countries a month to gain flight time and experience different weather conditions and different bases. This was in addition to our normal training syllabus. The CO wanted us all to be more than just comfortable in our aircraft. One week four of us 1st Lieutenants decided to take a cross country to the West Coast. By this time in the squadron, we were all qualified division leaders. When the Skipper saw the flight schedule, he called us into his office and said, "You are my four best Lieutenants, don't embarrass me." We thought we could do anything. We had a procedure where the flight lead for the leg would file the flight plan, the number two would fuel the jets, number three would get the weather brief and number four would check the NOTAMS. We were flying a leg into NAS Dallas and our lead called Dallas tower for landing. The tower responded, "NAS Dallas is NOTAMed as closed, what are your intentions?" Since we were down to 1300 lbs. of fuel, we told the tower that our intensions were to land. We got out of our aircraft and lined-up smartly with our fore and aft caps on, showing our shiny 1st Lieutenants bars. A Navy staff car pulls up and a Navy Captain in Dress Whites steps out and asks, "Who is leading this flight?" The Navy Captain did a double take and said, "What, four 1st Lieutenants? Your skipper let you fly together?" We all responded, "Yes sir." The Captain shook his head and said, "No Wonder!" and walks back to his staff Car. Lesson: OVER CONFIDENCE CAN BE A KILLER; HOWEVER, YOUNG LIEUTENANTS NORMALLY GET A BREAK WHEN THEY DO SOMETHING STUPID!

I was selected to go to the Naval Postgraduate School in Monterey, CA to earn an advanced degree in Aeronautical Engineering after two years in the squadron. This was 1965 and my biggest worry was that I would miss the Vietnam war. The course was three years long and I entered the school as a 1st Lieutenant and graduated as a temporary Major due to the build-up of the Armed Forces.

After Monterey, I was ordered to MCAS El Toro for A-4 refresher training in VMA-214, the Black Sheep Squadron. When I checked into the squadron, the Skipper was delighted because I was a second tour A-4 pilot. This squadron was used to train nuggets and helicopter re-treads (helicopter pilots who were transitioning to fixed wing aircraft) and the CO had almost no experienced A-4 pilots. He made heavy use of my experience. After only one FAM flight, I led a four-plane night in-flight refueling mission. In the two months of refresher training I accumulated 110 hours of flight time training new Marine pilots. I had a great relationship with the Skipper and this relationship was responsible for me getting command of a Marine Aircraft Group many years later. Lesson: RELATIONSHIPS WERE VERY IMPORTANT IN THE MARINE CORPS. I FOUND THIS TRUE ALSO IN POST-MILITARY ENDEAVORS.

I finally got to the war in September 1968. I was assigned to VMA-211, Wake Island Avengers, at Chu Lai, RVN. My job was Assistant Ops Officer. After three weeks, I had flown 20 missions, earned 1 Air Medal and I was ready to go back to the States. However, I still had 12 months and one week left on my tour. Lesson: ACTUAL COMBAT IS NOT THE HOLLYWOOD DEPICTION OF THE "GLORY" OF WAR. IT WAS DIRTY, UGLY AND DEFINITELY NOT FUN. There were four A-4 Squadrons and two A-6 Squadrons in our Air Group, MAG-12. A-4s flew days, nights and alerts. A normal day was one squadron on days, one squadron on nights and two squadrons on alert (five-minute alert) from 0600 to 1800. The A-6s flew nights 1800 to 0600. Squadrons rotated between days, nights and alerts every three or four days. Days blended into weeks, and weeks blended into months. You lost track of what day or month it was as the routine was always the same: wake-up, eat, fly, head to the O-Club and finally to your hut to sleep. As an ADHD kid I had an advantage. I was able to completely focus on the mission and not think about anything else. I never worried about getting shot down or what was happening back in the States. I flew 350 Combat missions, was awarded four DFCs and 24 Air Medals. Most of my DFCs were on missions with troops in contact, bad weather and heavy enemy fire. My time at the Basic School and the bond I had with my brothers on the ground gave me an extra incentive to ensure that my weapons were on target.

The Marine Corps taught me to do the right thing, even if it presents a problem. One of those times came when we were using the short crosswind runway. This runway required a Jet Assisted takeoff (JATO). The Group policy was: if your JATO did not light, you were to shut down the engine, drop your tail hook and catch the arresting wire at the end of the runway. On this blustery day, I launched and my JATO did not light. I kept the power at 100% and continued on. I could see that with the strong wind I could made a normal takeoff. I got airborne and flew my mission. When I returned, my Skipper wanted to see me ASAP. As I stood there, he told me that I was either the best pilot or luckiest pilot in his squadron. He chewed me out, grounded me and assigned me to be Squadron Duty Officer for three days because I violated Group Policy. I told him that the policy was flawed, why would you shut down a perfectly good engine and have no option if you had a hook skip. I did my duty, but weeks later the Group changed the policy.

After Vietnam, I was ordered to the Attack Weapons Branch in Test Operations at the Naval Missile Center, Point Mugu, CA. This was a test community, so there was no restriction on how many aircraft you could fly. I enjoyed being a test pilot and project officer for missile test and development. At the end of the three-year tour, I was qualified in the A-4, A-7, A-6 and F-4 aircraft. The inter-service relationships that I established at Point Mugu were very helpful throughout the rest of my Marine Corps service.

The next tour brought me back to the Marine Corps at MCAS Yuma. I was assigned as the Ops Officer of the A-4 Training Squadron; more training of nuggets and lots of flight time. I was finally back flying with Marines and enjoying the camaraderie at the Yuma O-Club. At the one-year mark in the tour, the Group CO selected me to command the Tactical A-4F Squadron at Yuma, VMA-223. I was still a major; however, the Commanding General of the Wing concurred with the CO's selection and I was now a Squadron Commander. This was a good time to be at YUMA as the Air Combat Maneuvering Range (ACMR). was just being established. The A-4s at this time, could not carry the ACMR pod. However, using my contacts at Point Mugu, I had them modify Walleye cables so that our A-4s could carry the pod on the Walleye station. Since the A-4Fs in the squadron had the A-4M engine with 1000lbs more thrust, our A-4s were in demand for ACM. The squadron quickly gained the reputation as a tough ACM adversary. Because of this, we were requested by VF-1, the Navy's first F-14 Squadron, to give them Air Combat Maneuver

(ACM) training. We were also the first squadron outside of the Air Force to fight the USAF aggressor Squadron. VX-4, the Navy's air-to-air tactics development squadron, also wanted an experienced adversary because they were working the Agile missile tactics. We were happy to comply. This missile was the forerunner to the AM-9X. Most of these ACM missions were flown by experienced pilots so the lieutenants were showing some displeasure. It was obvious I needed to do something to make them an integral part of the squadron. I had the Ops Officer challenge the Air Force A-7 Squadron in Tucson to a bombing derby, Lieutenant to Lieutenant. The squadron deployed and the Marine lieutenants took-on the Air Force. When we arrived, the Air Force wondered how we could just pick-up a squadron and deploy. I responded, "Because we are Marines and I did not ask for permission." Our lieutenants flew to the range as a four-plane flight of lieutenants, while the Air Force had a major or captain lead three lieutenants to the range. The A-4 has no weapons system, just an iron sight, while the A-7 had the best weapons system of any aircraft at that time. We were not the best and we were not the worst. Our hits were tightly grouped while the Air Force hits were all over the map. Score one for Marine lieutenants. The last thing I did as CO of the squadron was qualify every pilot with the Sidewinder missile. Since the Sidewinder shoots are conducted at Point Mugu, I knew how to make this happen. No, I did not ask for permission and knew there would be some "flack" afterwards. A week after the shoot, the Wing Commanding General called me to chew me out and told me that Sidewinders are for fighter pilots. I simply explained that I was just following the A-4 Training Syllabus.

After Yuma, I had a 12-month overseas tour with the grunts, the striking 9th Marine Regiment. Initially I was assigned as the Air Liaison Officer (ALO) and later as the G-3. Every time the Commanding General flew to our base, he asked me why one of his Regiments has an Aviator as the G-3, and I would always remind him that every Marine is a rifleman. Returning stateside, I had several staff tours, one in OPNAV R&D and one as the head programmer for the Marine Corps POM. This job was affectionately known as- "Prince of the POM," a really tough and important job. I scored one small victory for the Marine Corps while I was a Development Coordinator for attack weapons and aircraft, OP-982. The two-star general came to my desk and told me I had two hours to put a Laser Maverick Program into the POM. Using my experiences at Point Mugu and talking to contacts I made at China Lake, I came up with a development program which resulted in a strike weapon that the Marines and the Air Force have relied upon for CAS and interdiction missions to this day. You have to stay ready, remain flexible and be innovative, especially in Washington, when you are threatened by a two-star general.

I attended the Naval War College for senior level school and the National War College. While at National, I was selected for Colonel. I quickly sent a letter to my old Skipper of the Black Sheep Squadron, who was now Commanding General of the 2nd MAW. I reminded him how well we worked together when he was Squadron CO and requested that he select me to command one of his Aircraft Groups, MAG-12. He responded "Marty, you've got it." MAG-12 was the highlight of my career. The Group was made-up of two A-4M Squadrons, one A-6E squadron, an EA-6B detachment, a HQ and Maintenance Squadron that had OA-4M aircraft and a Marine Air Base Squadron. This was a 12-month overseas tour in Japan. Halfway through the tour, one of my A-4 squadrons was replaced with a Navy A-7 squadron, VA-105, the Gun Slingers. This was the first time since WWII that the Marines controlled a Navy squadron. The biggest concern of the Navy Skipper was how a Marine Fitness Report would look in his record.

My final Marine Corps job was in Washington, DC at HQMC. I was the head of the Plans, Programs, and Budget Branch of Marine Corps Aviation. My main responsibility was the Marine Corps Aviation Plan. Near the end of this tour, the new Commandant of the Marine Corps requested a brief on the Marine Aviation Plan. The hour brief turned into five hours with the Commandant telling me and the three-star, Deputy Commandant for Aviation, that he wanted to, "...turn in F-18 aircraft for more helicopters." Since the Marine aircraft and weapons are bought with Navy "Blue Dollars," the Navy would gladly take F-18s off our hands, but we would not get more helicopters. It took three years of hard work by myself and my three -star boss to harmonize the Navy and the Marine Corps Aviation Plans. At this point, the unending politics of Washington got to me and I put in for retirement. I asked for a small ceremony with only the Aviation Department in attendance. Who shows up, but the Commandant with the Secretary of the Navy - not a bad way to exit active duty.

Looking back, the Marine Corps took a directionless Chicago kid and gave him the training and opportunity for a lifetime of excitement and success. The Marines taught me a most valuable lesson - ALL MARINES ARE RIFLEMEN - we are the quintessential "band of brothers" - every Marine has ALL Marines' back - our country could learn a lot from that lesson.

CHAPTER SIXTEEN

EARTH TO THE MOON
by Jim McDivitt

I taxied-out to lead a group of 48 F-80s on a mission in the Korean war. I was 23 years old and a Lieutenant. I only had 400 hours of flying time but I had more combat time than anyone else in the squadron.

Such was the nature of Korea. Just like Pearl Harbor, we were a nation unprepared for the war we entered. The North Koreans alone had almost pushed the South Koreans and us into the Yellow Sea from the Pusan perimeter. We played a pickup game until MacArthur pulled off the Inchon landing, encircled much of North Korea's fighting forces and pushed the rest back to the Yalu River. It looked like we had won, and MacArthur was once again a hero, but China came to the aid of North Korea: GAME ON! Lesson: THE ENEMY ALWAYS HAS A VOTE.

I was an Irish Catholic kid, born in Chicago, raised and finished high school in Kalamazoo, MI. I was a Boy Scout soaring to the rank of "Tenderfoot." Growing up in Michigan was a great life. I was a post-Depression kid being born in 1929 and never noticed our poverty because most people had the same things, enough to eat and a warm house, what else would one need? I probably noticed the moon when I was a kid, but I was not mesmerized by it. Little did I know it would play a major part in my later life.

I was always a good student. My life growing up included jobs such as newspaper boy, grocery store clerk, bowling alley pin setter, mowing lawns and shoveling snow. My father worked as a Railway Express clerk in Chicago. Later, he became a Railway Express truck driver delivering packages and we moved to Wisconsin, then back to Chicago, then to Michigan where I graduated from high school in 1947, I worked for a year in a water heater factory, then went to Jackson Junior College because I didn't have the money for four years of school.

When it came time for me to enter the workforce, Korea was on the map, and the Air Force had become a separate service. I applied for the Air Force Aviation Cadet program, was selected and went to Moultrie, GA to await pilot training. I had never been in an airplane before. We flew the new T-6Gs with civilian contract instructors. Then, I went to Williams AFB and flew the old T-6s because the T-28s were shedding props. We also got three hops in the T-33, then soloed and finished training in the F-80. I graduated and was commissioned a 2d Lt. in 1952.

After pilot training, I went to Luke AFB, AZ and trained for gunnery in the F-80. We also got 10 hours in the F-84, "The Lead Sled," as it was called. After I had been at Luke for two weeks, I contracted mononucleosis and washed back a couple of classes. I graduated from Luke with orders in hand for Korea in the F-84 even though I only had 10 hours in the airplane and had done my gunnery training in the F-80. Lesson: YOU DON'T HAVE TO BE AN EXPERIENCED PILOT TO GO TO WAR. YOU JUST HAVE TO GO. YOU'LL GET PLENTY OF EXPERIENCE THERE.

I was scheduled to depart from San Francisco and while waiting for the departing flight, I spied some pilots I had seen at Luke and struck up a conversation. We were all questioning why we were being sent to Korea in F-84s when our gunnery training was in the F-80, Catch-22. One of the pilots mentioned he had a cousin in personnel, a two-stripper, who was leaving on the same flight. He talked to his cousin, and soon we all had orders to the F-80 rather than the Lead Sled and were off to Korea to win the war. I was headed for K-13 at Suwon, 40 miles south of Seoul. Lesson: IT'S ALWAYS GOOD TO KNOW SOMEONE IN PERSONNEL.

The F-80 was instrumental in establishing air superiority over the North Koreans early in the war, but by the time we arrived in Korea, the F-86s were assuming the air-to-air role and the F-80s were relegated to air-to-ground interdiction and Close Air Support (CAS). I started out as a wingman, then progressed to element lead, then flight lead, then squadron leader and finally group leader. I was a group leader as a 1st Lt. leading as many as 48 airplanes because I had more combat time than most all the other pilots. I got about 80 missions in the F-80 and then checked out in the F-86.

The F-80s were being moved out and the F-86s began to cover both air-to-air and air-to-ground roles. My F-86 checkout was pretty perfunctory: here's a Dash One, study it; a couple of short sessions on the electrical and hydraulic systems; a crew chief showed you how to strap-in and start, and good luck, you were on your way.

I had some great mentors. One of the best, was a professional singer, Capt. Keeler. He was the best briefer and flight leader I saw in the war. I wanted to be like him. We also had one crazy squadron commander who came to us air-to-mud guys, told us we were crap and we needed to "GO KILL MiGs." He wanted us to all be Aces. He took us on dumb and dangerous flights 50-100 miles deep into China, an unnecessary risk. He climbed us to high altitude 45-48,000 ft. where we had no ability to turn, much less break. We never encountered MiGs, because they were behind and well below us near the Yalu, a total waste of time. Lesson: SUPPORT OF GROUND TROOPS WASN'T AS GLAMOROUS AS CHASING MIGS, BUT WAS EVERY BIT AS IMPORTANT; The Korean War tour was set at 100 missions, but every time I approached 100, my squadron commander needed someone qualified as a group leader and I was one of the few left in theatre. I finished with 145 missions. I flew my last mission two hours after the Armistice was signed.

Out of Korea, I guess they thought my Korean blood was cold enough for the extreme northeast U.S, so I went to Dow AFB, ME to fly F-86Fs in the air defense mission. I was an experienced combat pilot, a 1st Lt. and Assistant Ops Officer. I met Capt. Keeler once again. He had lost his spot promotion and was back to 1st Lt. He was now in Ferry Command, a total waste of the talent of a great combat leader. About all we did in the 86F was practice trying to intercept B-47s and B-52s. I went to Tyndall and checked out in F-86Ds, then to McGuire AFB NJ, still in air defense.

It was time to finally get my college degree and I was sent to the University of Michigan in Aeronautical Engineering. An interesting part of my career was about to begin. I finished first in my class, left college and went to Edwards AFB, CA, to the Air Force Test Pilot School. Lesson: IT'S NEVER TOO LATE TO GET A DEGREE.

This was a most interesting era of aeronautical research. The military was preparing for the next step up from the early Century Series fighters and I got to fly many of the developmental types. Also, Bob White was scheduled to become the lead X-15 pilot and I was to become the backup in the program as well as work development of the F-4, a full and interesting plate. Then, came my big decision: NASA!

My initial decision was not to apply for the astronaut program. I enjoyed flying airplanes and my opportunity to fly in the X-15 and F-4 programs was appealing. I was also involved in developing the curricula for the Advanced Test Pilot School at Edwards. It was the equivalent of a Masters degree for test pilots. I discussed the NASA thing with several people and decided to fill out the application. I actually sent it in late. When the Director of Flight Test found out, he stormed into the office, ripped up my application, threw it on the floor and called me a "deserter." I noted he did not seem pleased. He considered leaving the Air Force for the NASA program comparable to being a traitor. He took me off all programs and I had nothing to fly. I assumed my Air Force career was finished. My name was mud at Edwards, but I was selected for the astronaut program and headed for space. Long after he retired, the Director wrote me a letter, apologized and said he was wrong. The space program was well-underway by that time

President Kennedy was inaugurated in January 1962. He made his "moon speech" in September and I joined the second group of astronauts the same month amidst much hoopla. We completed the early round of press interviews at the Rice Hotel in Houston and stopped by a truckers convention room for free food and beer. I guess we didn't look like truckers, because we were thrown out. Our celebrity status was not yet widely appreciated.

Initially, the astronaut program was a disappointment for me; I wanted to fly, and we had nothing to fly. The Mercury Seven astronauts had performed six space flights designed to prove the U.S. could orbit the earth, function in space and safely recover, the building blocks. As the second group, we were assigned the responsibility for the next step, the Gemini program, but there were no spacecraft.

The Gemini program was to take the next steps towards fulfilling President Kennedy's vision to "...land a man on the moon within this decade." Kennedy was assassinated in 1963. Gulp. We had no idea what would happen to NASA, but Lyndon Baines Johnson picked up the moon mantel. We met him. He was larger than life, a real character. We liked him and he liked us. He gave me a "spot promotion" from major to lieutenant colonel, then I really liked him. I was a lieutenant for a long time. I made captain at Edwards and was a captain for a long time. Promotions did not come rapidly at NASA.

He sent us, no-notice with wives, to Paris with VP Humphrey to tout the U.S. space program. Lady Bird loaned clothes to our wives for the trip. It was a heady time for all, of us.

Our specific mission with Gemini was to develop the technology to test astronauts' ability for long duration missions, up to two weeks; develop rendezvous and docking ability in orbit around the earth and moon; perfect re-entry and recovery; and develop understanding of issues for future long-term space flights. Ten missions were scheduled between the Mercury and Apollo moon-landing flights. We had to prove man could exist for long durations in space. Some scientists predicted our hearts would stop after a few days as the heart muscles weakened from reduced gravity. There was so much we didn't know, and we were the guinea pigs to find out.

The Mercury capsules were launched on Redstone and Atlas rockets. In Gemini, we were to boost out on Titan IIs, bigger, faster, further, and from a one man to two-man capsule. It was a busy and ambitious program, much to be done in a hurry. I flew Gemini 4 with my close friend, Ed White. He and I had been at Michigan together. I was the mission commander and our duties included a long, for the time, four-day flight and our first Extra Vehicular Activity (EVA) spacewalk. Ed flew tethered outside the capsule for 20 minutes, an American first, and we encountered a potentially serious problem that demonstrated the dangers of space activities.

For Ed to exit the capsule, we had to depressurize and open the hatch. The hatch handle was stubborn and potentially faulty, a red-light warning. I had seen support crews on the ground encounter the same problem and watched them fix it. The issue was clear: if we got the hatch open and could not get it closed, we would burn up on re-entry, dead meat. Ed and I discussed the problem. I was confident I could perform the same procedure used on the ground to relatch. After discussion, we decided to "give it a go." The hatch, opened, the hatch closed, we lived. Lesson: THE CORE OF EXPLORATION IS RISK VS. REWARD. SERIOUS RISK SHOULD INVOLVE CONSULTATION AND AGREEMENT BY EXPERTS. That is exactly what we did. We came. We saw. We conquered, but we did not take action until we had input from two experts, us, and we both understood the risk. We made an intelligent decision to proceed. When Ed and I splashed down in the ocean, I looked at him and asked, "How do you feel?" He said, "Fine," and I said, "So do I, so I guess the doctors were wrong. We're not dead."

Our next challenge after Gemini was the Apollo program to train for and execute the moon landing. The crew for Apollo 1 was Roger Chafee, Gus Grissom and my friend, Ed White. Unfortunately, on 27 January 1967, Ed White, my dear friend, superb test pilot, brilliant engineer and astronaut, was killed along with the rest of the crew during a tragic accident. A fire swept instantly through the pure oxygen environment in the command module during a training session. The saddest day of my life was visiting Ed's family.

When the Apollo program regrouped after the accident, I flew on Apollo 9 as mission commander along with Dave Scott and Rusty Schweickart. The mission was delayed because we all had colds, but we finally launched on the powerful three stage Saturn V rocket. With the thrust of the more powerful engine, we experienced eight and one-half G's as the fuel burned off and our speed increased. On re-entry we were subjected to as much as 10 1/2 Gs.

Our mission was the first with the fully mated Apollo assembly, the Command Module, the Service Module and the Lunar Module. It was a low earth-orbit mission to qualify the Lunar Module for operation in preparation for the moon landing. We had to show we could separate, fly and dock with the Lunar Module. Rusty Schweickart also performed an EVA. I flew the Lunar Module along with Rusty. We separated from Dave in the Command Module by 115 miles, the first American untethered separation in a vehicle that could not return to earth on its own if it could not redock. It was a high-pressure event, and no one had ever accomplished it before. Lesson: SPACE INVOLVES INHERENT DANGERS, BUT WE DID NOT TAKE FOOLISH RISKS. WE TRAINED INCESSANTLY

FOR DIFFICULT TASKS AND ALWAYS HAD CONTINGENCY PLANS FOR FAILURE. Apollo 9 was my last space flight.

In May '69 I became manager of Lunar Landing Operations and then Manager of the Apollo Spacecraft Program in August, managing Apollos 12, 13, 14, 15 and 16. Apollo 11 was the ultimate reward for all our hard work. Three days after launch on 16 July 1969 they entered lunar orbit. On 20 July the Eagle landed on the Sea of Tranquility. Neil Armstrong was the first human to step on the moon, and Buzz Aldrin joined him 20 minutes later. They spent two and one-half hours picking up 50lbs. of rock. Meanwhile, Michael Collins, operated the Command Module in lunar orbit. TV watchers worldwide held their breath as the "Eagle" lifted off after 21 hours. Neil and Buzz used the same procedures developed by Rusty Schweickart and me on Apollo 9 to rendezvous with Collins. 30 more orbits, and Apollo 9 jettisoned the Eagle and fired engines to return to earth a little over eight days after departure. They splashed down in the Pacific and were picked up by crews from the Navy carrier, Hornet, a crowning jewel of accomplishment for America.

"HOUSTON, WE'VE HAD A PROBLEM." It was a problem indeed, a BIG one. One of my greatest challenges as Apollo manager came with Apollo 13. The incident called upon everything I had learned about tests, engineering, management and leadership. I was on the floor in Mission Control when it happened. The crew, Jim Lovell, Jack Swigert and Fred Haise were the seventh Apollo mission and scheduled to be the third moon landing. Swigert was inserted as a backup for Ken Mattingly who had been inadvertently exposed to the measles. Lesson: BEING A BACKUP IS OFTEN AS IMPORTANT AS BEING ON THE FIRST TEAM.

The Apollo 13 crew was in the Command Module (CM) mated with the Service Module (SM) and Lunar Module (LM), when the explosion of an oxygen tank occurred in the SM. Oxygen was required for breathing and generating power to operate systems for re-entry. This was not just a problem. It was an immediate CRISIS. The CM had to be shut down and the crew moved into the LM that was designed to support two men for two days. Now, it had to be jury-rigged to support three men for four days on the return trip. Further, we now had to remove cartridges from the CM to facilitate removal of carbon dioxide from the LM. All this required consultation with expert engineers and other astronauts to structure improvised solutions. There was no manual for this emergency. The overall objective was to design innovative work-around solutions to conserve oxygen and power for re-entry. This left conditions in the LM miserable for the crew, cold, wet and cramped. The journey home required four days and a carefully timed movement of the crew back into the CM from the LM for re-entry. During the crisis I met with the crew's families. I told them I thought we had a very good plan for recovery. I explained the plan. I could not tell them I was certain we would be successful. They understood.

The lessons I learned from Apollo 13 are not new but deserve repeating: Lesson: WHEN A CRISIS OCCURS, YOU MUST HAVE CREATED A TEAM. A CRISIS INVOLVES COLLABORATION AND A PROCESS FOR LISTENING AND DECIDING WHO YOU CAN TRUST BEFORE MAKING A FINAL IMPORTANT DECISION. I had a team of 400 experts available. I couldn't listen to all, but I knew who I wanted around me.

As Astronauts our career patterns did not fit the standard mold. I got my Bachelors degree later than most and did not attend intermediate or senior service schools; however, my astronaut and NASA experience was recognized and I retired as a Brigadier General in 1972. Lesson: ONE CAN TRY TO HANG ON FOREVER, BUT AT SOME POINT, IT IS TIME TO PASS THE BATON. We passed the baton from the Apollo program to the Space Shuttle.

My post retirement experiences included senior executive positions with an electric power company and the Pullman Car Company. I was a railcar salesman. I also learned many lessons from the civilian sector, but those are different stories for another time.

I am 91-years old. We have a summer home in Michigan and a winter home in Tucson. On Fridays I lunch with the Friday Pilots. It's a good way to spend part of my day with guys like me that learned to manage risk-reward and took "measured" risks under difficult circumstances.

CHAPTER SEVENTEEN

ROGER BALL HORNET – COMMAND, NOT STAFF

by Daniel E. Moore, Jr.

> We believe in <u>command</u>, not <u>staff</u>. We believe we have "real" things to do. The Navy believes in putting a man in a position with a job to do and let him do it — give him hell if he does not perform — but to be a man in his own name. We decentralize and capitalize on the capabilities of our individual people rather than centralize and make automatons of them. This builds that essential pride of service and sense of accomplishment. If it results in a certain amount of cockiness, I am for it.
>
> *Personal papers collection of CNO Admiral*
> *Arleigh A. Burke*

Turn out your living room lights. Sit in your living room chair. Close your eyes. Let all the images behind your eyelids settle into darkness. Open your eyes. Everything is pitch black. Even though it's too dark for you to see, extend your right arm with your thumb pointing up. For the next 15 minutes every external light you see will fit inside your extended thumbnail. If you sit up and fly right, those tiny lights inside your thumbnail will explode in size — in less than 20 seconds — becoming large enough to swallow up you, your living room, your house, and most of the houses on your block. If you miss the arresting wire, the flight deck feels like an ice-skating rink as you slide across it — lights flash by in a couple of seconds and instantly disappear behind you. Everything is pitch black. Every external light you see fits inside your extended thumbnail. If all goes well, you'll make it aboard on your second pass. With each missed approach or landing, the degree of danger increases. You're quickly running out of gas and there's no other place to land. If the weather and sea state are bad, you may find yourself descending in a parachute into 30-degree water with 15 to 30-foot waves. You start to remember the videos from your initial flight training at NAS Pensacola showing pilots who "make a play for the deck." Red flashing wave off lights illuminate the underside of a jet with the pilot desperately pulling its nose up just before it hits the back of the ship (the ramp) and explodes into five or six flaming pieces that go skidding down the flight deck.

Welcome to night carrier landings.

Among carrier pilots it's well known that stress levels for carrier pilots increase the most during carrier landings, even more than in combat.

My fellow Friday Pilots unanimously applaud NASA's wisdom in selecting from the ranks of carrier aviation five out of the six astronauts that successfully landed on the moon: Neil Armstrong, the first man to land and walk on the moon, Pete Conrad, Alan Shepard, John Young and Gene Cernan, the last man to land and walk on the moon.

Take O'Hare Airport's runway of 13,000 feet with 50 airplanes. Stuff it onto a 1,000-foot-long postage stamp in the middle of the ocean. Fill it with over 100 airplanes in continuously changing states of flight and readiness. Some are taking off in afterburner and landing simultaneously every 45 seconds. Hundreds of people are scurrying within inches of airplane afterburners and jet intakes at full power. This ballet goes on 24 hours a day, 7 days a week, 365 days a year. It succeeds because all 5,000 of the people aboard have a job to do: boiler technicians, propulsion engineers, mess cooks, laundrymen, coop cleaners, yeoman, meteorologists, intelligence officers, helmsmen, signalmen, boatswain mates, navigators, aircraft maintenance, aircraft troubleshooters, the air boss, catapult and arresting gear crews, shooters, weapon handlers, weapon loaders, plane captains, taxi directors, dentists, doctors, pilots and the commanding officer. They stay calm and carry on – day, night, sun, rain, snow or ice –on the world's oceans, seas, fjords – on flight decks coated with sea spray, salt, oil, jet fuel, soap, and sometimes, blood.

A hundred things I have no control over could go wrong and wreck my career. . .but wherever I go from here, I'll never have a better job than this. This is the best job in the world.

Aircraft Carrier Commanding Officer

"The Self-Designing High-Reliability Organization: Aircraft Carrier Flight Operations at Sea" Naval War College Review, Autumn 1987

The crucible of the aircraft carrier molds and produces some of the world's finest leaders, enlisted and officer. There's no place to hide, just perform, no excuses. When you're with your shipmates 24/7 for months at a time, you get to know a person's character.

When an arresting wire jerks an aircraft to a stop, responsibility for the aircraft shifts from the pilot to one of the rottweilers of the flight deck, an enlisted yellow shirt. The pilot is now an overpaid brake rider. Failure by an officer pilot to immediately see and heed hand and head signals from enlisted yellow shirts is first met with a yellow shirt hand signal that has a fist pulled down from an extended palm, telling the officer pilot to pull his head out of his a**. This isn't missed by the watchful eyes of the commanding officer, air boss, fellow pilots and other yellow shirts. If needed, the level of involvement instantly elevates to the air boss sitting in the tower overlooking the flight deck. Responsible for everyone and everything on the flight deck, it's really bad when the air boss is compelled to make a radio broadcast with hundreds of people listening in, telling a pilot to pay attention to the yellow shirt. If this fails to correct the situation, the pilot brake rider is fired, at least temporarily, when a tow bar and tractor are attached, and the pilot and aircraft are dragged across the flight deck for a very public ride of shame.

While the air boss is responsible for everyone and everything on the flight deck, the landing signal officer (LSO) is responsible for safe and efficient landings during the last 20 seconds of approach and landing. This begins at three-quarters of a mile from touch down. The pilot transmits over the common radio landing frequency the side number of the aircraft, the type of aircraft and that the pilot sees the visual glideslope indicator or "ball," and the aircraft's fuel state — *"101 Hornet Ball 5.2."* The LSO responds with — *"Roger Ball Hornet"* confirming that the pilot is currently within safe landing parameters and may continue the approach and that the aircraft carrier's arresting gear engines have the proper weight settings for a Hornet. Interestingly, the tone of voice used by the pilot and the LSO during those two brief transmissions significantly impact whether the following approach and landing are a "ho hum" routine or a "white knuckle on the edge of seat" kind of affair. During the remaining seconds before arrestment, the LSO has the final say in determining whether the aircraft and flight deck are safe for landing. If needed, the LSO provides the pilot with visual and radio cues or commands necessary to maintain a safe approach to landing. The LSO waves off the aircraft if the approach or flight deck become unsafe.

Central to this is a bond of honesty and trust between the LSO and all the air wing pilots, the air boss and the carrier commanding officer. This honesty and trust build over months, years and decades involving tens of thousands of landings, first in field carrier landing practice (FCLP), then day, and then night carrier qualifications and finally in deployed carrier flight operations. The performance abilities of both pilots and LSOs are constantly recorded and on display for continuous learning and feedback.

In the early days of carrier landings, LSOs used paddles to signal or "wave" to the pilots during their final approach. Hence LSOs are often called "paddles" and are "waving" airplanes as they land.

Seventeen of my 29 years in uniform, involved mastering and teaching the art and science of global carrier flight operations. During those years, we conducted safe and efficient carrier flight operations in the Pacific, Atlantic and Arctic Oceans, the Mediterranean and Adriatic Seas and the Persian Gulf — day, night, rain, sleet, snow, fog with pitching and rolling flight decks. Our six carrier deployments supported several conflicts: Iranian Hostage Crisis; Reflagging of Kuwaiti Tankers in the Persian Gulf; Operations Desert Shield and Desert Storm; Operation Deny Flight over Bosnia-Herzegovina and enforcing the no-fly zones of Operation Southern Watch in Southern Iraq.

Three types of leaders emerged during my 29 years of active duty. The first two were best described by General Dwight D. Eisenhower shortly after WWII in his address to the Reserve Officers' Association:

> Lack of leadership cannot be compensated for by rank, front, or any of the surface qualities that gain a man the reputation of a winning personality. Soldiers apply an acid test to their officers that only the true leader can survive. Our men invariably recognize and repudiate pretense, selfishness, evasion of responsibility and dodging of effort. The officer who fakes or shirks or dodges is an open book to them. His position may compel them to obey his orders, but he cannot lead or inspire them.

> The officer, however, who puts his job and his men first, who helps them over the hurdles, who knows their problems, who shares their ups and downs without ostentation or pretentiousness, who wins their confidence, inspires an eager will to follow him. Moreover, he himself learns from them and in this process of mutual help the whole unit achieves maximum efficiency and morale and becomes an elite unit.

From the moment I was born, I've been surrounded by and inspired by the second type of leaders to include my Dad, Richard (Dick) Leopold, William S. Sims, John (Spider) Lockard, Mike (Wizzard) McCabe, Jim Stockdale, Daniel (Doc) Zoerb, Phil (Salami) Anselmo, Jerry (Hook) Singleton, Leon (Bud) Edney, Joel Collins, Ben Kohlmann, Tom Blackburn, Adrian Marks, Ira (Ike) Kepford, and Jim McDivitt. Each of these leaders embodied Admiral Burke's vision of command, not staff.

"Caretaker" describes the third type of leader. They show up on time, do their job, keep their hair cut, shine their shoes, and press their uniforms. They view positions of increasing authority and responsibility not as an opportunity to make a positive difference but rather as steppingstones for promotion — to be crossed as quickly as possible. They have neither the time nor interest in learning and practicing the skills of the second type of leader. They stay in their lane. They don't rock the boat. They go along to get along.

Only in retrospect did I fully understand and appreciate FIVE LEADERSHIP LESSONS. The first is distilled from *Naval Command and Control* doctrine, NDP-6, published in 1987.

To strike a balance between freedom of action and synchronized operations, naval commanders use two types of control: *mission control* and *detailed control*. Mission control allows commanders to exercise a "loose rein" approach to maximizing individual and team performance so they can flourish and exploit during periods of chaos, confusion, uncertainty and time compression. Commanders define mission requirements to guide subordinate actions and then permit them freedom of action – expecting them to use initiative and creativity to achieve the highest possible levels of performance. Orders and commands are necessarily succinct – reduced to words or sentences. Spontaneous cooperation and horizontal communications across the team produces unity of effort and continuous learning. Everyone focuses outward on the enemy and situation rather than inward and upward awaiting orders from above. Mission control offers commanders high degrees of resiliency during combat and danger and is less vulnerable to disruption than detailed control.

Detailed control is preferred when time is not a critical factor and safety is paramount. Commanders adopt a "tight-rein" approach. They centralize command and control. Orders and plans are detailed and specific. Information flows vertically up the chain of command and orders flow down. Close adherence to process and procedures is essential for safety reasons in running a nuclear power plant or restrictive rules of engagement. Detailed control seizes up when confronted with fluid situations or uncertainty. It's dysfunctional when vertical information flows are disrupted. Detailed control is not preferred under conditions of uncertainty or time constraints.

First Lesson – IN PRACTICE, COMMANDERS CANNOT RELY SOLELY ON MISSION OR DETAILED CONTROL. IT DEPENDS ON THE CHARACTER AND QUALITY OF THEIR PEOPLE, THE ENEMY, AND THE NATURE OF THE OPERATION OR TASK. Detailed control may be more appropriate in performing precise or technical tasks like airspace control but not in the conduct of high-tempo operations that require experience, judgment, initiative and creativity. As the more ambitious form of control, mission control demands more from leaders at every level.

Second Lesson – MY GREATEST OPPORTUNITIES FOR PEAK PROFESSIONAL LEADERSHIP PERFORMANCE OCCURRED DURING MY MORE JUNIOR LEADERSHIP POSITIONS – VA-25 squadron pilot and LSO, VFA-125 flight instructor and training LSO, senior airwing LSO and pilot. During those years, as long as I met performance expectations, I was given extraordinary freedom, authority and responsibility by my squadron commanding officers, carrier air wing commanders, carrier commanding officers and battle group admirals. My most productive and fun tour was as air wing LSO. We worked hard and played hard – flying and waving almost every day enduring the most challenging environments above the Arctic Circle with pitching and rolling decks at night and no diverts.

Third Lesson – MOVING UP THE CHAIN OF COMMAND REDUCES YOUR ABILITY TO HELP THE TEAM ACHIEVE PEAK PERFORMANCE. This is often due to increasing numbers of internal competing centers of gravity that have nothing to do with mission accomplishment. The hubris of remote professional politicians and senior officers detached from the realities of combat and deployed operations often convinces them to impose detailed control when mission control is necessary to compete and win against capable and determined enemies in rapidly changing environments. This syndrome is succinctly described by the British as, "lions led by donkeys."

Fourth Lesson – With nearly 5,000 people, an aircraft carrier is arguably the largest span of control that a single person, the commanding officer, can directly impact. THOSE WHO EMPOWER AND DELEGATE WERE THE MOST SUCCESSFUL. Even on a carrier with clear lines of authority and responsibility a lot of internal friction builds up. One of my favorite carrier commanding officers had a "No No Policy." This meant the only person on the carrier that could say no to a request or a proposal was the commanding officer and everyone knew it from the most junior sailor to the crustiest Old Salt. Consequently, it produced a carrier where "yes" was the most likely answer to getting things done.

Fifth Lesson– EVERY NIGHT I COUNT MY BLESSINGS AND THANK GOD FOR MY FAMILY, SHIPMATES, FRIENDS AND THE DAILY OPPORTUNITIES TO LEARN, TEACH AND RE-LEARN THE LEADERSHIP LESSONS OF <u>COMMAND</u>, NOT <u>STAFF</u>.

I close my eyes. It's night. We're in the Arctic Ocean out of range of the nearest divert field — 1,500 miles from the nearest land. We have 40 aircraft airborne and the ceiling and visibility are rapidly and unexpectedly dropping to minimums. On the LSO platform I feel the flight deck rolling and pitching beneath my feet. The seas are heaving with 30-foot swells. We're drenched in salt spray. The lights of the mast on the destroyer "plane guard" one mile astern of the carrier gives us our only reference to a horizon as we stare into a black void. Because of the swells, the mast lights bob and sway like a drunken cork. Sometimes they disappear for five to six seconds. Just above the mast lights the lights of an F/A-18 on approach fade in and out of the fog and a ragged ceiling. It's showtime.

"101 Hornet Ball 5.2"

"Roger Ball Hornet."

I was fortunate to serve during the Golden Age of Naval Aviation from 1977 to 2006. My wonderful days at sea include:

- VA-25, an A-7E Corsair II squadron pilot and LSO
- VFA-125, among the first Hornet (F/A-18) flight instructors and training LSOs responsible for training the first 100 USN/USMC and Royal Australian Air Force (RAAF) instructor pilots. Our small VFA-125 LSO team spent countless hours learning and developing a syllabus, night carrier flight simulators, and the thousands of night practice landings — often after midnight — necessary to night carrier qualify pilots and LSOs for the first seven F/A-18 Hornet squadrons: VFA-125, VFA-131, 132,

VMFA-314 and 323 on USS Coral Sea (CV-43); VFA-25 and 113 on USS Constellation (CV-64)

- Senior LSO Carrier Air Wing FOURTEEN (CVW-14) responsible for all airwing aircraft, F/A-18, F-14, A-6, EA-6B, E-2, S-3, and SH-3 during three months of workups and six months of deployment. First west coast deployment of F/A-18 Hornets.
- VFA-131 F/A-18 squadron operations officer aboard USS Dwight D. Eisenhower (CVN-69)
- VFA-81 F/A -18 commanding officer aboard USS Saratoga (CV-60)

"Roger Ball Hornet" is one of the several chapters intended to be included in *Aviator Sketchbook* — © 2020 All Rights Reserved — a book by Daniel Moore, Jr. It is made up of a series of factual penetrations behind the misty veil of the past and forms a definitive link in the ever-lengthening chain which is the aviation story, to be published in 2021.

CHAPTER EIGHTEEN

STUFF HAPPENS

by Chuck Ogren

I was born in 1941 at Walter Reed Medical Center in Washington DC, four months before Pearl Harbor. My father was an Army dentist and was stationed at Fort Meyer, Virginia. As an Army brat, we moved every two to three years. After Fort Meyer, I lived in Santa Fe, New Mexico; Germany as part of the US occupation after the World War II; Washington D.C.; Fort Belvoir, Virginia; Schofield Barracks, Hawaii; Fort Sheridan, Illinois (Highland Park HS) and Fort Sam Houston, Texas (Thomas Jefferson HS). I have a number of good memories through these years, especially from our three years in Hawaii and a few not-so-good that are related to moving and leaving friends and familiar locales for the unknown.

The best (worst) example was the move from Illinois to Texas in the middle of my junior year in high school. I was actually looking forward to the move since I had heard so much about Texas sports. As I was checking into my new school, the football coach came up to me and asked who I was and where I was coming from. After I told him, his next words were, "Well, you can't play for me." Texas rules were that if you transferred into a new high school you could not play varsity football or basketball for one year. Needless to say, I was crushed. I got to play JV and then varsity basketball my senior year as well as track, where the rule did not apply. However, I did miss playing football. Lesson: STUFF HAPPENS — OFTEN WHEN WE LEAST EXPECT IT. WE CAN RECOVER AND LIFE WILL MOVE ON, OFTEN FOR THE BETTER.

I had always assumed I would attend West Point, then go into the Air Force and fly, as two of my uncles had done. My grandfather was a member of the West Point Class of 1915. His two sons were also graduates (Class of Jan 1943 and Class of 1949), and they both became pilots and served full careers in the Air Force. At some point, I learned of the plans for a new Air Force Academy. I knew then that the Air Force Academy was the place to go if I wanted to fly.

I was accepted into the Class of 1963 and reported to the Academy in June 1959. We were the first class to spend all four years at the Academy's new campus and were the fifth class to graduate. I was convinced that flying was definitely the way I wanted go and admit that I was attracted to the Strategic Air Command (SAC). They had a strong story about how they were saving the free world, and I bought into that story. I got rides in a T-33, an F-100 and an F-104 while at the Academy and on summer visits to "real" Air Force bases. These were very motivational, but it was not until pilot training at Williams AFB, Arizona that I changed my mind and became an aspiring fighter pilot. The key determinate was formation flying, first in T-37 and then in the T-38. It helped to have an old fighter pilot as my T-38 instructor. He was cool and calm and even added a few events to our instruction that were not in the syllabus.

During our T-38 four-ship formation phase, he took four of his students out together. He was in the back seat of the lead aircraft with three solo students on the wing. The only briefing was a review of rejoins after takeoff. Then he spent time on the formations he wanted us to fly and on how to conserve fuel while in the various phases of the flight. He wanted us to fly an extended fingertip with two to three ship widths between aircraft. He also wanted us to maintain a constant altitude even on turns into the two aircraft on the left wing. He never did say exactly where we were going or what we were going to do

After takeoff, we joined up and climbed out to the north of Williams (the usual formation areas were out to the east of the base). The only radio calls all day were to check the flight in, get periodic fuel checks and to tell the wingman when to select afterburner. We climbed out to 40,000 feet (well outside of the training area) leveled for a short period and then started a slow descent. As we started a left turn, I saw a large dam under lead and it finally dawned on me that we were over the Glen Canyon Dam and were descending into the Grand Canyon.

We leveled just above the bottom canyon that the river flows through and then followed the river to the west for a considerable distance. Then, Lead called for a left turn, selected afterburner and established about a 30 degree climb to the south. As we left the canyon, we passed right over the South Rim tourist area. I hope the canyon visitors were impressed with this four-ship flyby, I was.

Lead maintained the afterburner climb all the way to 50,000 ft. After a short level off, he pulled the power almost to idle and started a descent. He had it timed so we leveled out about five miles out on initial at Williams where he called for four full stop landings. Needless to say by this time, all the wingmen were well under bingo fuel. Fortunately, everyone landed safely the first time. After the flight, we had a very short debriefing. The IP told all of us, "Good flight — does anyone have any questions?" I think we were all in a state of shock and awe; no questions.

This was the same IP that teamed up with another ex-fighter pilot IP and took the students like me that were going to fighters. Instead of practicing close formation maneuvers and pitchouts and rejoins, we were introduced to basic fighter maneuvers (BFM), air-to-air fighting, for the first time. Great fun! Lesson: WHEN INSTRUCTING STUDENTS, NOTHING BEATS GIVING THEM EXPERIENCE, BUT YOU MAY HAVE TO DEFEND YOUR METHODS OF INSTRUCTION.

I was fortunate to get a fighter our of pilot training, even if it was the back seat of the F-4C. After checkout at Davis Monthan AFB, I reported to George AFB and the 497th TFS as my first PCS assignment.

Approximately 10 months later, the squadron was moved PCS to Ubon RTAFB, Thailand. I spent eight months flying combat missions (100 counters), mostly at night (497th Night Owls) into southern North Vietnam (Route Package I) and Laos trying to disrupt the supply lines on the Ho Chi Minh Trail.

I was very fortunate to have excellent front seaters, good pilots, experienced in other tactical fighters before the F-4 and with outstanding judgement. They worked hard to accomplish the mission, they appreciated and used crew concepts to maximum advantage and, most important, they didn't try to get us killed doing stupid things. Two incidents stand out where I flew with other pilots where the opposite was true. Lesson: THERE ARE GOOD AND BAD MENTORS. BOTH TEACH YOU SOMETHING.

The first, was a night mission into Route Package 1 to hunt trucks or boats. We had not sighted any targets, so we dropped our bombs on a suspected truck park (read large grove of trees) on the main road by the coast. All was well until my front seater decided to shoot our gun pod at the same trees. Since it was just starting to get light, he elected not to use any flares and rolled in for a low angle pass from the east over the water (ies, right out of the morning sky). All went well until the pull out at low altitude over the trees, when we found ourselves bracketed by 37mm rounds. How they missed us I will never know. I'm sure I could hear them passing by the aircraft. It felt like I could reach out and touch them as they went by the canopy. Then, the guy leveled out and started to head west at low altitude. I hollered at him and helped him pull up and turn toward the water in case we had any battle damage. He decided that was a good plan.

The second, was another mission on a very dark night, this time over Laos. After our first bomb pass, the front seater was in the pull out and getting ready to reposition for another run. Unfortunately, he was trying to acquire the target and let the aircraft nose get very high with low airspeed and then, started to pull into a hard turn. This is a textbook way to get the F-4 to depart controlled flight. At our altitude, the only option would be to eject since recovery would be impossible. Fortunately, I was watching the situation develop and called out a warning. When the front seater did not unload the aircraft, I grabbed the stick as the aircraft started to shutter and held it in the center as I pushed forward to unload the aircraft until we had good flying speed. The front seater was really pissed that I took control, and I don't think he ever realized or admitted how close we were to losing the airplane. I declined to fly again with either of these front seaters for the remainder of the tour. Lesson: SOMETIMES, YOU JUST GOTTA' TAKE THE RISK AND DO WHAT YOU THINK IS RIGHT.

Two additional events are worth a few words. One pilot flew a daytime sortie and was determined to get under the clouds to try and accomplish his mission. He didn't find any targets but came home with some fence wire caught on his wing and dirt inside a broken forward wing tip light. Of course, we all had to go out on the flight line to check out the bird. Unfortunately, a few months later this same pilot was trying to evade some anti-aircraft fire at night. He egressed out over the water at low altitude and flew into the Gulf at high speed, taking his back seater with him. Lesson: IN FLYING THERE ARE SOMETIMES EARLY WARNING SIGNS THAT SHOULD NOT BE IGNORED.

In the second incident, a wingman was following his lead with a standard two-mile trail across Laos to RP 1. He missed a radio call, so lead turned back and saw a fire on a mountain side that was under their route of flight. The only conclusion was that they were not paying attention and descended into the mountain. Regretfully, two of my classmates were in the rear cockpits and did not survive.

One common element in my two incidents and in the two unfortunate loses was that all of the front seat pilots involved were ex F-102 aircrews out of Air Defense Command or from Europe. We had some very skilled and dedicated pilots that flew air defense prior to the F-4 but we also had too many that, I believe, looked down on the tactical fighter role, did not take combat seriously and did not adapt to and take advantage of having a second crewman for mission success. Lesson: DON'T LET SOME A__ HOLE KILL YOU. THIS IS REALLY THE ULTIMATE CASE OF, "IF YOU SEE SOMETHING, SAY SOMETHING AND DO SOMETHING!!!"

At the end of my first tour, I went back to Davis Monthan for a front seat checkout before moving to Ramstein AFB, West Germany in Dec 1966 with an assignment to the 417th TFS flying the F-4D. Our primary mission was nuclear alert. After 18 months, the 417th transferred to Mountain Home AFB, ID. I remained at Ramstein and moved to the 13th Air Force Tac Eval Team.

I returned to the CONUS in Dec 1970 and attended the University of Arizona in Tucson, AZ to get a Masters degree in Aeronautical Engineering before reporting to the Air Force Academy in May 1971 to be an instructor, and then, Assistant Professor. I also flew the T-41 and T-33 supporting cadet programs. Lesson: EDUCATION OPENS FUTURE DOORS.

After the Academy assignment, I went back to the F-4 for a second tour in Thailand (Oct 74 - Aug 75) at Udorn RTAFB (F-4E). With the flying war over for the U.S., our primary job was to sit air defense alert. We had two missions that were still involved with the war.

The first, was overhead standby air support during the emergency evacuation of the U.S. Embassy in Saigon. The concern was that some of the South Vietnam pilots would try to disrupt the evacuation. Fortunately, we never had to leave our holding pattern and we got to watch all the activity from 15,000 feet.

The second, was air support during the Mayaguez Incident, when the Cambodian Khmer Rouge took over a U.S. cargo ship in the Gulf of Thailand and the Navy/Marines went in to free the crew and ship. Although a number of our Udorn flights did deliver ordinance to support both the insertion and withdrawal of the Marines from Koh Tong Island, my flight was scheduled after the extraction was complete. Lesson: THE EARLY BIRD GETS THE ACTION — SOMETIMES.

After the Thailand tour, I was assigned to Luke AFB, AZ as an F-4 IP and Squadron Operations Officer for a Tactical Fighter Training Squadron responsible for checking out new pilots and weapon system officers (WSOs) in the F-4. Things were going well when the stuff hit the fan.

One of our IP flight leads briefed a four-ship ground attack tactics mission. IPs were in the front seats of #1 and #3 with student WSOs in the rear cockpits; two student pilots, with IPs in the rear cockpits were at the #2 and #4 positions. On the way to the range the IP lead briefed for the flight to do a "controlled SAM break." On his call from tactical formation, all aircraft were to do a minus one G pushover to approximately 30 degrees nose low. Again, on his call, all aircraft were to recover with a straight ahead 4 to 5 G pull up. This maneuver was not included in the syllabus for this phase of training; however, it was part of the student academic training and the syllabus called for the flight lead to add events to increase mission realism.

The flight and SAM break maneuver were flown as briefed. After recovery, a smoke column was observed behind the flight and #4 failed to check in. #4 had crashed in the desert. The crew attempted to eject but too late for survival — a very sad day for everyone connected to flying operations.

One immediate result was the relief of the Squadron Operations Office, yours truly, the Squadron Commander and the Wing Deputy Commander for Operations. So, although the maneuver was within the aircraft performance limitations and there were no restrictions to performing it, the command structure was held responsible for the accident and relieved. I was reassigned to a wing staff position, the Squadron Commander retired from the Air Force and the Wing Deputy for Operations was reassigned to another base. Lesson: LIFE IS NOT ALWAYS FAIR. MILITARY FLYING IS A TOUGH BUSINESS AND COMMAND EVEN TOUGHER.

Needless to say, this incident and the resulting fallout was career limiting. I received a poor Officer Effectiveness Report (OER) that specifically referenced the accident. Although I was able to get the OER removed from my file, I was subsequently passed over for Lieutenant Colonel. Fortunately, I had some friends who helped me get a new job in the Air Staff at the Pentagon. With this vote of confidence, I was promoted the following year. Since I was out of the running for further advancement in the fighter community, I elected to retire after my Pentagon tour at the 20-year point.

My weapons requirement job in the Air Staff provided considerable exposure to the weapons development industry. This led to a high level job in program management at Hughes Aircraft in their Missile Systems Group. I spent over 30 years with Hughes and all of the various missile company combinations that evolved through mergers and acquisitions. These included, General Motors buying Hughes and then spinning it off, acquisition of General Dynamics Missiles and then Raytheon buying Texas Instruments Missiles and then Hughes.

I was fortunate to be involved in two major weapon system improvements, one for AMRAAM and one for Standard Missile 6. It was extremely satisfying to take a program from early technology development and demonstrations all the way through incorporation into a missile system and into production. Each of these developments provided a major contribution to our war fighters.

Lesson: ALTHOUGH STUFF HAPPENS, THERE ARE ALWAYS ALTERNATIVES THAT CAN PROVIDE SATISFYING RESULTS. NEVER GIVE UP! I consider myself fortunate to have had two very satisfying careers. I am a happy man.

CHAPTER NINETEEN

LIFE LESSONS FROM OLD GEEZERS

by Earl O'Loughlin

In the summer of 2019, my bride, (age 82), and I, (age 89), spent the summer building a new home after activating part of my trust and having a son take over the farm. I told all my kids that at our age most people are looking at nursing homes not starting something new. But age definitely affects people differently, as do life experiences. I realized in 2020 I am 90 years old and have a new house. I now actually have a lifetime roof guarantee. In addition, if I shoot someone, it doesn't have the impact it once had. Now, I would have a private room, three meals a day, free TV and health care. Lesson: TREAT GEEZERS WITH CARE, AND BEWARE.

The purpose of my story is to tell you some of what it was like to be a four-star Air Force General in the old days — the preparation, the climb and what it was like when I arrived. I love the United States Air Force. I would never do anything to hurt the institution or the people in it. I have chosen to leave out names to protect the innocent and the guilty. Lesson: ALL OF THEM HELPED ME GROW.

Raised in a small town in Northern Michigan and with blue collar parents, it was always clear in my mind where I was going after retirement. What was the big draw? - comfort, closeness of town folks, integrity of the people and the work ethic, HARD work ethic. Not surprisingly, having spent nearly 37 years in the USAF, when someone asks, "What do you miss most about your career?" My immediate answer is, "the people," for all the same reasons I returned home.

When I ask military people, "How do you feel when you enter the main gate returning from TDY or leave?" The most often reply is, "I'm home," or one of relief because they are safe, among friends, and back with the disciplined people they consider colleagues. Compare that with recent events in our cities across this nation. Without a doubt, one's environment growing up is very influential and not completely under one's control.

I was born in 1930 had and grew up with several influences outside my control. A series of events, the crash of 1929, followed by the Great Depression, and then WWII, were all major events that shaped my life. Fortunately, my Dad and Mom were people from tough circumstances. I learned what to do, what was tolerated and lines not to cross on a daily basis. My townspeople were always a good influence, there to correct me, guide me and cheer me on as I grew up and life became more complicated. If I could have picked one place or time to grow up, I don't think I could have done better than Tawas, MI. A good grade school and high school with all the activities I wanted to participate in, were right there for my taking. My Dad had a steady job. We certainly weren't well off, but in those days, not many were. Lesson: A WARM BED, PLENTY TO EAT AND A GOOD FAMILY ARE A GREAT START IN LIFE.

Living near an Army Air Corp Base was a motivator to help me set goals for my future. I wanted to fly, but how to get there was a problem. I worked hard throughout school, summers and during vacation time. Finding jobs was easy because so many young men were off for service during the 1940's. As high school graduation neared, my sights were set on being a pilot. Since I was still eligible for the draft, I needed to get into college quick. I had saved summer job money and applied for scholarships to our nearest Junior College. I got a scholarship and headed off. I lived free with my grandparents and that helped immensely because my parents had no money to help. Upon completion of Junior College, I took the Air Force qualifying tests at Selfridge AFB, MI, was accepted and later enlisted to await a pilot slot.

Upon graduation from pilot training in class 52-D at Enid, OK, I was assigned to the 98th Bomb Wing, Yokota, Japan flying B-29s over North Korea. Combat was a meaningful and exciting growth experience for a young kid from Tawas. Upon completion of my Korean tour, I was assigned to Lockbourne AFB, OH and spent 10 years as a B-47 pilot, Instructor Pilot (IP) and Operations Officer.

I learned from my many jobs during high school that in addition to flying as a crew member, volunteering for additional duties paid off. Working hard and pulling additional duties in the squadron grows your reputation as a team player. If you do well, better jobs and recognition come your way. I became one of the first 1/Lt. Aircraft Commanders in the Bomb Wing and maybe all of SAC. After attending Command and Staff College, I went on to B-52s, became an Aircraft Commander, an Instructor Pilot, and after a one-year stint in Vietnam, went back to my old wing at Wurtsmith AFB. I was sent back to Wurtsmith on a humanitarian assignment to assist my family after my father as killed in a tragic car/train accident. At Wurtsmith I was offered several staff jobs. I chose maintenance and my serious vector into Air Force maintenance began.

I hit the road charging and six months later was named, Deputy Chief of Maintenance, then Chief. All of this time, I worked 12-14-hour days learning and applying people skills. Watching the effects on subordinates was astonishing. Giving people under you the capability to innovate within the rules proved highly successful. Our maintenance performance made the Wing solid during all the evaluations. As we performed well, so did the Wing. I learned again that working with your people to help them become better is a key to success. Lesson: IT IS EASY TO FIRE SOMEONE, BUT HARDER TO MAKE THEM BETTER. The reward is seeing them enjoy their success because they are doing better.

As my career progressed through the rank of Lt. Colonel and as Chief of Maintenance for the Bomb Wing, I had visions of someday becoming a Wing Commander, God willing. My experience in maintenance helped me be better at judging people and their potential. This ability to judge people became a very important asset as I was given added responsibility. It is not hard to understand that your best and most important leadership skills are caring for the people under you and getting the best out of them. My big Lesson: SET GOALS, ESTABLISH PRIORITIES AND MAKE ALL OF THEM ORIENTED TOWARDS THE MISSION.

Lesson: A MAIN INGREDIENT THAT ANY ORGANIZATION MUST HAVE IS AN INFORMATION FLOW. I often observed the Wing Commander would have a weekly staff meeting. The meeting would be attended by key personnel, squadron commanders and senior staff. Very often as a worker bee we never got any feedback about what was discussed at the staff meeting. Often, if I asked my supervisor who attended the meeting, "What's new?" he would reply that a lot of sensitive info was discussed but he was not at liberty to reveal any of it. People hold the items close to make themselves feel important. When I became a Wing Commander, I had my secretary compose an "O'Gram" that discussed the agenda of the morning' staff meeting in brief detail and encouraged the troops if interested in any subject to ask their supervisor. This worked and the usual one-page O'Gram was distributed to all unit personnel, and the close hold crap went away. Lesson: AN UNINFORMED BASE IS NOT DESIREABLE, YOU WANT EVERYONE ON YOUR PAGE!

With added rank and responsibility, you must be aware that as you become part of the hierarchy, you represent not only your unit but what you do reflects on your boss. When I became Vice Commander at a Depot, I had my first experience being between the dog and the fire hydrant. My boss didn't know (or maybe care) what went on in the depot, so people found out what they wanted to know about engine status, aircraft delivery, etc. by calling me, the Vice Commander. This was uncomfortable for me. I wasn't trying to make him look bad, but our four-star Commander called me, not my boss, for info. It didn't take long until the boss was replaced, and I was promoted and went to the headquarters working directly for the four-star. Later, we became better acquainted and traveled throughout the major commands working issues together.

One issue we worked was at Sacramento ALC, the prime depot for the A-10. We were scheduled for an A-10 Weapon System briefing. It just so happened that the four-star being briefed had been the Project Officer for heading the transition from Systems Command to Air Force Logistics Command (AFLC) for the A-10. The Colonel doing the briefing was a West Point grad, like the four-star. As the Colonel was explaining the problem with the aircraft "white area," the area between the pilot's legs where the cannon and flight controls cables traveled, he was calling the four star's baby ugly. The event took on the complexion of a West Point 4th Classman briefing a West Point lst Classman, and it was ugly. On return home, my boss, flying the T-39, came back in the aircraft and said, "You know, I didn't like that briefing." I assured him everyone knew that, and he said, "I want you to fire that Colonel." I replied that I could do that and also included, "Is there anyone else you want me to fire that's telling you the truth?" Needless to say, I realized I could be next. He went back to the left seat and flew us home. The next morning at 0700 my intercom rang as I suspected and he said, "Okay you can keep the SOB, but you know I didn't like that briefing." I assured him he would not get another one soon. This all happened in October. In January, he promoted the Colonel to Brigadier General. Lesson: KNOW YOUR BOSS, HAVE FAITH IN HIS JUDGEMENT BUT TRY TO PROTECT PEOPLE YOU RESPECT, RISK OR NOT.

Similarly, while I was Vice Commander of Air Force Logistics Command, a situation occurred with the Secretary of the Air Force that nearly spun out of control. The Secretary wanted my four-star boss fired. The Air Force Chief of Staff was rightfully reluctant to do so, because he had no real cause. So, the Secretary would only do business with me (dog and the fire hydrant again), not my boss. As a result, rumors flooded the Headquarters. In an effort to put a stop to some of it, I scheduled a staff meeting at 1200 hours because I knew the four star left for lunch at 11:45. My first question to the entire staff of general officers was, "Who here has heard that our boss was going to be fired?" As I expected, all raised their hands. I said to all of them, "If I hear after this meeting, any more rumors, I will track down the source and hell will pay!" I was pleasantly surprised, when all rumors stopped. Lesson: IT IS NEVER A STAFF'S ROLE TO CONTRIBUTE TO THEIR BOSS' DEMISE. What a boss does is his business. Your job is to do your job as best you can and let the higher powers make personnel decisions. Lesson: NO ONE GAINS WHEN THE BOSS IS FIRED. Needless to say, how you handle situations like above, is a lesson in maturing as a leader. You always want to be loyal to and truthful with a boss, but you can be put in uncomfortable positions and pulled in two different directions by high-ranking people. Lesson: BEING CAUGHT BETWEEN THE DOG AND THE FIRE HYDRANT IS SOMETIMES THE PRICE OF HIGH LEVEL LEADERSHIP.

Interestingly, when promoted to senior ranks, power plays become more visible, and you find yourself involved in "WTF" situations without being warned. One such situation occurred while I was assigned as the AFLC Vice Commander. I received a phone call from a longtime friend and compatriot that he and his wife were coming on a Friday afternoon and wanted to have dinner at my quarters with me and my wife. No one was to know of it, especially my four-star boss. At dinner, he advised me that he was going to be the next Air Force Chief of Staff, and I was to become the next AFLC Commander. All these events were to happen in the next year. His desire was for me to get my staff lined-up so we could hit the road running. He knew the risk I faced with my present boss and the uncomfortable position I was in with divided loyalties. He said to keep him advised.

My boss was completely non-communicative with me and others, except for the command Chief of Staff, who he directed to make changes on a daily basis without any consultation with the senior staff. The main problem for me as the Vice was how to get "my people" in place to "hit the ground running" at the behest of the new Chief of Staff who had not yet been appointed "without" open confrontation with my present four-star boss, an uncomfortable dilemma.

The command's Chief of Staff was a personal and long-term friend of mine from the old SAC days. I figured he was the key to the success of any plan, so I decided to consult/confide in him what the new Chief to be had in mind. My instruction to him was "Don't do anything our boss tells you to do until you clear it with me, especially personnel changes." Now we were both uncomfortable. Believe it or not we escaped chaos and held things together pretty well. We had to divert some efforts, but never got caught. The current USAF Chief of Staff would call me with concern and ask, "How are things?" He was concerned and also part of the new, yet to be appointed, Chief's plan.

Then, the crap really hit the fan, the Commander of Tactical Air Command, who was to be the next Chief, and I were talking and I asked him if he had yet checked out in the Lear, C-21. He said he hadn't had time to think about it because of everything he was involved with, and I told him he should do it. The Lear was everything the T-39 wasn't, especially hydraulics. He explained his daughter was threatening a miscarriage and he had to fly down and pick up his wife in Texas Friday and to be in Pennsylvania for a speech Saturday. If he could schedule a Lear checkout Monday, he would. Saturday night I was speaking at Plattsburg in a dining-in. The current Chief tracked me down and said, "Bad news. The next Chief, going into Wilkes-Barre-Scranton Airport just ran off the end of the runway, hydraulics." I asked what was the result? He said, "The fire's too big to get close." I commented, "Then he's gone, Chief." After 20-30 seconds he said, "You are probably right." He didn't want to believe it either.

The loss was a disaster for the USAF for several reasons, the biggest being our leadership change. It destroyed the logical succession of players, and we paid for it. I am not sure we have recovered yet.

The last major event in my career: before the sitting Chief retired, and due to the new potential Chief's death, he called me 11 months before I was to retire and wanted me to go to Omaha and become CINCSAC. Needless to say, having spent 25+ years in SAC, I was qualified and this would have been my dream retirement job. However, I explained that if I went, he or the next Chief, would be disrupting the command twice in two years and I didn't think that was fair to the command. He must have agreed with me because he didn't offer to extend me past my mandatory retirement date at 35 years commissioned service. I would have gone to be CINCSAC if he had said go for two years. I loved SAC, its discipline, its people, the its mission to accept responsibility for nuclear security. Unfortunately, the overall impact that General LeMay created by his total emphasis on and promotion of SAC at the expense of other commands, created a negative and unhealthy low-level climate of internecine warfare within the Air Force. At times it bordered on open and public warfare that lasted for years. The rest of the Air Force did not easily forget and we suffered when our collective goals should have been to knock off the BS and produce the effective combat capability needed in all commands to support our national security strategy. Lesson: WARFARE IS NOT ABOUT THE DOMINANCE OF ONE COMMAND BUT ABOUT THE ABILITY OF THE NATION TO FIGHT WHEN AND WHERE NEEDED AND WIN. The rest is history.

I must conclude that I loved my service with the Air Force and I experienced events in combat I would not have experienced anywhere else. During the Cold War, I overflew Russia, deep into Soviet territory being chased by MiGs and defying the people I associated with Communism. I had pride in my mission accomplishments. My time in SAC was all far above my dreams as a young boy. Lesson: I HAVE BEEN BLESSED. I got to fly the B-29, KC-97, B, RB, and EB 47E, the KC-135, B-52D, E, F, G and H, the FB-111 and the B-1, just to name a few. Yes, I have been blessed.

In a long career to four-star general, one receives many awards and honors. The one that meant most to me was The Order of the Sword. It is bestowed by noncommissioned officers of a command on those they hold in high esteem. When I received this award from those who had worked so hard for me, I had a lump in my throat and tears in my eyes. It meant more than anything else they could have done.

Another memory I shall always treasure: in the last promotion board for general officers before I retired as commander of Air Force Logistics Command, five of my brigadier generals received promotion to two-star, unprecedented for one board in one command. I cannot describe my joy at seeing those under my command be so successful.

I want to pass on one final lesson. I am old and gruff but I loved my people. Lesson: IF YOU ASPIRE TO COMMAND AND LEAD, BECOME A PEOPLE PERSON. GOOD LEADERS ACT AS MENTORS AND CREATE ORGANIZATIONS WHERE EMPLOYEES CAN INNOVATE. WHEN YOUR PEOPLE FEEL FREE TO INNOVATE, THEY WILL DELIVER BEYOND YOUR WILDEST EXPECTATIONS - MINE DID.

CHAPTER TWENTY

SWINGING WINGS

by Phil Osterli

I grew up in the Central Valley of California where my father was a specialist in the Agronomy and Range Science Department at the University of California Davis campus. Davis, located 15 miles west of Sacramento, was a small town, an ideal place to grow up in the post WWII era.

It was a carefree life, participating in Boy Scouts, Little League baseball, basketball on the school playgrounds, school activities (studies were optional) and family gatherings. It was just a short bike ride into the country with buddies to practice shooting our Daisy BB guns and sneak up on waterfowl in the local creeks. Competitive sports, cars, girls and academics, in that order, became the norm during high school. As the eldest child and only male, even though occasional conflicts over parental boundaries occurred, life was good. School was no problem, and there was time and the opportunity to participate in interscholastic basketball and tennis. Encouraged by my parent's work ethic, I found summer employment on campus in the research fields around the university airport and was intrigued by all the flight activity, thinking what a neat thing it would be to learn to fly. About that time, I accompanied my father in a university single engine Cessna piloted by a former WWII bomber pilot. We flew into SFO and taxied to the United Airlines concourse, where Dad climbed out, grabbed his bags and walked to the airliner. Imagine that in today's environment! I was given the controls for most of the flight back from SFO to Davis, and I was hooked! All I needed was a way to make this a reality!

After high school, I attended UC Davis, majoring in plant science and was required to take two years of ROTC (my first exposure with the military). Since I was single and facing the draft upon graduation, the opportunity to be an officer was appealing, so I enrolled in upper division ROTC. I learned that there was an Army ROTC flight program at the campus (one of only a few in the country), applied for admission and after passing some introductory tests, was accepted into the program. During my senior year, I received 40 hours of private fixed wing flight instruction in a Piper Tri Pacer. I was now officially a pilot and received my commission January 1963 with a three-year active duty obligation: SOME DREAMS DO COME TRUE.

I also developed an interest in pursuing graduate studies in Plant Genetics and applied to several schools for admission. Fortunately, my scholastic record had improved, and I was accepted in several graduate programs, including the University of Minnesota, where I began a new experience (icy roads, below zero wind chills, apartment living, and a focused curriculum using xerox copies of newly-published research as textbooks). The Army granted my request for a delay to active duty for three years: HARD WORK, STUDY AND PERSISTENCE PAY OFF.

Time flew by in Minnesota. The delay expired, and I was called to active service. I was off to Transportation Branch School followed by Flight School; an eight-month combination of classroom and hands-on flight instruction, graduating November 1966 as an Army Rotary Wing Aviator (the third oldest in our class). I reconnected with, and married, a lady from Canada via Minnesota while in flight school, starting a family (later to grow to four children). Upon graduation I received orders to Vietnam: GOALS OCCASIONALLY HAVE UNEXPECTED CONSEQUENCES.

While on leave a new set of orders arrived assigning a classmate and me as emergency replacements for the 335th Assault Helicopter Company (Cowboys) in Bien Hoa, Vietnam that was attached to the 173rd Airborne Brigade (SEP). Arriving in Saigon in January 1967, we were welcomed to the unit by the CO who had two vacancies, one in the gun platoon (the Falcons) the other in a lift platoon (slicks). Since I had been in the inactive reserve during graduate school, time-in-grade resulted in my promotion to 1Lt. and the CO gave me first choice. I immediately responded, "I'd like the guns, Sir!" Looking back, being assigned to the gun platoon, which provided armed helicopter escort and firepower for various airmobile operations and requests from ground troops in contact turned out very well for me! I could shoot back: RECOGNIZE AND CAPITALIZE ON AN OPPORTUNITY!

The Cowboys had been in-country with the 173rd since mid 1965. I met my platoon leader who arranged for a quick walk around one of our gunships and a review of the starting procedures to include a hydraulics off hovering demonstration. Later that day, while I was getting acquainted with my hooch-mates, I was asked to move one of our ships from maintenance to a revetment. I accomplished the flight in Bermuda shorts and flip flops: THINGS WERE A LITTLE LESS REGIMENTED IN COUNTRY!

The next day, my section leader (an Aircraft Commander, or A/C) gave me an orientation flight (my first experience in an armed helicopter) over a free fire zone called War Zone C. As we flew over a large clearing at 1000' (our standard admin altitude), we heard a "pop-pop" out my side window. The A/C asked the gunner who was on my side of the aircraft where that came from? Gunny answered that he couldn't tell, so we turned around, dropped 100' closer to the ground and retracked our path over the clearing; "pop-pop," still no joy. We repeated coming lower and altering our flight path two more times until the door gunner finally spotted the source and returned fire silencing the threat…welcome to Vietnam! It took a while for me to comprehend that someone was actually shooting at me! This college boy was naïve no more and reality finally set in! I also found out my anti-ballistic seat wasn't big enough to hide behind! Later in that flight, I was offered the controls, firing my first rockets from 1,000 ft. then dropping to 50 ft. to fire at targets in tree lines in the free fire zone: THEY DON'T CALL IT HAZARDOUS DUTY PAY FOR NOTHING.

Thus began my transition: flying with the various A/Cs on real missions while learning the nuances of flying cover for slick operations (behind and below); staying out of the 0-1,000 ft. "dead man's zone;" when on the deck altering your flight path continuously to confuse accurate enemy gunfire; communicating and flying as a fire team by being in a position to provide mutual fire cover for each other; providing preparatory fires and marking LZs for airmobile troop insertions; firing the various weapons systems; various aerial attack procedures and getting used to the flight characteristics of the various gunship configurations; and, ultimately being awarded Aircraft Commander status: BE OBSERVANT: TRUST YOURSELF AND YOUR TEAM.

I soon learned that the 173rd was General Westmoreland's reaction force, meaning we would be tasked to move into the next tactical "hot spot" that required additional troops. As a Pilot, Aircraft Commander and Platoon Leader, I logged 582 combat hours escorting Combat Assaults, Eagle Flights, Long Range Recon Patrol team insertions/extractions, Medevacs, ground troop close air support and various miscellaneous requests. My first mission as an A/C involved providing gunship escort for the first battalion sized combat jump since WWII; another request to cover a "people sniffer" slick, a special device that measured ammonia from the air proved fatal for some water buffalo instead of the NVA; answering a "Mayday," orbiting around a scout helicopter that had an engine failure and was waiting for a "slick" to arrive; running low on fuel and deciding to land my aircraft and pick up the pilot, reinforcing the fact that an extra few hundred pounds on a hot afternoon really taxed that old engine and my control touch when departing that confined area!

While there was no "normal" day, we generally were up, fed, briefed, and in the air each morning before sunrise. This was partially due to the fact our aircraft with full fuel, crew and armament was over max gross weight. The cool mornings allowed us to take off while burning enough fuel en route to safely land at a forward fire support base ready to provide rapid reaction firepower to the units in the field. During my 358 days in country, I received a DFC, 20 Air Medals, Army Commendation Medal, the Presidential Unit and Meritorious Unit Citations and the Vietnamese Cross of Gallantry: CONDUCT EACH MISSION TO THE BEST OF YOUR ABILITY.

In mid-1967 we were told of LBJ's "Pacification Program" that emasculated our ability to respond to immediate threats and forced us to abandon proven tactics that maintained survivability of flight crews and had proven successful in combat situations. That single act caused me to seriously question continuing active military service once my obligation was complete. The senior officers in the unit were mid-career. Most, knew that Vietnam provided an opportunity to serve in combat, demonstrated exemplary leadership, while a handful were wary of making a mistake that might reflect poorly on their record. Most of our pilots were 19-20 year-old warrant officers, new to the military and eager to complete the assigned missions, survive and get back home in one piece.

We all were appreciative of good leadership. ADAPT AND APPLY YOUR TRAINING TO THE SITUATION. YOU CAN LEARN FROM ALL TYPES OF EXAMPLES.

Looking back, 1967 was an unforgettable experience that made an unmistakable impact on my life. However, my experiences don't compare to those of the "grunts" who spent countless days out in the jungle searching for and finding the enemy; engaging in close combat; being on the receiving end of automatic weapons fire, incoming rockets and mortars; seeing their buddies hit by enemy fire. In short, the grunts experienced the horror of war up-close and personal! Being expected to provide support to those on the ground was a big responsibility....and very rewarding! I was busy flying the aircraft, conducting the mission, communicating via the various radios to other aircraft as well as the grunts, reacting to the situation and returning or directing fire where needed. But, after all this, unlike the grunts, I was able to fly back to relative safety, unwind, debrief and prepare for the next day. My bed was a cot in a tent but significantly more comfortable than the grunts in a poncho on the jungle floor. APPRECIATE YOUR GOOD FORTUNE.

I went to Vietnam because my country asked me to serve. My experience was similar to most veterans. War was not something I wanted to be involved with, but if you're involved, you've got to use everything at your disposal. You absolutely need to be in it to win...it's not something to be micro-managed from afar! It still confounds me that we keep repeating this insane approach to armed conflict. We ask our young to risk it all without providing them everything needed to win, namely a strategy with a defined purpose. NEVER FORGET THE PAST.

Returning to CONUS on Christmas Eve 1967, I was met by my parents and my wife and son at Travis AFB CA celebrating a memorable Christmas back home. I was assigned to Fort Stewart GA serving a year in the Department of Tactics as assistant flight commander and instructor pilot. During this time, married with a second child on the way, I was working towards a career in commercial aviation at a local FBO, adding to my fixed wing time during off-duty hours. As a long shot alternative, I inquired about the possibility of a full-time research associate position at the University of California, Davis campus. My job during high school in the research fields really paid off! I was offered a position with the opportunity to re-enter graduate school in Plant Genetics establishing a Rice research facility on campus. At the end of 1968, my little family departed Georgia for California and a new career! EXPERIENCE AND RELATIONSHIPS ARE INVALUABLE.

The three-year break from academia showed what I had learned on the "cutting edge" of genetic knowledge was now being taught in basic undergraduate genetics courses! I had lots of catching up to do. Additionally, being a Vietnam Veteran on a college campus in 1969 was a unique experience. Fortunately, the Davis campus wasn't as vociferous as Berkeley in protesting our Vietnam involvement, but there was no organized support group on campus either. I answered a TV advertisement for helicopter pilots in a Sacramento unit of the California Army National Guard, becoming the first Vietnam veteran to do so in Northern California. This provided an opportunity to continue a parttime career in Army Aviation as well as a break from the campus environment. In fact, while I was in the process of signing up, the unit was activated for a student occupation of "People's Park" on the Berkeley campus. I accumulated another 1500+ hours of flight time through another 10 years in aviation, including commanding the 126th Air Ambulance Company, followed by six years on the staff of the 175th Medical Brigade, four years as XO of the 352nd Evacuation Hospital, and three on the staff of the 2nd Hospital Center. I transferred to the inactive reserve before retiring in 2000 as a Colonel with over 37 years commissioned service.

Overall, the military was good to me and my family. I was able to swear-in my son as a 2Lt. and later joined him in pinning gold bars on his son (my grandson) and also welcomed a West Point graduate stepson and an Air Force son-in-law to our extended family. STAY FLEXIBLE, ALWAYS GIVE IT YOUR BEST EFFORT.

That last lesson paid off again! While at Davis, I was offered an academic position with UC Cooperative Extension to conduct an applied research and education program working with growers, commodity associations, agricultural consultants, food processors (dehydrators, freezers and canneries), regulatory agencies and environmental organizations to maintain an economically viable agricultural industry in the Central Valley of California. Being at the interface between cutting edge research and its application in the field was a very interesting and rewarding job. I later served in the dual capacity of University Administrator and County Department Head providing leadership in water quality, public policy/land use and serving on several state and national committees and organizations that represented the agricultural community. SURROUND YOURSELF WITH OUTSTANDING PEOPLE.

During the latter part of this tenure, I fortunately crossed paths with my current spouse and partner, adding two more sons to the family, that has grown to include 14 grandchildren. Three sons served in the Army overseas in Iraq, Saudi Arabia and Afghanistan. Our oldest grandson served with Special Forces in the Philippines. We suffered the anxiety of having loved ones in harm's way while sitting in the comfort of home. I am reminded that I only called home once during my year in Vietnam and now can understand their concern for me and the frustration of not knowing and living in fear. TREASURE AND CULTIVATE FAMILY.

After retiring from 34 years at UC, it was time to enjoy other interests: boating in the Pacific Northwest; actively participating in various boating organizations in Washington; serving in several leadership positions over the next 10+ years. As the years passed, the cold, wet winters began to affect our aging bones. We became "snowbirds," enjoying our motorhome in the relative warmth of the California Coast. We finally relocated to Arizona. I fortunately found the Friday Pilots, who graciously extended an invitation to join this impressive group of aviators. Always in awe of their valor, professionalism and accomplishments while serving our country, I look forward to our informal Friday luncheons with these heroes!

Our extended family is scattered around the country providing an incentive to continue traveling as long as we are able and the kids put up with us.

FINALLY, BE GRATEFUL FOR EACH DAY. LIVE LIFE TO THE FULLEST!

CHAPTER TWENTY-ONE

THE PLAN
by Bill Pitts

"Life is not a journey to the grave with the intention of arriving safely in a pretty and well-preserved body, but rather to skid in broadside, thoroughly used up, totally worn out, and loudly proclaiming, WOW - WHAT A RIDE!!!"

My roots were in rural Alabama. I was a normal kid with normal parents - at least for most of my formative years. In high school, many of my friends knew who they would probably be when they grew up, following in their parents' footsteps - I envied them. That wasn't me. My Dad owned a jewelry store in a small Alabama town of 12,000. I had no intentions of being a jeweler.

When I look back on what I now perceive to be "The Plan," I realize that as you age, who you choose to grow up and be friends with, makes a tremendous difference in who you become. All of my peers were planning to go to college. No one in my family had ever done that. In my senior year, my parents had asked a local judge to help get me an appointment to the Air Force Academy. I never quite knew why or how they picked the Air Force because I had never voiced an interest in that service or the Academy. In fact, I was positive that I would either go to the University of Alabama or Auburn. To my surprise, I received a letter from a U.S. Senator from Alabama giving me a first alternate appointment to the Academy. "The Plan" was set in motion.

The individual who received the primary appointment accepted, so I enrolled in Auburn University in the fall of 1964. As a land grant college, ROTC was mandatory. Because of my first alternate appointment, the Air Force ROTC department accepted me immediately. Virtually all of my friends ended up in Army ROTC. I had dodged the Army during the heart of the Vietnam war, obviously part of "The Plan."

I believe that some of us know who we want to be when we grow up and plan college accordingly. I did not. As I entered Auburn, in order to be enrolled in courses that might lead in a positive direction, I chose a pre-dentistry curriculum. Bad choice! I floundered in my very first chemistry course and switched to Business Administration where chemistry had no applicability. The bad side of that decision was that I had no idea, once again, what or who I wanted to be when I grew up.

One day, about midway through my sophomore year, Staff Sergeant McGrath called me into his office. He said, "Cadet Pitts - you did quite well on the Air Force Officer Qualification Test and especially well on the aviation portion. Have you ever considered being an Air Force pilot?" I grew up in a small country town in the middle of farms and textile mills. Not once had I ever been close to an airplane. I didn't have a relative who had flown in any of the previous wars. I had never been to an air show where I looked up and said, "I want to do that someday." My answer to Sergeant McGrath even surprised me. I said, "no I haven't, but it sounds like fun." Lesson: NOT HAVING ANY IDEA WHAT YOU WANT TO DO, THEN SUDDENLY GETTING A GLIMPSE, IS A GREAT EXPERIENCE.

In April 1969, I entered Air Force pilot training at Craig AFB in Selma, AL, 100 miles from home. Toward the end of my pilot training year, my good friend, Harry Hayes, who had gone to West Point, graduated as a 2nd Lieutenant, went to Vietnam as an infantryman, was killed by a sniper at the end of his first month. That gave me a whole new mindset. I now knew the airplane that I wanted to fly when I graduated. I wanted to be a Forward Air Controller (FAC) and fly the OV-10. I wanted to go to Vietnam. Finishing in the top 10 in my class, I got my first choice of assignments and was on my way to Vietnam as an OV-10 pilot.

My year in Vietnam was definitely eye opening. In many respects, my experiences caused me to mature ahead of my normal timeline. In others, it caused me to regress back to my college days where partying was half the fun. I believe that both FACs and fighter pilots went out every day with a sense of immortality. I don't know of anyone who flew a mission thinking that "today's my day to die." Every day carried that possibility.

Many of our squadron members did not return. I remember thinking on many occasions that "I was not on the list today." The saying was, "If you're on the list, there's nothing you can do about it." The corollary is, of course, "If you're not on the list, there's nothing you can do about that either." Lesson: NOBODY EVER GETS TO SEE THE LIST. MANY OF US, IN SELF-REFLECTION, WHEN FACED WITH THE LOSS OF A FRIEND OR SQUADRON MATE, WOULD ASK, "WHY HIM AND WHY NOT ME?" By the way, I am confident that I did manage to remove several snipers from the war during my 12 months there.

As I evaluate my life from then to now, I can see that "The Plan" included me returning alive. How else could I fly through an Arc Light with bombs exploding all around me, 324 500lb. bombs dropped from 3 B-52s flying at over 30,000 feet above me? How did I manage to recover from an inverted spin, at night, over Laos, in mountainous terrain, when I had never spun the OV-10 before? How did I manage to land on a 3,000 feet long perforated steel planking runway with emergency fuel, at night, with total power outage on the base, therefore no runway lighting, with the field under rocket attack? Why did I not crash after falling asleep in my OV-10 for nearly 15 minutes over the Ho Chi Minh trail? How did I manage, during 196 combat missions, to never be hit by the tens of thousands of anti-aircraft artillery rounds fired by the NVA, when as a FAC, we spent three hours over the Ho Chi Minh trail on every mission being shot at?

Lesson: WHAT I DISCOVERED AFTER MY VIETNAM TOUR IS THAT I WAS NOW WHO GOD INTENDED FOR ME TO BE. I loved being an Air Force pilot, a career that I had never imagined until Staff Sergeant McGrath asked that question.

Returning from Vietnam, the next phase of "The Plan" took effect. I requested to fly the F-4 and return to the war - not going to happen. I requested to be an OV-10 instructor - not going to happen. What happened is that I was assigned as a T-38 instructor back at Craig AFB. I was back in Alabama as a 26-year old bachelor who did want to get married someday. That actually happened in September 1972. The marriage lasted over 18 years and produced three wonderful sons.

While at Craig, I saw an Air Force Magazine with an A-10 on the cover with over 16,000 pounds of assorted munitions triangulated in front. I really wanted to someday fly the "Warthog," its affectionate nickname. In 1976, as my time at Craig was coming to an end, the war had ended, the Air Force was downsizing, and there were very few airplanes for pilots to fly. Rated supplement, or career broadening assignments, were rampant. My research into non-flying career fields produced a short list of jobs that I might find interesting. That was not to be. "The Plan" took hold once again. I was assigned as a "strong" non-volunteer to the Officers' Open Mess career field. I was going to be an Officers' Club Manager. The only good news was, I was on my way to Myrtle Beach AFB, SC, an A-7 wing that would be the first to convert to the A-10.

I spent over two years managing 25 employees at a club with more than 550 members. I knew from the beginning that the only way I would ever fly my dream airplane was to succeed at this job. The odds were definitely stacked against me. At that time, approximately 50% of the club officers in the Air Force were fired each year. After several very challenging months, the club seemed to make a turn around. Business picked up, wing officers, and their wives, seemed to be happy with the food and service, and the club was profitable. The Wing Commander and his senior staff frequented the club and seemed to think that I was managing well.

In March 1978, the Military Personnel Center released me from the club assignment back to flight duty. I received a very strong recommendation from the Wing Commander to be selected to fly the A-10. My assignment came down in May, and I was on my way to training at Davis-Monthan AFB (DM) to be an A-10 pilot in the third operational squadron at Myrtle Beach. "The Plan" had placed me in the right place at the right time for my next adventure in life.

The A-10 was literally a dream come true for me. There was nothing about the airplane that I did not love. I learned to fly it well, finishing at the top of my class in 1978. I quickly certified in all areas, becoming an instructor, a combat search and rescue pilot, and one of the first to qualify in Joint Air Attack Team tactics with the Army. My squadron additional duty was as the training officer. This led to another part of "The Plan." After two years flying at Myrtle Beach, I was selected to be the Chief of Training as part of the initial cadre to convert the England AFB A-7 pilots to the A-10, back-to-back operational flying assignments, unusual at that time.

The 23ʳᵈ Fighter Wing was home to the Flying Tigers with rich heritage dating back to the American Volunteer Group flying P-40s over Burma and China during World War II. Being a member of the Flying Tigers was special and different than any of my previous assignments. I truly felt as though I had found a home. With shark's teeth prominently displayed on the A-10, Warthog pilots flew around the world with pride.

My assignment at England AFB was extremely rewarding. During my two-year stay, I had been: the training coordinator for the wing's conversion from A-7s to A-10s; a flight commander in the 74ᵗʰ Fighter Squadron, the first to convert; assistant operations officer in the 74ᵗʰ; 9ᵗʰ Air Force Top Gun in September 1981; and a member of the 1981 Gunsmoke team that finished second in the worldwide gunnery competition.

It was now time for me to head overseas to complete a staff tour. After several job offers, I settled on Alaskan Air Command (AAC). Little did I know how important a part this assignment would play in "The Plan" as I progressed through life. The first three months of my "non-flying" staff job were spent as a "guest help" instructor flying the A-10 at Eielson AFB when they converted from F-4s. I, along with two lieutenants, delivered the first three A-10s from the factory to Eielson in February of 1982.

Now, it was time to settle into a desk job in the war plans division of AAC. My time there was very rewarding as I coordinated with the Pentagon staff during the Air Force's manpower study. I also worked on a team that developed the command strategy and plan for an all-out war with the Soviet Union. I worked directly with the Commander, AAC, to develop a briefing to be given at Corona, the Air Force's four-star conference.

Just as I settled in comfortably, the Director of Operations requested that I be reassigned to his directorate. He needed a fighter qualified pilot with FAC time to be in charge of the FAC program for AAC. In the middle of a non-flying staff tour, I was off to Patrick AFB, FL to learn to fly the O-2. I was now in charge of overseeing the FAC program as well as being the Chief of the Standardization/Evaluation Division.

My three-year non-flying staff tour, where I flew for more than 20 months, was coming to an end. I was offered the opportunity to fly the F-16, but my love for the Warthog was just too strong. I couldn't wait to be a Flying Tiger again so in July of 1985, I was driving the Alcan highway toward Louisiana.

I had just been promoted to Lieutenant Colonel. "The Plan," being multi-faceted, was integral to this event. I was one of a few renegades who had not toed the line and gotten a Masters degree, an important part of an officer's portfolio. I was told that my successes as a Club Officer had made the difference. In other words, my success as a Club Officer, where I was a "strong" non-volunteer, was critical to me getting an A-10 assignment and being promoted. Who could have predicted that?

The next five years as a Flying Tiger were by far the best of my flying career. While going through the A-10 refresher program at DM, having not yet pinned on my Lieutenant Colonel rank, I was informed that I would be the new operations officer in the 75th Fighter Squadron, a job normally reserved for a more senior LTC already in the wing. I was shocked, apprehensive, but delighted. That job, filled with challenges, rewards, and many more experiences to round out my flying career, lasted 14 months.

The Wing Commander called me into his office and explained that he needed a seasoned officer to be his Chief of Safety. I interpreted that as being fired from my current position since, during my career, the Chief of Safety position had normally been given to a pilot who was on the verge of retirement. He explained that now the chief had to be on the squadron commander's list, which was the first time that I realized that I was actually on that list. I held the safety position for just over one year and then assumed command of the 76th Fighter Squadron Vanguards.

Early as a fighter pilot, I had established a mediocre set of career goals. At the pinnacle of my list was to someday be a fighter squadron commander. I had achieved my ultimate goal with lots of time left for more, and more was yet to come. As I was nearing the conclusion of a fabulous two-year tour as commander, I was informed that I had been promoted to Colonel, a rank that I never expected to achieve. The great news to go along with that promotion was that I would remain in the 23rd Fighter Wing as the Assistant Director of Operations (ADO), and I would continue to fly the Warthog!

Now, after four years, the family was solidly entrenched in the Louisiana lifestyle, and it appeared that I had at least another year to go.

After many months had passed, I was interviewed for a lateral job at DM. I politely declined the Wing Commander's offer, but he hired me anyway. I wasn't too keen on going to the training wing after being an operational A-10 pilot for eight years, but I was one of those fortunate colonels who got to continue to fly, so stop your whining and pack!

But wait, "The Plan" had a say in all this. With only four days until moving day to Tucson, the 23rd Wing was called into action for Desert Shield. After the emergency meeting to notify the senior officers, I approached the Wing Commander and requested that my DM assignment be placed on hold and that I be part of the Wing's deployment. I said, "Only five pilots in this wing have ever been shot at before, and I am one. You can't go to war without me." I was the senior officer on the advanced party deployment in August of 1990 and the first Flying Tiger on the ground at King Fahd International Airport in Saudi. It was a hot, grueling, and very productive three months stay for me. My immediate boss replaced me in November, and I was now really on my way to DM.

Lots had changed in those three months. "The Plan" had delayed my assignment and given me time to reorganize my future. I departed for DM in December 1990 without my family. Several months passed, and I became a single parent with two teenaged boys living with me. Lesson: BE CAREFUL WHAT YOU WISH FOR, YOU MIGHT GET IT.

I spent two years as the ADO at DM and finally received my "over the hill" speech. I was now pretty much looking for a place to go until retirement. I had been chosen to be the Chief of Safety for Special Ops Command, but a few days later, that position was placed on the Air Force's chopping block. I eventually reported to Warner Robbins AFB, GA as the chief of the inspections division for the Air Force Reserve Inspector General. My boss retired shortly thereafter, and I spent my last year and a half as the Inspector General for the Air Force Reserve.

As I approached my retirement date, the Deputy Vice Commander of AFRES asked me my retirement plans. Sadly, I had none. He said, "Have you considered flying for UPS? The person in charge of hiring there works for me in the Reserves, and I can put in a good word." Once again, "The Plan" made sure that I was in the right place at the right time. Six weeks after retiring, I was working for UPS as a flight engineer on the 727.

While I was at DM, I met a wonderful Arizona lady. We dated for more than a year and married in August 1993. Upon my retirement in September 1994, we settled in Tucson. She was an incredible entrepreneur, starting her own commercial office furniture business in June of 1994, selling primarily to federal agencies. This became my third career, as I was in charge of the operations and finance departments. She grew the business from just she and I, to 25 employees in five states over the next seven years. At that point, I left UPS to be COO/CFO of a multi-million dollar company.

We closed our business in 2008 after nearly 15 years of success. Our plans were to travel as much as we could over the remainder of our lives. On an early morning in October 2014, she said goodbye as she left to ride her bike, practicing for the 40-mile segment of the Tour de Tucson. She never returned. She had a cycling accident that morning severely damaging her brain and died six days later. Lesson: NOT ALL PARTS OF THIS "LIFE PLAN" ARE UNDERSTANDABLE, BUT THEY ARE WHAT THEY ARE, AND LIFE GOES ON.

The remainder of my tale about "The Plan," actually revolves directly around The Friday Pilots. This is the part that made me clearly see just how I've been directed and redirected throughout my life.

After Lt. Gen. Jim Record retired here in Tucson, he and I became lifelong friends. He was a member of a lunch group that called themselves the "Luncho Buncho." These were the foundation members of who are now called "The Friday Pilots." For the record, The Friday Pilots are incredible American patriots who have fought for our country and survived to tell their amazing tales of courage and bravery. Most would never actually talk about their own courage or bravery, but trust me, these are extraordinary Americans. Gen. Record invited me to join him at lunch on several occasions, so I met the group. I was a bit younger than the original cadre, but they accepted me anyway. After Gen. Record died in 2009, and after his memorial service, several of the members asked me to join the group for lunch each Friday. I made a very wise decision and accepted.

Years passed and the group continued to grow. On one Friday, a new face appeared. This awesome pilot was Eric Erickson. Eric had been a FAC in Vietnam flying the same OV-10 from the same base as me but three years earlier. After a year there, Eric became a Raven FAC flying in support of CIA operations. While a Raven, Eric flew with another terrific pilot named Lloyd Duncan. Dunc just happened to be the leader of our A-10 Gunsmoke team in 1981, 13 years after he had flown with Eric, different faces, different places and different times. Dunc told Eric to stop by The Friday Pilots' lunch and introduce himself - Eric would be a perfect fit. Eric and his wife had just moved to Tucson. Eric had attended maybe eight or 10 lunches, when one day his heart stopped. He survived for six days before passing and heading West. This was in October 2015, exactly one year from my wife's death.

Proceeds from The Friday Pilots' original book go to a military charity organization here in Tucson. Eric and his wife, Frieda, supported the same organization in Alaska. At an event hosted by that group in January 2016, I met Frieda. I explained who I was, and she knew me simply from Eric talking about meeting me at lunch. Through a series of communications concerning our similar losses, we decided to meet for a "happy hour" where we could share grief and also maybe smile a bit. That happy hour lasted two hours, and I believe that we smiled more than we cried that day. We agreed to meet again and that turned into one happy hour each month for five months.

As Frieda and I shared life experiences, we discovered several commonalities. Our birthdays are the same day. Frieda had lived in Alaska for 16 years. I had lived there for three but went back for 13 summers to fish. Alaska is her favorite place and mine as well. We both have strong faith in God and very similar political views. After our five happy hours, I had fallen "in like." She let me know in no uncertain terms that I was a year ahead of her. I let her know that in 20 years, I would still be a year ahead of her. We saw each other more and more as time passed, and we were married in April 2018.

The events that led up to my becoming a Friday Pilot, led to me meeting a beautiful lady who loves life. We both love to travel and have committed to doing as much of that as possible over our remaining lifetime.

I wish that I could find a way to explain "The Plan", but I can't. I simply hope that I have explained my understanding of what became "My Plan." I certainly don't profess to know what lies ahead, but I love my wife, enjoy my life, and look forward to the adventures that "The Plan" has in store.

Lesson: GOD'S PLAN IS AMAZING AND WOW - WHAT A RIDE!!!

CHAPTER TWENTY-TWO

REFLECTIONS

by George Allan "GAR" Rose

How did George Alan Rose achieve the honor of being labeled "an old geezer?" How did I survive 30 years of defying gravity as a fighter pilot in the USAF and an airline pilot? Good questions, and I do not have a hard and fast answer for the questions. In the course of my 78 years on this beautiful planet, several people have provided guidance, advice and criticism for and to me.

I'll mention a few of them: At the top of the list is my Father. Dad was born in 1905, the fourth of five children in a hard scrabble meal-to-meal family. My grandfather passed away when Dad was five years old. Life became even tougher, but my grandmother was able to eke out a living as a seamstress, taking in laundry and cleaning other's homes. Dad was a big kid, excelled in the classroom and on the athletic field. He was offered an athletic scholarship to the University of Arkansas which he readily accepted. He was a varsity player from the outset in football, baseball, track and basketball. His size at six feet five inches and 225+ pounds gave him an advantage on the basketball court which he used to lead the Razorbacks to several conference championships and garner him recognition as the first All-American round baller in Arkansas history.

Dad joined the U.S. Army ROTC program and was commissioned as a 2nd Lt. when he graduated. Glen Rose possessed natural leadership ability and was comfortable in that role. He became a coach and an officer in the Arkansas National Guard but during the depression era, he had to take on other jobs for income. He was supporting his Mom and younger sister as well as his new bride, Lois. Dad learned a valuable lesson as a young coach and a rising Army officer while dealing with his players and enlisted men. He preached, "If you undertake a job, do it right!" He had to fire men for slacking because of the shoddy work. A Lesson from Dad: "THE PEOPLE WHO WORK FOR YOU MAY NOT LIKE YOU BUT THEY WILL RESPECT YOU IF YOU ARE FAIR WITH THEM!"

Another valuable Lesson from Dad: "IF YOU ARE GOING INTO THE MILITARY, YOU WANT TO BE AN OFFICER!" Fast forward a few years, and Dad suggested I might want to take an aptitude test for ideas that would possibly point me in a career direction. A pilot, a forest ranger or accountant were the results. I had a great interest in airplanes since the age of five according to my Mom. When I enrolled at the University of Arkansas in 1960, I signed up for the USAF ROTC program with the idea of becoming an Air Force pilot then transitioning into the civilian side of flying. That plan cost me one girl friend whose dad was adamant his daughter would not be involved long term with a guy with such notions. Oh well! Turned out to be a blessing in disguise when I met the love of my life, Rebecca, while enrolled in USAF Pilot Training at Laredo, TX.

My initial instructor in pilot training was Captain Carroll B. Arnold. He was an F-86 fighter pilot who transferred to the Air Training Command when the F-86 was being retired from the active duty forces. The first morning when my class reported to the flight line operations building, we all discussed our flying career aspirations with Capt. Arnold. I told him I was thinking about an assignment in a large transport or refueling aircraft to gain the experience required to be an airline pilot. "Hmm!" was his response. A few days later "Arnie," as he came to be known to us, came into the ops room, called out my name and told me get my gear and meet him out front. We were to fly the weather scout mission for the morning and determine if the areas were suitable for training without too much hinderance from clouds. Arnie quickly determined that the low clouds and spotty rain showers in the area would preclude any student flights at least for the morning. Then he said, "Hang on, let's play around a little bit to burn off some fuel before we go back to the base and land, after all, it is your 'dollar ride' and the last flight you will have without a grade." So, we yanked and banked between cloud layers, made tight turns around and into the rain showers, then popped up above the clouds into bright sunlight and Arnie demonstrated some aerobatics, and then I did my first aileron roll. Hey, this is fun stuff! Then we returned to base and landed. I was successful at landing, albeit, pretty rough. As we were taxiing into the parking area Arnie tapped me on the shoulder and said, "You cannot do what we just did in a transport!"

One Sunday afternoon, Arnie invited a few of us over to his place for hamburgers and beer and what we flyers call "Hangar Flying." In the course of the afternoon he offered this piece of advice, "When you strap into an airplane, you are strapping it onto you. You are in-charge, but you are as one. Think how you want to perform a maneuver, then you and your mechanical partner, perform it in concert!" Lesson: MY NOTION OF FLYING A TRANSPORT VANISHED AND I DECIDED I WANTED TO FLY JET FIGHTERS AND BE A FIGHTER PILOT BY TRADE!

After my first tour in Vietnam in F-4s, I was assigned to a fighter squadron in Germany. There, I met Lt. Col. Felix C. Fowler, commander of the 9th Tac Fighter Squadron. Colonel Fowler was a combat veteran with WWII B-24 pilot experience, had been a police officer in Cleveland, OH, then was recalled to active duty and sent to Vietnam as a squadron commander of an F-4 squadron. He was a bear of a man in stature. He was a "people person!" He made it his goal to know each of his pilots and the enlisted men in his maintenance section too. He truly cared for each of us. And in turn, we respected his position of squadron commander as much as we respected him as our leader and would follow him to "the gates of hell" if he requested such. Lesson: IF YOU TAKE CARE OF YOUR PEOPLE, THEY WILL TAKE CARE OF YOU AND YOU SHOULDN'T HAVE TO WORK AT BEING A CARING PERSON. IT SHOULD BE A NATURAL TRAIT OF A GOOD LEADER! And, Colonel Fowler was just that, and I hope I took that lesson from him. I know several other 9th TFS pilots who were later commanders in their own right, and we tried to emulate Felix!

My second war tour to Southeast Asia was in 1972. My unit, the 334th Tac Fighter Squadron, based in North Carolina, was ordered to Thailand in April in response to the North Vietnamese invasion of our ally, The Republic of Vietnam. The U.S. involvement in the Vietnam War was coming to a close and major North Vietnamese forces were flooding into the South. Under the command of Lt. Col. C. O. "Shock" Shockley the squadron was ready to get to work as soon as we arrived at Ubon RTAFB. Each unit on the base seemed to have a specific mission that was their specialty. Our squadron was assigned the mission of attempting to deter surface to air missiles (SAMs) by creating a layer of radar confusing chaff (strips of aluminum foil) that was contained in a fiberglass bomb case designed to open shortly after release from the aircraft. The precision munition-laden tactical bombers ingressed to the target above the chaff cloud, attacked the target then egressed the area, once again above the chaff cloud. This was one of the most demanding missions of the air war, not to mention, downright unnerving. Shock was the leader on most of these hazardous missions. Lesson: HE WOULD NOT SEND HIS MEN ON A MISSION THAT HE WOULD NOT UNDERTAKE HIMSELF! And, he did undertake the missions, far more than anyone else. Shock led countless missions into the flak and missile filled skies of North Vietnam to deliver the chaff and create corridors the bombers needed to complete their mission. To this day Shock deserves any claim to accolades for a job well done from his "guys!" He is very highly respected as a role model of professionalism and courage. He is what a leader should be.

On a chaff mission 21 June of 1972, the longest day of that year, (literally and figuratively) the aircraft I was flying was mortally wounded by a missile from a North Vietnamese fighter. My weapon systems officer, Lt. Pete Callaghan, and I were forced to eject from our F-4, or die, when the plane blew up. We were both captured by enemy forces and transported to the notorious Hoa Lo prison (Hanoi Hilton) where we were isolated from each other, interrogated and held in some pretty filthy conditions. After several days, Pete and I were reunited and with another F-4 crew and moved in the dead of night to another prison on the southern side of Hanoi called The Zoo. Fortunately, for most of us shot down in 1972, the torture endured by so many of our predecessors had ceased as the enemy bowed to international pressure for more humane treatment of their prisoners. They realized we might be more valuable alive than dead. But, one never knew, and we kept a wary eye on our guards for any sign of a change to their policy on any given day. We spent our days exercising to maintain some semblance of conditioning, contemplating when we would be released and relating various war stories (and/or lies).

Hours and hours of boredom, then came the heavy bombing campaign of December 1972, Linebacker II, as the Paris Peace Talks fell apart. Our morale was cautiously raised as our guards appeared to be scared out of their wits with the incessant attacks by fighters during the day and B-52s at night. When the bombing ceased, we were positive we were on our way back to the USA. And so, we were. My release date was March 28, 1973 in the next to last group.

So where am I going with this? I cannot count the number of people, be they hardened combat veterans, or members of my high school class at a reunion, that have said, "I could not have endured what you did in captivity! I just couldn't! I wouldn't make it!" My answer has always been, Lesson: "YOU WOULD SURPRISE YOURSELF!" As I was descending in my parachute into the jungle there were thoughts racing through my brain at a ferocious pace, and some of them were not good. But, in retrospect I think I was already entering "my new world" and how to cope with the situation. I had thoughts of rescue while I was hiding in what I thought was a pretty well concealed position. These hopes were buoyed when Shock led a flight back to my shoot down area in hopes of making contact but by then it was too late for me. I was too deep in enemy territory for a rescue attempt!

Oops, gun in my face and any notion of escape went away instantly. In short order I was being paraded across fields in my skivvies by a really angry mob of civilians and I knew my survival depended on them, a precarious situation at the moment! And so, one event led to the next, but I dealt with each event as it came, one at a time. "I must concentrate on what's in front of me and not the what ifs," was my thought pattern at the time.

New event, a militia soldier arrives on the scene to take charge of me pending turn over to the regulars, whenever that may be. The issue of mutilation by the angry mob goes into a compartment hopefully to not be reopened. Now, to communicate that I'm really thirsty. Somehow, I made the point, and an old lady gently offered some hot tea. Good stuff. Let me reiterate, Lesson; WHEN IN DEEP TROUBLE, TAKE THINGS ONE AT A TIME AND TRY TO KEEP A SOMEWHAT CLEAR MIND BY NOT MULTITASKING.

"How did you survive?" is another question. Each event was a new problem to solve, so, Lesson: I JUST TRIED TO TAKE EVENTS ONE AT A TIME. Each interrogation seemed to have a different theme or plot to it. Did I lie to the interrogators? You bet your bippy! What are targets in the future? "Hanoi!" Did I exaggerate? You bet. Think of a question about the number of aircraft at your base. "Hundreds!" the response. Was I concerned about my responses? Yes, indeed but what else were they going to do? Kill me? They've tried that already and most thankfully failed! Maybe a little haughty for a 29-year old, but really, what were they going to do? I never lost faith in my country and the promise to leave no man behind. I never lost faith in myself. Lesson: BELIEVE IN YOURSELF! - YOU CAN DO IT! If you give up on yourself, you're done, because who is going to bring you back? I never lost faith in my fellow prisoners. Lesson: AS POWS WE WERE ALL IN THE SAME LIFE RAFT AND NEEDED EACH OTHER TO ROW. And, if I lost faith in myself, I would have to fall back on the fact that they would rescue me. And lastly, faith in my family that they would not abandon me. And, they didn't.

In reflective moments while incarcerated, and believe me, there are lot of those moments, I thought of people who had faith in me through the years: Dad, who launched me into adulthood; Arnie, who taught me how to really fly by becoming one with your machine and planted the seed of flying fighters; Felix who was a strong leader of men by his caring and gentle manner; Shock, who went to the front of the line before he would send his men to do something he wouldn't do and returned to a very hostile environment to search for a lost crew; and a host of others I've encountered in the course of my journey. And, Lesson: I SURE AS THE DEVIL DIDN'T WANT TO FACE THEM IF I HADN'T GIVEN MY BEST TO THE TASK I WAS GIVEN, WANT IT OR NOT!

CHAPTER TWENTY-THREE

GROWING UP ITALIAN-AMERICAN AND CONTINUING TO GROW AS A FIGHTER PILOT AND GENERAL OFFICER

by Gene Santarelli

I am dividing my story into two parts: my early years growing up in an Italian American immigrant household, and my professional life as a USAF fighter-pilot and General Officer. I will attempt to capture a few lessons for life that old men, especially we fighter-pilots, remember the most. They involve flying, but the lessons are far broader.

My early life memories revolve around family, first and second-generation Italian immigrants in the mid-20th Century, and of course, food. The "family" included our father, mother, older brother, younger sister, plus aunts and uncles and their families, most of whom lived in Canton, Ohio. I was told by my father there were cousins still in Italy, others who also immigrated to the U.S and settled elsewhere, plus more who migrated to South America and who knows where else. I suspect this is similar to many other Italian American immigrant families.

My father and World War II were significant factors in my growth. Most of my uncles served in WW II, but my father having been too young to serve in WW I, then found himself too old to serve in WW II. He was trapped by age. Instead, he worked as a steelworker in our local mill, making steel that went into military equipment. I mention this because it had a significant impact on him. It was a major factor in how he raised us and an influence on my decision to make the military a career

My father was the oldest of his generation of our family in America. This meant he was the Patriarch: provided the home for grandmother, when Grandpa passed, and the location for most of our family get togethers. These included weekly and holiday family meals, usually in the afternoon, where all aunts and uncles would gather. This seemed to always evolve into the evening "snack," mixed with card games and a lot of talk.

The talk was usually in Italian and loud among my parents' generation. The rule seemed to be when someone didn't understand, you got closer and spoke louder. I also witnessed this later in life when two people who spoke different languages often resorted to that tactic when the language barrier interfered. I thought I outgrew this shortcoming but find myself up to this day slipping back into the habit. The lesson holds, Lesson: IF THEY DON'T UNDERSTAND, GET CLOSER AND SPEAK LOUDER.

A more vivid memory is amongst all the loud Italian chatter in our household on Sunday afternoons and evenings. The chatter ceased in an instant when one of my generation entered the room. The silence was followed immediately by my father, the Patriarch, saying, "Speak English." The chatter immediately resumed, but in English. It was amazing to watch people in deep conversations or arguments in one language, pause, then pick up in another without dropping a thought. For years I thought this was the norm in all immigrant families. The importance of this memory was that language was key to insure the children grew up "American" and did not linger in the "old country." It was the core to education and growing beyond being an immigrant. It demonstrated my parents' generation's fierce loyalty to being American and wanting to insure their children grew up with the same loyalty to America. They lived through the prejudice most every ethnic group in our country experienced. They did not want their children to suffer the same.

The next memory of growing up Italian was food. Before most holidays, my mother and aunts would gather for what I would call "the cookie or pasta brigade". This was usually at our house, because this is where one of the Grandmas resided, and an entire day was spent making cookies and/or pasta. There were enough cookies or pasta of a mixed variety for each participant to carry home a stash of sweets or the Italian staple for their next few holidays, plus the Sunday afternoon family get-togethers at our house. The pasta took several shapes, plain spaghetti, sewer pipes (Rigatoni), swirls (Fusilli), etc. I did not learn until much later in life that each shape had an Italian name. In our house they were all called spaghetti or pasta.

The other staple of the kitchen needed for the pasta was the Sunday tomato sauce. The sauce was always tomato base with meat (Bolognese). The pasta was accompanied by meatballs. For variety, chicken would be an added meat, but always in addition to the meatballs. On Fridays, the meatballs may be replaced with tuna fish, or some other fish variety, but usually the meal was just pasta covered with oil and pepper.

One Thanksgiving, around my 10th, one Uncle Chuck, who was of Spanish descent, could no longer stand it and announced the previous Sunday that he was bringing a turkey. He would bake it earlier but would need the kitchen oven to re-warm. This almost caused panic in the kitchen, but my uncle and mother made it work. That was the first time something other than meatballs or chicken were the main meat dish. The turkey was at the center of the table, but of course there were pastas and meatballs as side dishes. Before that day, turkey was a mythical dish. The "national bird" in our house was chicken or the meatballs in tomato sauce.

In addition to family and food, I learned the importance of education. My father did not complete elementary school, having dropped out to feed the family. He never resented this, it was just the way it was. However, he impressed upon his children the necessity to complete high school and to go on and get a college degree. My parents nearly went broke trying to get my older brother and myself through college. They drained their savings both times. Lesson: MY PARENTS THOUGHT COLLEGE IMPORTANT ENOUGH TO DRAIN THEIR SAVINGS FOR US.

My brother dropped out of school to join the Air Force, which was a major influence on me. My college education was at the University of Notre Dame. During my freshman year, I joined AFROTC, which paid $27/month, but only during my Junior and Senior years. I was also fortunate enough to get an educational grant and loans. Upon graduation I was commissioned a 2nd Lieutenant in the U.S. Air Force. Lesson: GROWING UP IN AN ITALIAN IMMIGRANT FAMILY LED TO MY CONSERVATIVE VALUES, RESPECT FOR THE MILITARY, AND SET THE FOUNDATION FOR MY MILITARY CAREER.

Following my graduation in 1966, I proceeded to and completed pilot training at Laughlin AFB, Texas. When I went through pilot training, the

Air Force produced what was called the Universally Assignable Pilot. Your follow-on aircraft was determined by your selection of an aircraft from the list available to your class. I wanted to be a fighter pilot, so fighters were at the top of my "dream sheet." I got the F-4 Phantom, the workhorse fighter of the Air Force. More than 5000 were ultimately delivered to the USAF. Vietnam requirements drove pilot production, due to the establishment of the "One Tour" policy for Vietnam tours. However, the retirement of WW II and Korean War pilots created a pilot shortage. A solution was to put pilots in the backseat of the F-4. This created the makeup of squadron manning on my first Vietnam tour.

Part of my story in Friday Pilots, Book 1, tells of my time on this first tour, but I will try to not repeat my stories from that writing effort. However, the memories overlap. Vietnam was a lasting impression on my professional Air Force career. Lesson: I WAS AND STILL AM A FIGHTER PILOT. IT IS A STATE OF MIND MOLDED BY FLYING EXPERIENCES. Vietnam combat naturally is at the core of many of these memories.

The Vietnam war was a virtual testing ground for the requirements and development of later aircraft such as the single mission F-15 and A-10, plus the multi-mission F-16, all of which I have flown. Vietnam also brought the beginning of precision guided weapons, air and space integration, realistic training, aggressor training, Red Flag and many other developments that led to the Air Force we have today. The technology advancements in these weapon systems proved themselves 20 years later in Desert Storm One. I will not repeat these impacts on my fighter pilot career, but will look at another aspect, personnel policy.

My Vietnam experiences were based on two combat tours in the F-4C/ D, back to back, and assigned to the 497th TFS, Nite Owls, Ubon, Thailand. My first combat tour, 1968 –1969, was as a GIB (Guy in the Back), the pilot F-4 Weapon System Officer. I spent 12 months on that tour flying almost exclusively night combat missions, roughly 240, a total 67 of which, were in North Vietnam. Our missions included Armed Road Reconnaissance along the Ho Chi Minh Trail in Laos, or in southern North Vietnam, Route Package 1. The other most frequently flown mission was escort of AC-130 gunships which patrolled the Ho Chi Minh Trail. The AC-130s possessed night vision equipment and were much more effective at finding North Vietnamese trucks, supply areas and other targets. They needed armed escort to suppress enemy anti-aircraft fire. That was the mission of the two F-4s that accompanied them.

The Nite Owls were manned at that time by a mix of front seaters, mostly majors and lieutenant colonels who came from every other command and staff except Tactical Air Command, to which most of the fighter pilots were assigned. This meant there was little fighter or combat experience in the front seat. The back-seaters were young lieutenants and some captains on their first combat tour. The policy of the Air Force was: all non-volunteers must have one tour in Vietnam before the Air Force would assign pilots back for a second, non-volunteer tour. The other Air Force policy that impacted my first tour was the end of the tour length defined by 100 missions over NVN. The standard Vietnam tour length became one calendar year.

As a backseat pilot my only future was to volunteer for a second Vietnam tour in the F-4 or move to a non-fighter aircraft. I volunteered to upgrade to the front seat and a second combat tour. This was at the time the Air Force was running short of pilots who had not served in Vietnam and decided to send upgrading F-4 Aircraft Commanders (ACs) right back to Vietnam, a policy they tried to avoid until other pilots were not available. My fate was sealed. I would get to be an F-4 Aircraft Commander, but in Vietnam again. This led to two observations: fighter pilot experience was in short supply and Lesson: THE "UNIVERSALLY ASSIGNABLE PILOT" WAS A FAILED POLICY. I'll explain as we go forward.

I returned to the U.S. for upgrade training, after which I volunteered to return to Ubon, and the 497ᵗʰ Nite Owls. On arrival, I noticed one distinct change. Most of the F-4 ACs were like me, young captains on their second combat tour. The GIBs were predominantly Navigator Weapon System Officers, mostly young and on their first combat tour. The Nite Owls though had a mix of these young WSOs, a few pilot WSOs who had to serve a combat tour but opted to not upgrade because they planned to separate from the Air Force when first able, and a few senior grade Lt. Col. and Major navigators who needed a combat tour. It proved to be a good blend.

The missions remained the same as the first combat tour, AC-130 escort, armed recce, and working with Forward Air Controllers (FACs).

We added one mission of Night Forward Air Control, having acquired F-4 aircraft, with precision navigation equipment. As Night FACs we identified the target and directed other aircraft to attack it. We also could lead other aircraft in formation, in bad weather, to drop on our radio call. The aircraft with precision navigation equipment led these missions.

On my first tour, the Nite Owls lost nine crew in combat. During my second tour, the squadron lost only two, and there were fewer aircraft with battle damage. In my view, this can be credited to the higher level of combat experience in the squadron. Lesson: THE VIETNAM "ONE TOUR ASSIGNMENT POLICY" WAS FAIR, BUT OPERATIONAL EFFECTIVENESS WAS SACRIFICED. Moving forward to the current day, Combat requirements will need the Air Force to continue to balance operational and personnel needs. The Vietnam model is not the answer.

Lesson: AFTER VIETNAM, DEVELOPING THE F-15 AS A SINGLE MISSION AIRCRAFT PROVED TO BE SHORT SIGHTED. As was experienced in Desert Storm, we had too many F-15s without bomb dropping capabilities when bomb droppers were needed. Earlier F-15As possessed air-to-ground capability, but the capability was removed to expand air-to-air capability. I flew the F-15C at Bitburg AB, Germany and thoroughly enjoyed the dedicated air-to-air mission as a Major. Later, as a Major General operational commander, I had a much different perspective. The result of our F-15 experiences was the development of the F-15E, a multi-mission capable aircraft. This was an expensive path to a multi-mission fighter force.

I will now move you to my time as the 17th AF Commander, in Europe. Most of my units supported Operation Northern Watch, patrolling the "no-fly zone" over Northern Iraq. I frequently visited Incirlik Airbase, Headquarters for Northern Watch and flew F-16 combat air patrol missions. This was a successful operation for more than 1000 days. Then, 14 April 1994, Northern Watch suffered one of the most disastrous "friendly fire incidents" on USAF record. Two F-15s, ultimately under my command, mistakenly identified two US Army Blackhawk helicopters as Russian made Iraqi aircraft. They shot down both, with 26 military and civilians aboard, all fatalities. There was a Safety Investigation Board (SIB), with a fellow two-star general serving as the SIB President. Its purpose was to develop findings and conclusions that would help preclude such an event from happening again. These findings and conclusions are close hold. I was named President of the Accident Board, a Uniform Code of Military Justice (UCMJ) established investigation to provide a publicly releasable report and determine appropriate judicial actions for seven people assigned to USAFE. Parts of the SIB investigation findings were made available to the Accident Board, but my investigation was separate and independent. There was a counterpart Accident Board investigation in Air Combat Command that did the same for people assigned to ACC. This experience as an Accident Board President, was one of the worst periods of my life.

As an Accident Board President, you are isolated and not permitted to seek advice from commanders who had been through similar experiences, or anyone else. The only people I could discuss the accident with were members of the staff provided to help conduct the investigation. Then there was my wife, Kay. Her support and willing ear were a critical part of getting through this difficult period. She was there when all others could not be. Even though she might not have understood what I was talking about, she listened to my dilemmas, frustrations with the isolation and whatever else was on my mind. Kay provided some personal advice, but usually was there to listen. I cannot say enough about her.

Because of the publicity of this accident, there was quiet political pressure for me to complete the investigation quickly, and "get the story off the front page". I could understand the desire for me to complete the investigation quickly, I could not accept the motivation to stop the publicity. I felt it was wrong to rush this investigation,

Although isolated, I was lucky to have an opportunity to privately meet with the Desert Storm Air Commander on his visit to USAFE, in between assignments. The conversation with him started with a discussion about our restriction from being able to talk about my Accident Board Investigation. We discussed friendly fire incidents in general terms, and he provided me the best advice he could: Lesson: "THERE IS A WELL-ESTABLISHED PROCESS FOR INVESTIGATING THESE KINDS OF EVENTS. LET THE PROCESS WORK." I could not have asked for anything more. I must protect the process.

There is one other lesson from this experience. During my time in leadership positions, I learned that people who get into trouble either commit mistakes or crimes. Lesson: MISTAKES ARE FORGIVABLE;

CRIMES MUST BE DEALT WITH STERNLY. In the Northern Watch Blackhawk shoot down incident, there were enough mistakes to go around. However, everyone involved followed the Rules of Engagement (ROE), and procedures were in accordance with Operational guidance. However, the obvious significant error was mis-identifying the Blackhawk helicopters. It is questionable whether the mis-ID was the only cause, but it was most definitely significant.

As with most accidents, "the stars just line up one day," and that day becomes the worst of your life. The isolated Army unit in Eastern Turkey planned and flew their fateful Blackhawk mission as it previously had but failed to confirm this day's mission with the Northern Watch Headquarters. This had happened previously with no problems (more than 1000 days of successful operations). The AWACs aircraft was only minutes behind schedule, as had happened previously, with no problems (more than 1000 days of successful operations). The F-15s arrived on station and began their sweep of the area In Accordance With (IAW) the rules for "first in the area." They received earlier intelligence reports that the Iraqis were planning a violation of the No-Fly Zone. During the initial sweep, the F-15s saw on radar, unidentified aircraft. IAW the ROE they proceeded to visually identify the low flying aircraft. One pass by the Blackhawks, one radio call, "Bandit, Bandit, Bandit!!" and the result was, two Blackhawks down and 26 fatalities.

The lessons for me were Lesson: 1000 DAYS OF SUCCESSFUL OPERATIONS CAN EASILY LEAD TO COMPLACENCY, WHICH IN FLYING COMBAT AIR PATROLS CAN BE DEADLY. Some mistakes that are egregious cannot be forgiven and must be dealt with sternly. Lastly, Lesson: AS YOU BECOME MORE SENIOR, YOUR PROBLEMS DO NOT GET EASIER. THE DECISIONS REQUIRED BY YOU WILL BE DIFFICULT AND REQUIRE COURAGE. OUTSIDE PRESSURES WILL LIKELY BE PRESENT, AND YOU MUST DEAL WITH THEM COURAGEOUSLY. I did what I thought was the right thing. That is what is expected of a general officer, and you accept what comes with your decisions.

Lesson: GROWING UP IN AN IMMIGRANT FAMILY PROVIDED A STRONG BASIS FOR UNDERSTANDING WHAT IT MEANS TO BE AN AMERICAN. It also provided me the foundation to follow a military career. Being a fighter pilot strengthened the principles of good leadership, maintaining fairness in dealing with subordinates, maintaining courage when dealing with difficult decisions, and respect for others, your wingmen. Lesson: YOU ARE NOT INDEPENDENT, THERE ARE OTHERS IN YOUR FORMATION WHO WILL HELP YOU THROUGH DIFFICULT TIMES.

Postscript: To the Friday Pilots:

"On a more personal note, I've been in another battle with serious cancer for 3+ years. My formation has some of the best specialists in their field: many supportive friends, my dear wife, Kay, and a loving family. I cannot say enough about her and the Friday Pilots being in this formation. Thanks to all of you from the bottom of my heart, I will be forever grateful."

CHAPTER TWENTY-FOUR

IF I HAD IT TO DO OVER AGAIN

by Don Shepperd

The phone rang. It was the morning of 27 June 1958. I was to drive with my parents from our home in Denver to Lowry Air Force base and report to the Air Force Academy as a new cadet.

The call was from a neighbor. Their nephew, Don Watson, was also reporting to the Academy, and they wondered if he could get a ride? Of course. We were 17 years old. Little did I know we were about to embark on a life of adventure beyond my wildest imagination. Don and I completed the four Academy years with the class of 1962, the fourth class to enter the new Academy. We went to pilot training together, then went to F-100 training together at Luke. I went to Hahn AB in Germany. Don went to Cannon AFB NM. On that bright June morning in 1958, little did I suspect that two years after graduation, my friend and classmate, Don Watson, would become the first classmate on the Vietnam Wall. Lesson: FRIENDSHIPS ARE IMPORTANT. HOLD FRIENDS CLOSELY. THEY MAY NOT LAST FOREVER, BUT MEMORIES OF THEM WILL.

The fourth class, "Doolie" Academy summer, was physically excruciating. Apparently, I couldn't do anything right and saw more of my Element leader Hank Canterbury's tonsils than I wished. I did more pushups, polished my shoes more and memorized more useless knowledge than I ever anticipated.

The academic year arrived, and we all took "placement" tests to put us into academic sections. The problem was, there were no dummies. I did well in math and ended up in the upper section. The professor came into the first class and said, "Gentlemen, I see by your placement scores you are all math whizzes. We will do a quick review of advanced Algebra and then move rapidly into calculus. Let's start on page 265." We opened to calculations and formulas I had never seen before. Lesson: YOU MAY NOT BE AS SMART AS YOU THINK YOU ARE. COLLEGE IS DIFFERENT FROM HIGH SCHOOL.

I dreamed of being a pilot since I was five years-old near the end of WWII, when my dad bought me my first ride in a light aircraft from the ramp at Randolph AFB at the end of a War Bond rally. I only had one other airplane ride with a family friend in a Luscombe on a muddy, rain-soaked runway when I was 12. Our friend was a WWII B-25 pilot. The flight was fun once we got airborne, but even I could tell thick mud and small wheels made for a long and dicey takeoff as we weaved back and forth and struggled into the air. Our friend killed himself and another passenger two months later. Lesson: ALL FLYING IS SERIOUS. LIGHT AIRPLANES CAN GO JUST FAST ENOUGH TO KILL YOU.

I remember getting two T-33 orientation flights from Lowry and we got to do a roll. Later, on a summer field trip I went supersonic on an F-100 backseat ride and got a Machbuster's pin. WHOOPEE! I was almost a fighter pilot, just a couple of hurdles to go. We all had to have 20-20 vision, but we had no flight programs at USAFA in the early days. We could elect to take Navigator training in the T-29, even leading to Navigator wings. I wanted no part of anything but being a pilot. A professor tried to convince me to take Nav training as a backup just in case I washed out of pilot training. "WASHED OUT???" What are you talking about? There is no way I'm going to wash out of anything." He was a Navigator, looked at me askance and shook his head. Lesson: PLANNING FOR CONTINGENCIES MAY NOT BE A BAD IDEA. Fortunately, I did not need a backup plan, but some classmates did and had successful careers as Navigators.

My only other flight experience was on Operation Third Lieutenant. We were sent on two-week tours to Air Force bases to learn about the "real Air Force." It was the Cold War and I was sent to a B-52 base and flew on three 24-hour "Chrome Dome" nuclear airborne alert missions with "real" nukes on board. I think they did it to get me out of their hair. I learned one thing about the "real" Air Force. I did not want to be in Strategic Air Command. My desire to be a fighter pilot intensified. Lesson:

IT IS IMPORTANT TO LEARN WHAT YOU WANT TO DO AND EQUALLY IMPORTANT TO LEARN WHAT YOU DO NOT.

My four-year journey through USAFA was difficult but fulfilling. I had some very interesting experiences involving famous people. Three of the experiences were pleasant, the fourth, not so much: I was invited to have a private lunch with Russian aviation pioneer Alexander P. de Seversky; the second lunch was with Wernher von Braun, the WW II German rocket scientist; the third was a dinner with the legendary Gen. Curtis LeMay. I could write a book about each encounter. With the fourth celebrity, I was chosen to escort Madame Chiang Kai-shek, the First Lady of the Republic of China. At the end of the event the Commandant of Cadets asked me how the visit went. My smartass reply was, "Well I think she was a pretty hot chick." The Commandant was not amused. With a stern face, he spoke in a firm voice, "Cadet Shepperd, I expect cadets to be more professional than to refer to the wife of a world leader as a hot chick," and gave me two weeks restriction. Lesson: IF YOU DECIDE TO BE A SMARTASS, TIME IT CAREFULLY.

Looking back, the four years at USAFA passed in a flash but sure didn't seem like it at the time. The Academy looked really good in the rearview mirror as my new bride, Rose, and I sped out the exit gate. My father had given us some good advice, "Marriage is a serious thing. Don't rush into it." We didn't. We waited two whole hours after graduation, left with the top down on our new Chevrolet Impala convertible and headed for a month honeymoon in Mexico. While in Acapulco, we met and had drinks with Yolanda Espiritu, John Wayne's mistress. She looked at us sweetly and offered, "Espero que no se haya apresurado a casare. Es una cosa seria." Translated, "I hope you haven't rushed into marriage. It is a serious thing." Lesson: MARRIAGE IS A SERIOUS THING. DON'T RUSH INTO IT. We've been married 58 years. We agree it's a serious thing and think it's going to work.

Air Force pilot training at Williams AFB AZ in the T-37 and T-38 was absolutely the most fun a young man can have. We flew every day learning new things with old friends, takeoffs, landings, aerobatics, formation flying, night flying, navigation, flying solo and lots of it in the supersonic T-38. We didn't make much money, $445.18 second lieutenant's pay per month, BUT someone else was paying for the gas and we always had enough for Friday night beer call in the O-club. Rose and my dad pinned on my pilot wings. They were both intensely proud. We waited for assignments. Our class was "SACumcized," 95% SAC assignments, B-47s, B-52s and KC-97s. But, life was about to get good for me as we headed across town to Luke AFB for F-100 training. Lesson: DREAMS DO COME TRUE.

My first act across town was to go to Friday night beer call at the Luke O-club Stag Bar. Wow! These are real men, real fighter pilots, chugging beer, eating goldfish, singing raunchy songs, playing "DEAD BUG!" and no women permitted! This is going to be great but requires some practice and a very patient new wife. Lesson: THE PATIENCE OF A NEW WIFE CAN BE TESTED, BUT SHOULD BE DONE WITH GREAT CARE.

The first day of academics started with the "Sabre Dance" movie of the behind-the-power-curve fatal F-100 crash followed by the question, "Does anyone want to quit?" No one did. This had been a lifetime dream for most of us. My first flight was in the two-seat F-100F and I remember starting and taxiing, feeling the power and thinking, "I am finally a fighter pilot!" I was soon to learn there were a few more steps to go; one was the first takeoff. I wobbled into the air with a heavy wing rock wondering, "I thought I was a pilot. What the hell is going on?" It took a couple of takeoffs to master the hydraulicly-boosted controls of the Hun. Soon, came a mix of gunnery, air-to-air, low-level navigation and aerial refueling off KC-97s. Gunnery was a gas, composed of dive-bomb, rockets, strafe and skip-bombing that simulated napalm drops. We had to qualify in all events. I was an Ace at dive bombing, pretty decent at rockets, superb at strafe and absolutely lousy at skip bombing, the easiest gunnery event in existence.

We dropped four 25lb. practice bombs on each gunnery mission for skip-bombing. We flew at 100 ft. and to qualify, one had to hit two of four (50%) on two out of six missions, or 100% on one mission on a 50ft. X 200ft. target, easy peasey. On my first five missions, I had two total hits. That meant I had to hit all four on my last mission. Everyone else in the class had qualified. I was the class goat. I began thinking about the Navigator who told me I should get navigator wings at USAFA as a backup. What if I washed out? I hit all four for 100% and was a full-up round, qualified in all events and heading for an assignment in Germany. I will never know if I actually hit all four or if the squadron commander called the Range Officer and said, "Give this kid four hits and let's get rid of the dumbass because anyone can eventually learn to skip-bomb." And, I did. I don't think I ever missed another skip bomb in my entire fighter career and I used it a lot in Vietnam. Lesson: ANY DUMBASS CAN LEARN TO SKIP-BOMB. I PROVED IT.

I cannot begin to explain how enjoyable our first assignment to a fighter squadron in Germany was. I had been to Europe twice, both times riding backwards in a windowless C-121, once on a 30-day cadet field trip, once on a two-week exchange at Cranwell, the English Air Force Academy. Now we were PCS and the deutschmark was 4:1; deposits on beer bottles more than the beer; Mosel wine country at Hahn Airbase; Swiss Ski School; weekends in Paris; nuclear alert at home station and in Italy and Turkey; gunnery in Libya; aircraft deliveries for maintenance to Getafe, Spain, the Plaza Mayor and the Casablanca, Botin's, Casa Paco's. But, there were things to learn. There are few things as humbling as being a young, green bean fighter jock in a squadron of grizzled veterans, some from Korea, a handful from WWII.

My flight commander sat me down for a serious talk, "Son, all you young guys are the same. You think you are great pilots because you went to pilot training, finished high in the class to get fighter assignments and finished high again to get Europe. Let me tell you that you are NOT a great pilot, BUT, you better become one QUICK. You are flying the F-100, a tough airplane in the worst weather in Europe at Hahn. You either become a GREAT instrument pilot or you will be dead very soon." Gulp. Holy cow, this was worse than the Sabre Dance movie. Lesson: IF YOU ARE A YOUNG PILOT AND THINK YOU ARE GREAT, YOU PROBABLY AREN'T.

I finished a three-year Europe tour as an Air Liaison Officer with the Army and headed for Vietnam. I made a quick stop en-route to buy a house and drop off a seven-month old son that I would not see again until he was almost two. As I walked down the ramp at Stapleton Airport to depart, I looked back and my wife was crying. What could she be crying about? This was my lifelong dream, a real war for men with hair on their chests. There were missiles and MiGs and AAA, and our bases were attacked at nights with rockets and mortars. What was not to like? It was an important lesson. Families only sit, wait, wonder, worry and dread the sight of every blue car. We did not take care of families well during Vietnam, especially the POW wives. Lesson: WAR IS HARDER ON FAMILIES THAN THOSE WHO FIGHT IT.

I flew the Misty F-100 Fast FAC mission in Vietnam. It was a difficult and dangerous mission. We flew in Route Pack 1, the final funnel for all men and materials coming from North Vietnam into the South. We flew two seat F-100F aircraft on 4:30-6:00 hour missions, air-refueling and going back into North Vietnam three times on each flight to find and mark targets for bomb-carrying fighters. We changed seats every other mission. The frontseater flew the airplane, the backseater handled the radios, maps and a camera. We flew at 4500 ft., jinking and pulling Gs every seven-eight seconds to avoid gunfire. It was miserable and exhausting flying. We were in the heart of the AAA envelope for the 37mm and 57mm guns. We were not subjected to the heavy SAM, MiGs or concentrated AAA environment of Route Packs 5 and 6, but we were shot at ALL the time. We heard and felt it constantly as the shells passed close. It was unnerving and when we marked targets, we were the ONLY target for all guns. We had a high loss rate: 44 of our 157 Mistys were shot down, some twice. Our losses came from being subjected to constant gunfire at low altitudes throughout the mission.

In Vietnam I learned the difference between bravery and courage. Bravery is instinctive, momentary and impulsive. You either have it or you don't. You either do it, or you don't - you dive on the grenade, or roll away. Courage is much different. It is the ability to exercise bravery when you have time to consider the consequences. It was displayed in Vietnam by the Thud and F-4 drivers who went back into Route Packs 5 and 6 braving the AAA and SAMs every day and by the Sandys and Jolly Greens who came to rescue us in desperate circumstances and by the Misty FACs. The pilots knew what their missions entailed and went back day-after-day into the "eye of the tiger" and many paid for it dearly, ending up as POWs or names on the Vietnam Wall. LESSON: BRAVERY IS INSTINCTIVE, COURAGE IS A CHOICE. I saw lots of both.

Vietnam was a long and difficult war. We lost for many reasons, not the least of which was the failure to understand the purpose of engaging in the first place, the lack of a clear strategy, the failure to understand the enemy and the failure to have support of the American people. The courage of the soldiers, sailors, airmen and Marines who fought the war was never in doubt; the wisdom of politicians and senior military leaders who sent them was. The U.S. does not go to war to conquer the treasure or territory of others. We go, or should go, for things that are in our vital national interest or to assist an ally. Again, and again, we have made the mistake of mission creep and trying to stay and change the culture of another country. It is a mistake, one we have been making for the last 30 years in the Middle-East. Lesson: THERE ARE THINGS WORTH FIGHTING FOR, BUT WE MUST UNDERSTAND WHAT THEY ARE AND WE MUST HAVE THE AMERICAN PEOPLE BEHIND US IF WE ASK THEM TO SACRIFICE THEIR CHILDREN AND GRANDCHILDREN.

After Vietnam, I decided to get off active duty. I went with the airlines. It was a bad mistake. After my third furlough, I came back into the Air National Guard fulltime and ended up as head of the Air National Guard and a Major General, retiring in 1998 from the Pentagon. I swore as long as I was in command, I would fight to keep troops under me from going to war ill-trained and ill-equipped like we were for Vietnam. Lesson: WAR IS ABOUT SENDING YOUNG MEN AND NOW WOMEN, OUR KIDS, INTO COMBAT. THERE IS NO MORE SOBERING RESPONSIBILITY.

After retirement, I formed my own consulting firm and after the 9-11 attacks, I spent five years with CNN covering the wars in Iraq and Afghanistan on camera. Lesson: IF YOU ARE ON TV YOU MUST LEARN TO GIVE CONCISE 30 SECOND ANSWERS TO COMPLEX QUESTIONS AND HOW TO USE MAKEUP. I had a radio face.

Would I do it all again? You bet! The most important lesson I learned about leadership was: CARE MORE FOR THOSE UNDERNEATH YOU THAN YOU CARE ABOUT YOURSELF. It works for the family, in the military and in business.

Important life lessons for me: DO SOMETHING IMPORTANT. PREPARE WELL. WORK HARD. BE HONEST. ENJOY IT ALL. MAKE GOOD FRIENDS. BE THERE WHEN THEY NEED YOU. LIVE LIFE LIKE YOUR DAD IS WATCHING YOU. HE PROBABLY IS.

CHAPTER TWENTY-FIVE

THE LEARNING CURVE

by Ed "Moose" Skowron

MOOSE SKOWRON: "Tucson Approach. This is November 2358 Uniform. I've got at minor fuel problem. I'm going to land on I-19 south of the San Xavier Mission." TIA APPROACH: "You're what?"

Well, it was a nice weekend morning in August of 1987, and I was working an aerial photo job in my old but trusted Cessna 172. The assignment was to cover the pecan orchards along the Old Nogales Highway north of Green Valley in southern Arizona. My friend, Mike, and a part owner in the airplane, was flying the right seat.

My dreams as a boy were of airplanes and becoming a pilot. Paralleling that goal was a keen interest in photography. I would spend a lifetime in perfecting both to the limits of my capabilities. From my very first flight, the magical view of the earth from above opened my eyes to a totally new and exciting photo backdrop. There would be very few times I would not have a camera with me in flight, and what had started as a hobby in the Air Force, would become an actual business when I entered commercial and corporate aviation. The mix of flying and photos became "Aeroflicks," a 24-year stint in commercial photography.

Getting back to that morning in August '87, we had taken off from Tucson International Airport, TIA, and flew 10 minutes down to the groves. This was a short flight to what should have been a quick shoot. Well, that's what it was supposed to be planned as...I had a bit less than half a fuel load on the airplane, and from about 800 to 1,000 feet above ground level, using the lens and the camera equipment I had selected, I could get a well-framed view of the grove sections in which the customer was interested. With the left cockpit window latched up, and in a 45-degree banked left turn, I could stay reasonably stabilized over the target.

Now to keep the left wing strut and landing gear out of the frame, I'd hold a lot of top rudder and skid around with all the G forces pushing hard to the left, heavily cross-controlled.

I called out to Mike to roll into the turn, and I would jab in the right rudder and compose and shoot the pictures. We did this for about 15 to 20 minutes and error one cropped up: I ran out of film.

At the time, I was working at Learjet as a test and demo pilot, and my office was right at the approach end of runway 03 at TIA. I had plenty of film there. Five or ten minutes back. Land on 03. Taxi up to the office. Jump out, grab some film and back into the bird and return to the pecans.

I checked the fuel. Just short of a half tank in the left and a quarter tank in the right. This would take 20 or 25 minutes, and that's plenty of fuel. A short takeoff from 03, cleared for a right turn out, and we are on our way.

We got back into the ring around the groves and back to work. After about three turns, I'm racked up in a steep left bank, rudder full right, and, OOPS! the engine quits. Oh, no! Deafening silence.

Experience is the best teacher, but it can be very expensive. Immediately, the aircraft fuel system schematic floods my brain. I know the problem. The heavy cross control has forced all the fuel to the left ends of each tank. The right tank is now empty. The left is about half full but in the wrong place to draw fuel from the pick-up tube. I roll wings level, and we're gliding at about 800 feet.

The question is: how long will it take the fuel in the left tank to gravity feed down to the fuel selector, forward to the primer and into the carburetor? The fuel might make it before we contact the desert, but on the other hand, if it doesn't, things could get critical, real critical.

My decision: Land on I-19, hence, the call to Tucson Approach. We're heading north and parallel to I-19 and in about a downwind distance from a landing spot on the southbound lanes. That's the good part. At about 500 feet, I start a left base turn and pick a reasonable open area behind vehicles heading south. I roll out on a final at about 100 to 200 feet and about 100 yards behind a car. Good. I start to slow to landing speed, 45 to 50 knots, and I'm staying high out of the rearview mirrors of the car I'm following. I don't want him or her to see me, panic and cram on the brakes. I'm gaining on the car. It looks like a Chevy with a bobble head doll in the back window that appears to be laughing at me. I'm catching the car, and I start to hear my stall warning horn chatter.

The feds had just removed the national 55 miles-an-hour speed limit from the nation's highways. I'm thinking, "Push it up, buddy! Feel free to go 65 or more now!" With that, the car begins to move away, I drop down, flare and land.

On the rollout, there is a dirt crossover between the lanes, and I roll onto that, clear of all traffic, and the best part, I'm hiding behind a large bush. The driver following me must have been a pilot. He simply gave me a thumbs up, passed and continued on his way.

When I made the call to Tucson Approach of my intentions, they alerted the "off airport crash net." That includes all the local TV stations. I think the TV stations reached me faster than anyone else. As I was on final, there were probably TV trucks already behind me, cameras rolling.

The Arizona Highway Patrol had a car there in minutes. Fortunately, I knew the officer. He had been a security guard at Learjet. Always thinking, I had him verify there was fuel in the airplane because I knew I would be taking a lot of jibes from my fellow pilots, which, indeed, did happen. One actually mailed me a dead stick. The officer asked me my plan, and I told him: get some gas, take off and return to TIA. He was happy with that.

I wasn't sure there was positively enough fuel in the left tank to reach the stand pipe, so I called Jim Davis, who lives out on the west side of town, and told him that I was out of gas on I-19 and could he possibly bring me five or ten gallons. He said, sure. And, then I added, he would have to pick it up from the airport. Silence. And then, "Let me guess. You're in the 172?"… "Yup. And, please call my wife and tell her all's well and that she will probably see me on the local news."

Jim arrived with the fuel. We gassed up, and the Highway Patrol officer said he would do a slow rolling roadblock in the northbound lane and when he flashed his headlights, I would be clear to go. He did, and we rolled out onto the centerline and took off to the north.

I called Tucson Approach and told them in the most casual voice I could muster, "November 2358 Uniform is off I-19 and requesting landing." Approach cleared me to enter traffic and added, "That's a first for me." I told him, "Same for me."

Later that day, I checked in with the feds at the FAA office in Scottsdale and passed them the story. With no damage to property or to the airplane, they said, forget it. Good. No hits. No runs. No errors. Nobody left on base. Piece of cake.

For the next few months, every general aviation magazine I picked up had an article about the inaccuracies of light plane fuel indicating systems and the ease of un-porting of the fuel feed. I found out about that the hard way. More of the never-ending learning curve.

By the time this event took place, I had been actively flying for 35 years and would continue for another 17. How did this happen? Maybe, just a bit too complacent because even a Piper Cub will just barely kill you.

After all the jumping around between flying and photography, there were many lessons learned but two stand out for me. Lesson one: IN AVIATION, AS IN LIFE, ALWAYS HAVE A REAL PLAN "B" BECAUSE PLAN "A" CAN GO TO HELL IN A HEARTBEAT. Lesson two: IN PHOTOGRAPHY, ALWAYS SHOOT A LOT BUT ONLY SHOW A FEW. A BAD PICTURE, LIKE A BAD DECISION, CAN LAST FOREVER.

Oh, and the learning curve is always there.

CHAPTER TWENTY-SIX

ALTITUDE, AIRSPEED, BRAINS: YOU NEED TWO OF THOSE TO SURVIVE

by Jeff "Tico" Tice

"Number 66! Put your paw on the animal in front of you and march!" said a gruff voice tainted with a distinctly Russian accent. I could not see a thing with the black fabric bag over my head. I stuck my hand out to the guy in front of me, felt for his shoulder and we began to move. About 50 paces later, the same voice yelled, "Stop and turn to your left!" I did so and a pair of hands grabbed me and shoved me through a narrow doorway. A steel door slammed shut behind me. Before I could turn around, the door opened and the Russian accent said, "You will stand up until I come back!" I stood for what seemed hours but finally leaned against the cell wall. No sooner did I do that than the door flew open and a bucket of cold water splashed over me. This was about as far from "the wild blue yonder" as you could be and I thought, "I didn't sign up for this s**t!" This was Survival, Evasion, Resistance and Escape (SERE) School at Fairchild AFB, WA in April 1979.

I was born and raised in rural southeast Pennsylvania. I entered the world as number three out of four boys. My boyhood home was located about halfway between Philadelphia and Allentown in a picturesque shallow valley. The nearest neighbor with children was about a half mile west of our place.

My family was not wealthy, nor were we dirt poor. There were times when we'd have a few "meatless" days in a row, but they were thankfully rare. My formative years were typical of the late 50s and early 60s in a rural environment. There were no indoor distractions, no TV, computer games, etc. So, I spent most of my time outdoors, when not in school. It was common for me and my friends to walk miles along a nearby creek each day, looking for adventure. We knew we had to be back home before dark.

Entering junior high school, I had to get a physical before I could play sports. Our doctor discovered I had a heart murmur. The treatment was, "no strenuous activity for six-nine months." I was stunned, but my dad said, "Maybe now you'll finally get decent grades!" The doctor finally declared I was cured and could resume my normal activities. I played football, basketball and ran track throughout junior high and high school. I was good at track and held the state record for 100-yard high hurdles during my senior year in high school. My GPA ended up a respectable 3.8. Lesson: MY FATHER WAS RIGHT, "SOMETIMES YOU HAVE TO SLOW DOWN TO SPEED UP."

With my family's finances, I needed a scholarship to attend college. Few colleges gave track scholarships, so I tried to get an appointment to one of the service academies. That fizzled out, so I looked at an ROTC scholarship. I took the AFOQT and scored well. I was accepted into Penn State University with a full USAF 4-year ROTC scholarship and a pilot training slot awaiting upon graduation!

I arrived on the main campus of Penn State in September 1973. For a kid with a rural background, being dropped into "Happy Valley" with nearly 50,000 other young people was eye watering. In order to keep my pilot training slot, I needed to graduate with a "technical degree." I settled on electrical engineering. Little did I know how much classwork would be required. My freshman year I carried over 21 semester credit hours. My next three years were not much easier. I also had poor time-management skills. I discovered girls and beer. My grades suffered. I managed to regroup and graduated with a BSEE in 1977.

Vietnam drew to a close in 1975 and the USAF no longer needed a large pilot pipeline for the war. Upon graduation and commissioning as a 2d Lt. I was placed on inactive reserve status and told, "Don't call us. We'll call you." I was now unemployed and out of school. So I did what all young adults do when faced with this dilemma: I moved back in with my parents. Luckily, I found a decent job about 20 miles from home. The U.S. Navy hired me as a civilian electrical draftsman at the Naval Air Development Center in Warminster, PA. I got to climb all over every manner of Navy aircraft and catalog the "orange wire" in the test aircraft. A Navy test pilot strode by in full fighter pilot flight regalia one day and all of sudden, a personal goal landed in my lap! Now, I REALLY wanted to be a fighter pilot.

In early March 1978 an official package arrived containing orders for Undergraduate Pilot Training (UPT) April 1, 1978 at Columbus AFB, MS. An ROTC classmate friend from New Jersey had the exact same orders and we caravanned from PA to MS, 17 hours non-stop. When our UPT class began, the Wing Commander gave us the "Be No Brief:" There will be no fraternization, there will be no DUIs, etc. Near the end of his briefing, he told us all to look around and decide who wouldn't make it. He stated his job was to weed out at least 20%, preferably 30% of the class.

UPT was physically demanding, mentally challenging and required more personal discipline than I had ever demonstrated. The 20 other guys in class 79-04 were just as motivated as me. Competition over the next year was fierce, but friendly. However, the Wing Commander got his 20% wish as four guys washed out. I finished number four out of the 17 remaining in my class. As luck would have it, there were four fighter assignments.

On assignment night a 16-foot long table was lined from one end to the other with shot glasses filled with an unknown liquor. When your name was called, you picked up the next shot glass, drank it quickly and looked into the bottom. If there was no information, you stepped to next glass and kept drinking until an aircraft type showed up on glass bottom. The number of shots taken corresponded to the number of engines in your assigned aircraft. Poor bastards being sent into B-52s needed eight shots to get over their plight!

My turn came quickly, and I drank the first shot rapidly, no words in the bottom. The second shot went down a little slower, but there was something written on the bottom of the glass – F-111. I was thankful I didn't have to drink more, but what was an F-111, an Aardvark? I didn't ask because it had an "F" in front of the numbers, so I was on my way to being a fighter pilot! Lesson: DRINK CAREFULLY! YOUR FUTURE MIGHT BE IN THE BOTTOM OF A GLASS

The long road to becoming a fighter pilot involves many training courses including water survival, land survival, SERE, fighter lead-in training, to name a few. Each one is a pass-fail scenario. Pass, and you move on. Fail and you lose your wings and fulfill your seven-year military commitment as a ground pounder behind a desk.

I passed each course leading up to my F-111 assignment and went to Cannon AFB, NM as my F-111 Replacement Training Unit (RTU). After RTU, I got orders to RAF Lakenheath, UK in the F-111F. For a kid who hadn't been outside of a 100-mile radius of home until he was 17, it was mind-boggling and intoxicating. I was now on my way to England, all within 18 months of being called to active duty! My tour in the UK was an amazing start to a career and it was a great place for a 2d Lt. to "grow up." My career moved almost as fast as the 'Vark." But I didn't want to be stuck in F-111s for 20 years. I wanted to fly other aircraft and learn other missions. Swapping jets is expensive and not easy. I kept looking for a way into an air-to-air mission. Nearing the end of my four-year tour, I found the USAFE Aggressors were looking for volunteers to fly F-5s to replicate Soviet tactics and train the NATO air forces. I volunteered immediately but was rejected about as fast. I applied two more times and on my third try I got a call from the HQ USAFE personnel director. He said, "Capt. Tice, I've read your personnel file and your recommendation letters. Some ranking officers think pretty highly of you. However, you cannot even spell air-to-air and now you want to teach it! You must think you're a pretty damn good pilot, or you're just really stupid." I replied, "Yes, sir. I am one of those two things all the time, and the other one some of the time." Within two weeks I had orders to Nellis AFB, NV to attend the USAF Aggressor Training Program. Lesson: PERSEVERANCE MAY HAVE ITS REWARDS IF YOU HAVE THE SELF CONFIDENCE TO TRY.

The Aggressor Training Course is a subset of the USAF Weapons and Tactics School and essentially a PhD program in air-to-air fighter employment. The personnel guy was completely right: I couldn't even spell it. The program was, by far, the most difficult six months of my career. I nearly washed out twice. I managed to finish the course with the help of my classmates and the entire cadre of Aggressor IPs. I returned to England for back-to-back tours in Europe. The NATO Aggressors were all hand-picked, superb fighter pilots. Everything I learned about air-to-air from my squadron mates in four years would fill a book. I would do it all over again just to fly with that group of outstanding pilots. Lesson: FRIENDS WANT YOU TO SUCCEED. NEVER BE ASHAMED TO ASK FOR THEIR HELP.

My tour in the NATO Aggressors went by all too fast. I soon faced another assignment cycle and was due to return to the states in 1987 after eight years in Europe. At that time, the USAF faced mounting pilot attrition because the airlines were hiring. My squadron and wing commanders wanted me to get another air-to-air flying assignment and I heartily agreed. They recommended I be assigned to F-16s at Torrejón AB, Spain and the 3rd AF commander agreed. It made good sense and would save money, but the Air Force Military Personnel Center had other ideas. They ignored the common-sense approach and by-name request from the commanding three-star general. I went back to F-111s as an RTU IP at Mountain Home AFB, ID.

I was completely dejected. I reluctantly moved myself and my growing family back to the states. I relearned the F-111 systems quickly and began teaching "snot nosed" lieutenants how to fly the Vark. Almost all my old F-111 squadron mates were now IPs at Mountain Home. The camaraderie helped ease my disappointment at getting sucked back into the air-to-ground business. I was notified of my selection to Major but had about one year before I could pin on that rank and was contemplating leaving active duty and getting a pilot job at an Air National Guard unit. In fact, I seriously looked into the 162nd Fighter Wing in Tucson.

I was not very stealthy with my inquiries and the Deputy Wing Commander called me into his office. As I stepped in, he said, "Close the door and do not sit down." I quickly realized this was a "receive-only" discussion. He seriously upbraided me for even contemplating leaving active duty for the Guard. He mentioned how much money the USAF had invested in me, how many senior officers had gone out of their way to help me and he finally asked if I was serious, or was this whole thing a vicious rumor. I told him I was serious. He quietly said, "You are going to get an amazing deal within two weeks. I cannot tell you what it is now, but if you shut up and color within the lines for just a little while longer, I think your career will go where you want it." I told him I was starting two weeks leave on Monday to elk hunt in the Idaho wilderness. He said, "Expect a call when you get back. Remember, shut up and color!" I saluted, did an about face and left his office stunned, but curious.

Two weeks went by, and upon exiting the River of No Return Wilderness, elk-less, I found a pay phone and called my wife. She was beside herself. As soon as she heard my voice, she exclaimed, "Where the hell are you? Your squadron commander has been calling the house almost hourly for the last two days!" I told her where I was and immediately called him. He said the same thing as my wife, "Where the hell are you? I've been trying to get hold of you for two days!" I repeated my location and he told me, "Call AFMPC now!" I called immediately. The major on the other end was one of my old F-111 RTU classmates from Cannon AFB. He was excited, too. The first thing I asked him is, "WTF is going on?" He explained I had been selected by my Wing Commander to receive any assignment I wanted. I said, "Is this some huge practical joke? I've been here less than 18 months." He explained the USAF had just announced a new program to try to reduce pilot losses. Each Wing Commander was given one "golden carrot" per year and I was selected from my wing. Then he asked, "What airplane do you want and where do you want to go?" I responded, "I'd love an F-16! If you have a location no one wants, a remote tour or something like that, I'll take it." He told me he'd call me back the next morning and orders would be coming within 30 days. I hurried home. The next morning, I got the call that said I was getting orders to Torrejón AB, Spain in the F-16C. I pinched myself. Another dream had come true. Lesson: A SHARP TURN CAN LEAD IN THE RIGHT DIRECTION.

My F-16 RTU was MacDill AFB, FL. I was a major with over 2000 hours of fighter time, so I was given the "short course." It was another "drink from the fire hose" event. I was soon stepping onto the tarmac at Torrejón in August 1989. My family once again settled in to living off-base in a foreign country. It was a cultural challenge, but an enjoyable experience. My daughters learned reasonable Spanish within six months. I never did.

I signed into the 614ᵗʰ "Lucky Devils" squadron and went to see the commander. He invited me to have a seat and pushed two large notebooks across his desk for me to view. He then asked me, "What's wrong with this picture?" The documents before me were two USAF Form 5s–mine and his. The Form 5 is a detailed list of every flight you've ever made in the USAF along with a compilation of your total flight time. I quickly noticed my total fighter time was over 200 hours more than his. I responded to his question with, "Sir, it appears you've had less opportunity to fly than me even though your rank shows you are senior to me." He said, "Exactly! I am making you the squadron Chief of Scheduling to solve that problem." I said, "Thank you, sir. Do you want me to be the Chief of Scheduling to get you more flight time than I have?" He said, "Absolutely!" I left his office. I knew the squadron commander would never be able to keep up the flying schedule he wanted due to his other duties. I did what he asked and whenever he took himself off the schedule due to conflicts, I flew in his place. He never passed me in fighter time. Over 30 years later, we are still good friends. Lesson: EXECUTE YOUR BOSS' PLAN AND BACK HIM UP.

By spring 1990 I was a flight commander and soon after an assistant operations officer. In August, Iraq invaded Kuwait and the U.S. quickly responded. Our squadron got a warning order to deploy to an "undisclosed location" in the Middle East. We blasted off to Doha AB, Qatar, touching down August 26th at 10:00 PM local. It was 106°F and 100% humidity with the proximity to the Arabian Gulf. There was nothing at Doha but a hangar and a runway. We deployed as ordered with only the aviation package. No support team, no civil engineering, no food service, etc. The advance team had not yet arrived. The squadron commander called all the pilots together and asked if anyone had civil engineering experience. One of the pilots sheepishly raised his hand. The boss asked him, "What experience do you have?" He replied, "I helped build Israeli airfields in the Negev desert." He instantly became our civil engineer. Each pilot was assigned a support function and we set out to build a functional air base from nothing.

During this base building process, we flew local area training missions to become familiar with the weather and terrain. We also had four jets on 15-minute alert because we were about 450 miles from Kuwait. We fell into a routine of flying, working on base build up, and working out, no booze, no women, no fun. By November, we were ready to get on with this war. Our turn came on Jan 17, 1991 when Desert Storm began. The Iraqis had no chance of winning this war from the start. They were up against the collective might of the USA and one of the largest allied coalitions ever assembled. Plus, every single grunt, fighter pilot and support troop was pissed at being 10,000 miles from home over the holidays with no booze!

Since I was the maintenance officer, I did not fly on the first day of the war. I physically inspected every jet and every bomb loaded to make certain there were no errors on my troops' part. My first combat sortie was on Jan 18. I led an eight ship of F-16s to bomb Jalibah airfield just north of Kuwait. The weather was crappy with a thick overcast up to 15000'. The Rules of Engagement (ROE) at the time prohibited us from dropping bombs without visually acquiring the target. We ended dropping our ordnance on a secondary target near the Iraq-Kuwait border. It was the quintessential "milk run," no enemy fire, no secondary explosions. My next mission would be much different.

On Jan 19 I led another eight ship as part of a 74 aircraft package going to downtown Baghdad. My target was Daura oil refinery on the west bank of the Tigris River, another eight F-16s from my squadron were attacking an airfield to the northwest of Baghdad, another 48 F-16s were bombing several large weapons storage areas southeast of the city. Our plan was to feint towards Syria as if we were SCUD-hunting, then "student body right" to run-in on our respective targets. Timing was planned for all 64 F-16s to be over their targets simultaneously. Again, the weather was poor from the surface to about 12000'. The other 56 F-16s in the package aborted their primary targets but I could see my target from 40 miles away, the proverbial "Sucker Hole" was sitting over IP to target run in.

As we got to the clear area, the Iraqi defenses came alive. Every AAA battery in and around Baghdad began firing. Then the SAMs began to launch. The only good news was the AAA was barrage fire and well below our flight path, and the SAMs were ballistically launched with no guidance. A few SAMs got a bit close and we took evasive action. As we began the roll-in, I saw a SAM launch headed right for one of the F-16s egressing above us. I called out "CLAP 4, BREAK RIGHT!" He started to move but the SAM speared his jet and it disappeared in a fireball. Lesson: A "SUCKER HOLE" IS SO-NAMED FOR A GOOD REASON, AND IN COMBAT, THE ONLY EASY DAY WAS YESTERDAY.

I refocused on the refinery and put the pipper on my assigned target, a cracking tower in the northwest corner of the complex. As I pickled-off two Mk-84 2000lb. bombs, another volley of SAMs came up. We pulled hard up and out of the "Hot Zone" and turned to the egress point. Another SAM lit up my Radar Warning Receiver. This one was different than the other 8-10 shot at us in the last 60 seconds. I searched and saw a SAM arcing southwest towards me. I selected afterburner and put the missile smoke trail on my wingtip. As the missile closed to where I saw the rocket flame, I started a 6-G roll around the missile. The SAM went by so close I heard it "Whoosh" as it passed below my left wing trailing edge. "Damn, that was too close!" At the same time, I felt a bump not unlike a small pocket of turbulence. Then the electrics began cycling off and on. The F-16 is an "electric jet" and when the electrics go wrong, the jet goes wrong.

I looked back in the cockpit and noted the engine fire light on. About the same time "Bitchin' Betty" yelled at me, "Engine Fire, Engine Fire!" I told her, "Tell me something I don't know!" The jet was still flying so I pointed the nose up and jettisoned the fuel tanks. The left tank hung on the rear lug and rolled over the horizontal stabilizer putting the jet out of control for a brief moment. I got the aircraft back wings level and called to my wingman, "Stroke 1's been hit; lost the engine and electrics. Flow southeast, NOW!"

Large chunks of metal were missing from behind the cockpit. Flames were shooting out of some of them and the rest belched smoke. The jet was still flyable, but I knew that wouldn't last long. It didn't. About three minutes later, the jet began to pitch up and did not respond to my nose-down stick inputs. I pulled the ejection handle. Absolutely NOTHING happened!

Keeping the ejection handle stretched at its limit, I reached for the manual canopy jettison T-handle near my left hip. As I looked for that secondary method of exiting the jet, a gap grew between the canopy and the cockpit. The ejection seat had fired. The time from ejection handle pull to canopy separation is 0.3 seconds. In my mind it took an hour. Lesson: TEMPORAL DISTORTION IS REAL. EXPECT IT IN STRESSFUL SITUATIONS.

During the freefall and parachute descent the memory of SERE School came rushing back. I *did* sign up for this s**t! Suddenly, I needed every second of that training. I hit the desert sand and was quickly surrounded by Bedouin tribesmen. They had no shoes, very few teeth, but brand-new AK-47s. They were obviously not "Friendlies." After a night playing games with the tribesmen, I was turned over to the Iraqi Police in Samawah. They, in turn, handed me over to Secret Police later that day and I was on my way to Baghdad.

I spent 46 days as a "Guest of Saddam" and lost 45 pounds during my stay at five of his finest "hotels." The first two weeks of captivity were the most difficult, and I was pushed beyond normal human endurance. I am forever grateful to fellow Friday Pilot POWS, Bob Barnett, Marty Neuens and GAR Rose whose years in Vietnam POW camps led to the SERE School training I received 12 years earlier. That training kept me alive.

During my tour on the ground in Baghdad, my fellow pilots kept "bringing the heat" downtown. At night, if I had a window in my cell, I could watch the secondary explosions from their bombing. It was my only form of entertainment. The night of Feb 23 my entertainment "brought down the house." F-117 stealth fighters dropped four 2000 lb. laser-guided bombs on the building housing us POWs. The concussive power threw me around my 8' x 10' cell and leveled the western wing of the building. We were housed in the eastern wing and, miraculously, no POWs were seriously injured. It took over 24 hours for the Iraqis to dig us out of the rubble. Lesson: IT IS BETTER TO GIVE THAN TO RECEIVE.

Ten days later we were released to the International Red Cross and repatriated with our respective countrymen in Riyadh, Saudi Arabia. I never doubted I'd get released, because senior leaders allowed the military to prosecute a war with no direct political intervention. It was a glorious day descending the stairs of the Red Cross airplane and saluting Gen. Schwarzkopf as I stepped onto the tarmac. He had a tear running down his face. I knew exactly how he felt.

After recovery from my injuries, I resumed flying F-16s at Torrejon. The peace dividend was in full swing and forces were drawing down rapidly. My next assignment was a staff position at HQ ACC, Langley AFB, VA. From there, I went back to flying F-16s as the Active Duty Advisor to the Puerto Rico Air National Guard. My final assignment was to the 12th AF staff at Davis-Monthan AFB, AZ. I retired from the USAF in 1999 having flown 19 of 22 years.

My next career was with American Airlines. I was domiciled at LaGuardia Airport, NYC and commuted from Tucson to NY every week for 12 years. I was very lucky to fly with some fine pilots in the commercial world who taught me much about commercial aviating. Unfortunately, the airline business isn't run by pilots. After American filed for bankruptcy the second time, I retired from commercial aviation.

Since then I've been heavily involved with military-related charities, locally and nationwide. I've been supremely honored with an invite to join the Friday Pilots. I'd say my aviation life is complete when my heroes became my lunch buddies! Lesson: A POSITIVE ATTITUDE WILL GIVE YOU A POSITIVE LIFE.

CHAPTER TWENTY-SEVEN

GEEZER FLYING LESSONS
by Rob Van Sice

In 1966-67, as a flight-school qualified ROTC college senior, the USAF paid for me to get a private pilot's license through the local Bozeman Airport contracted instructors. At the same time, I was President of my Fraternity, carrying 18 credits in my Electrical Engineering course work, serving in a variety of campus roles, and, most importantly dating Lynne, the love of my life. The flying was fun but landed far down my list of priorities at that time. As a consequence, I was slow in getting time, constantly relearning what I already had done, and never really mastering what I should have. I did fine, got my hours, passed the FAA check-ride, and got my license. My instructor then took me aside and gave me a bit of a life lesson by saying "Rob, I have a feeling you'll probably be a pretty good pilot if you ever decide to give it your attention and focus your talents". Lesson: DON'T DO THINGS HALF-WAY…EITHER FOCUS AND DO THE BEST YOU CAN, OR QUIT, BUT DON'T BE SATISFIED BY DOING LESS THAN THE BEST YOU CAN.

– 1967-68, one of the challenging things to do in UPT was to learn the "rote" procedures associated with flying. Emergency procedures were particularly important for many reasons…for most of us young bucks that reason was immediate pride or embarrassment in front of the group. Someone (out of about 30 of us) was called on during the mass-briefing that took place each morning. "Lt. Van Sice, give me the EP for engine failure in flight". I was then expected to stand at attention and, from memory, give the checklist items verbatim and in the correct order, then respond equally flawlessly to follow-on questions and procedures as the emergency developed. One had pride in doing it exactly right and did NOT want to be embarrassed by screwing up. My wife, Lynne, was my tutor in learning verbatim responses, and in visualizing the cockpit actions and switchology to make it happen. We would rehearse every evening at home in the kitchen with a chair, an instrument panel mockup, and a broomstick. It worked! The confidence gained resulted in much better performance.... and I graduated near the top of my class, receiving my choice of assignments upon graduation. Lesson: BUILD "ALLIANCES" AND USE ALL AVAILABLE RESOURCES IN REACHING YOUR OBJECTIVES. Added benefit: Lynne remained fully invested in our career in the USAF...which could not have been a success without her help and talent.

– 1969, brand new 1st Lt. Aircraft Commander (one of two at Phu Cat) on my 4th or 5th combat sortie. Shortly after takeoff with a full load of 12 Mk 82 bombs and two wing tanks full of fuel, my nose gear would not indicate "up and locked." Upon inspection by my flight lead, the problem was identified as the nose-wheel being "cocked" about 30 degrees to the left (never heard of it happening before or since). So...this is really screwy, not a checklist emergency, what do we do and how do we land? After lots of chatter among ourselves and the Supervisor of Flying and Command Post, it was decided: First, fly out over the ocean with the landing gear all down and locked (but wheel still cocked), "dump fuel" and jettison the bombs, with a significant chance that one or more of the jettisoned items might collide with the landing gear/struts. We did that successfully. Second, how do you land with a nose-wheel cocked? We/they decided that the runway would be "foamed" with fire retardant urea foam which is very "slick/greasy," and I would engage the approach-end cable barrier while trying to hold the nose in the air to avoid damaging the barrier or tire (F-4s don't keep their nose up on landing), and hope we got stopped upright and on the runway. My back seater (an experienced navigator from Strategic Air Command bombers) was not thrilled by all this, particularly with an inexperienced Lt. driving. We did it all perfectly, ending up on the left edge of the runway with no damage to us or the aircraft. I "earned my spurs" on that flight. Lesson: REGARDLESS OF THE "NOVELTY" OF THE SITUATION, KEEPING YOUR COOL, USING YOUR HEAD WHILE LISTENING TO OTHERS, AND DOING WHAT YOU'VE LEARNED TO DO WILL PRODUCE GOOD RESULTS. (A little faith in the Good Lord, also helps.)

– 1970, newly assigned to Misawa AB, Japan doing a night intercept training sortie with the Squadron Commander as my flight lead. At some point during the flight I got an "engine fire" light in the cockpit, causing a lot of action in my airplane and among the flight members. We successfully performed all the checklist procedures, shut the engine down, declared an emergency, and headed back to land at Misawa…not an uncommon emergency in F-4s and the weather was ok, so it was "no big deal" from my perspective. As I recall, single engine called for half flaps, and an airspeed about 10 knots higher than normal, so that's what I did. Because we had not burned down all our fuel, the aircraft was heavy and required periodic afterburner to keep the airspeed from decaying because I had the gear down on final. I landed just fine, shut down with guidance from the emergency responders, and went in to do the normal maintenance and flight debriefings. When I got to the briefing room, much to my surprise, I was met by a pretty severe dressing-down from my Commander. "Why were you getting so slow that you had to use AB?" "Well, I was complying with the checklist sir!" "And what were you going to do if the AB didn't light?" Etc. etc. Lesson: JUST BECAUSE IT'S IN THE CHECKLIST DOESN'T MEAN YOU CAN'T BE SMART ENOUGH TO BUILD IN SOME ADDITIONAL CLEVER CAUTION. THINK!

– 1971 or '72, TDY from Kadena, Okinawa to Kunsan, Korea and training on the gunnery range with practice bombs. The visibility was terrible…dim light, no horizon, ocean the color of the sky, and generally a real challenge. Flying over water "up the crotch of the running man" using our radar to find and identify the target for us to deliver a simulated nuclear weapon from a LADD delivery profile kept us busy. Our run-in was planned at 300' and 520 knots and the WSO was having trouble getting his radar picture, so I'm "helping" on the front seat scope...not my usual role. I suddenly looked outside to realize we're about 50' above the water and descending. Our recovery was fine, but the fact is we were about a half second from becoming a ball of flaming protoplasm, and a statistic for the accident records. Lesson: WHEN FLYING (OR DRIVING, OR ANYTHING ELSE) DON'T FORGET <u>YOUR</u> JOB AND PRIORITIES. SPENDING A SECOND DOING SOMETHING OUT OF THE ORDINARY CAN COST YOUR LIFE. FLYING IS ONE "JOB" WHERE A SHORT ATTENTION SPAN IS VALUABLE!

- 1975-77, while teaching in the USAF F-4 Fighter Weapons School, I was doing the thing I loved most, in the most challenging peacetime flying environment that exists...and I was loving it. My flight commander called me in to let me know that it was time for me to attend Squadron Officers School (SOS), the first of several professional schools an officer is "expected" (required) to attend. You can take it by correspondence, but you were "expected" to physically attend. I begged off, saying I needed to fly more so that I could be a better fighter pilot and instructor. I did that THREE TIMES over the next couple years, never physically attending. At the time I was quite proud of myself for "getting out of going," but in fact, it was an extremely shortsighted and probably career limiting decision...I was never again given the opportunity to physically attend any of the senior service schools. Lesson: NEVER KNOWINGLY CLOSE DOORS TO THE FUTURE. Someone else, or the system, may do that for you, but don't make it easy for them!

- 1977, newly assigned to the 614th Tactical Fighter Squadron, Torrejon AB, Spain as an Instructor Pilot and Squadron Weapons Officer. I was in the back seat, completing my local checkout as an Instructor, with my friend and check pilot in the front seat. We had just completed a maneuver and were doing a very smooth recovery from an inverted nose-high attitude. During recovery, we rolled wings level and continued to accelerate nose low. Since we were getting quite low, I thought he was trying to "impress" me with something spectacular, so I said, over the intercom, "Joe, what the heck are you doing?" He responded by immediately "over-Ging" the aircraft as we descended below tree-tops…but recovered successfully. I thought he was flying, and he thought I was, so we mutually assumed ourselves into almost dying. Lesson: NEVER "ASSUME" ANYTHING WHILE FLYING, PARTICULARLY SOMETHING AS FUNDAMENTAL AS "WHO IS FLYING THE PLANE." HUNDREDS HAVE DIED BECAUSE OF ASSUMPTIONS.

Rob Van Sice Geezer Flying Memories:

— Special memories are there because of something really good/cool, or something bad/awful. I have lots of the former and a few of the latter:

- Good/cool:
  o First solo, winter 1966/7 in a Piper Cherokee from a snow-covered grass strip in Bozeman with 8 hours of total flying time
  o First jet landing in a T-37 at Vance AFB, Enid OK about a year later
  o First supersonic flight in a T-38 (wearing a "G-suit"!) about 4 months later
  o F-4E "dollar ride" at George AFB in early 1969… Mach 2.2! (the one and only time)
  o Spending a full year (69-70) flying combat in F-4s at Phu Cat Vietnam….and coming home
  o 1975, Sunrise, two-ship supersonic at 100' over a dry lake on the Nellis ranges…watching the sun rise through lead's shockwave
  o 1983, F-16 single ship, Kunsan AB, Korea, with nothing to do but fly aerobatics up and down the face of a thunderstorm ("…to reach out and touch the face of God!")

- o August 7-8, 1990, flying 16 hours non-stop from Shaw AFB, via Gibraltar, and multiple aerial refuelings, taking a total of 72 F-16s and 100+ pilots to the Middle East for Desert Shield/Desert Storm
- o March 1991, flying back from the Middle East having fought a war and not losing any of my pilots to enemy action
- o Getting old and having the privilege of retiring from the USAF!
- Bad/awful:
  - o Losing dozens of friends and comrades due to enemy action, bad weather, bad airplanes, bad maintenance, bad judgement, poor training, or poor leadership…or just plain "bad luck"
  - o Being the bombing range officer in Okinawa as an F-105 pilot "G-locked" as he pulled-off a strafe run, rolled inverted, and crashed into the sea…despite my many radio calls for him to bail out
  - o During Desert Shield, calling for one of my F-16 pilots, on fire, to eject, then watching every nanosecond of his successful ejection and the plane crashing into the desert
  - o Getting old and having to retire from the USAF!

It was a privilege and honor to be able to fly, learn, follow and lead through 27 years as an Air Force Fighter Pilot. Thanks to all the leaders, instructors, wingmen, mentors, friends and family that made it a successful endeavor and adventure! (That surely goes for the Friday Pilots, what a tremendous group!)

CHAPTER TWENTY-EIGHT

FIRST ATTACK OF A SURFACE TO AIR MISSILE SITE - 27 JULY 1965

by Russ Violett

I was a slick-winged captain in the 563rd Tactical Fighter Squadron, 23rd Tactical Fighter Wing, McConnell AFB, KS in 1965. Our days were filled with training flights in the F-105 aircraft. The squadron pilots were extremely tight. They liked being together and stopped by the stag bar on the way home for a drink with buddies on many days. The camaraderie was invigorating, and motivational to become the best of the best. Nothing was impossible, we felt we could do anything, and thought the F-105 aircraft was outstanding.

In April, at the morning briefing, we were told we were to deploy to a "classified destination" and no one was to know where we were going. A few days later, we took off as a squadron from McConnell and landed at Hickam AFB, HI. It was an uneventful trip; the next leg to Guam, and then Takhli RTAFB, we were in screened-in buildings, with tin roofs, built on stilts in 100 degree plus temperatures with high humidity and thunderstorms. And lots of bugs. And Rats. And Snakes. We slept on cots with a mosquito net. Our mission briefings started incredibly early. Our typical configuration was eight 750-pound bombs to attack roads, bridges, rail lines, and storage sites.

In early May, Billy Sparks, one of our pilots, said that Al Logan landed from a mission near Hanoi and reported that A SAM SITE was being built about 15 miles south of Hanoi. I flew a mission with Billy to that area in the afternoon and someone was indeed building a SAM site. We went to our boss, Major Jack Brown, and reported our concerns. Jack took a flight to the same area early the next morning and found the first of many sites.

He called all of us together and told us to get a plan ready to kill the SAM and left the next day for Saigon. He returned two days later with his tail between his legs, carrying a message to not fly within five miles of ANY SAM site. The word was to not "disturb" any activity that might anger the Russians who were doing the construction. A few days later, a directive came down from 2d Air Division ordering everyone to not over-fly or disturb any SAM activity in North Vietnam (NVN). The penalty for noncompliance would be courts-martial. Lesson: THIS SHOULD HAVE BEEN OUR FIRST WARNING THAT SOMETHING STUPID WAS COMING.

Takhli received a squadron of EB-66 aircraft in May who had the mission to track all electronic activity in the North. The EB-66 had four Electronic Warfare Officers (EWOs) sitting on downward-ejecting seats in the bomb bay that kept track of any and all electronic emissions. It was an underpowered, old, clunky aircraft, but they did a hell of a job that has never been properly recognized. Our EB-66 friends kept track of the SAM and all other radar activity and reported daily the progress in building missile capability in the North. We continued to receive directives not to bother the Russians. The number and activity of the SAMs continued to increase. One of our Flight Commanders was Captain Paul Craw, one of the absolute best, most aggressive, natural fighter jocks ever born. Paul was a firm believer in flying with the same people every mission. He was mean enough and strong enough to make it happen. We grew to be very competent, totally confident in each other.

The reports from the EB-66 EWOs convinced us that the SAMs were ready to shoot at any time. By the first week of July '65, the EWOs announced that all the SAM component systems were operating, had been checked out, and were fully operational. At that time 2AD issued a code phrase to be used when a SAM was being launched, "Bluebells are Singing." They also reiterated the ban on any attempt to take out the threat. To say that we were nervous is an understatement.

On July 24, Captain Craw was leading a four ship south of Hanoi after having hit a target nearby when an EB-66, on Guard channel, saying, "Bluebells are Singing! Repeat, Bluebells are Singing! south of Hanoi." The Russians had finished the checkout of their systems. The target for the SAMs was a flight of F-4C aircraft from Ubon that were in close formation penetrating the weather. The F-4 flight had switched off Guard channel and was hit with no warning. The F-4s were probably 60 to 70 miles in front of us in the clouds between 25-30,000 ft. when up comes the first missile of the war from one of the sites that McNamara made us draw a 30-mile ring around. We were not allowed inside of this ring because we might hurt a Russian. I like to point out that up to this day, Capt. Craw said, "I could have neutralized this site with two F-105s loaded with bombs and 20 mm cannons, especially the cannons, to rip up the radar control vans." Anyway, up comes the missile and down goes an F-4. They were in close formation and could well have lost more than the one aircraft. The backseater was picked up, but not the frontseater. One aircraft was blown away and the other three were damaged. The damaged birds managed to make it back to Udorn and land where one was written off. It is amazing that all were not lost.

The restrictions on hitting SAMs remained in effect and we were restricted from flying within 30 miles of Hanoi. Lesson: THIS WAS A TOTALLY STUPID REACTION THAT DESERVES TO BE QUESTIONED BY ANYONE WITH ANY KNOWLEDGE OF THE USE OF FORCE.

Two days later Captain Craw brought a clipping from a Bangkok paper quoting McNamara. "We can take out the Surface-to-Air Missile systems at any time we desire he said." The quote also contained the coordinates of two sites. In the same article McNamara stated that we had too many fighter pilots and that we should reduce the number. In rather foul language Craw pointed out that a good way to reduce the number of fighter pilots was to print where they were going. We also could not understand why TWO sites when only one had fired.

It was learned that a message was delivered to the South Vietnamese Headquarters by DOD directive on July 25 that listed, in detail, two SAM sites to be attacked, date and times, route of flight to and from each target, ordnance, speeds, and altitudes that would be flown. Lesson: I AM CONVINCED THAT ANY SUCH DIRECTIVE CONSTITUTES AT LEAST DERELICTION OF DUTY, IF NOT TREASON SINCE 2AD, AND EVERYONE ELSE IN SAIGON, KNEW OF THE LEAKS FROM THE SOUTH VIETNAMESE HQ.

Very early on July 27, 1965, someone woke me and said I didn't need to get up for my scheduled mission brief since I was now on the first SAM raid. I went to INTELL as soon as I could to find the order. It was a bunch of crap. The 563rd was to hit a SAM site, the one that had fired a few days earlier, using three flights of four F-105Ds in trail with only one minute spacing between flights. The ordnance listed was rear-dispensed bomblets (CBU-2) dropped from 50 feet and at 360 knots. The next two flights were ordered to carry napalm and drop from 50 feet and 360 knots. The idiocy of DOD was now apparent to all. If you tell anyone that you are going to hit him, and then give him almost a week's notice, any half-wit can figure out that the place will be empty and/or well defended. Lesson: TO OVER-FLY AN EXTREMELY WELL DEFENDED COMPLEX AT 50 FEET AND 360 KNOTS IS A SUICIDE ORDER. To exacerbate an already insane order, have all aircraft fly at the same altitude, airspeed and attack from the same direction, with close intervals. I may have been a slick-winged Captain, but I certainly knew better than that. HQ USAF, HQ PACAF, and 2AD all passed this frag down to us. We truly bitched, whined and moaned. Major Brown got on the horn and tried to talk to Saigon. The Yokota Squadron Commander gave it his best shot, all to no avail. Korat called as well. What we asked was to change the ingress and egress, change the altitudes, and increase our drop speed to at least 500 knots. At no time did we ever request not to hit the site. We were ordered to go as directed WITH ZERO CHANGES! The 563rd was to launch 12 aircraft to the SAM site. 12 aircraft from the Yokota squadron were to hit the "Supporting Barracks." Korat had the same order for a SAM site and support area a few miles from ours. The Times-on-Target (TOT) for both sites were the same, and the directed routes to and from insured that we would be almost head on with the Korat aircraft. It appeared that DOD also tried to schedule a mid-air collision.

We realized that we could either comply with this stupid order or mutiny, so we went to the squadron and briefed the insanity. Jack Brown stuck his head in the briefing room and told us to screw the airspeed restriction and to hold 540 knots from our letdown point to the target. We completed what little we could and suited up, we were not happy campers.

Tahkli was most fortunate to have an outstanding Chaplain, Father Frank McMullen. Father Mac started the Takhli tradition of blessing, complete with sprinkling, every aircraft that took off anytime day or night. This day Father Mac, who often attended our briefings and flew with the EB-66 guys, came to the line and blessed each pilot before takeoff. He climbed up the ladder just before start engine time and gave each pilot his blessing.

We flew into central Laos and then let down to about 100 feet above the terrain, and headed for our Initial Point (IP), Yen Bai, on the Red River. In July '65, Yen Bai had more guns than Hanoi; yet it was a mandatory checkpoint in the tasking message. DOD strikes again. We did not over-fly Yen Bai. But, almost immediately as we went by, we started to get 37mm flak burst directly over our flight path. 37mm guns do not have a fuse that will detonate on proximity, ergo; all the rounds had to have been manually set to detonate at a fixed time after they were fired. The time corresponded with the expected range from gun to target. It was obvious that they knew we were coming and at what route. The reason that the 37mm rounds were high was that the guns could not be depressed any lower. We flew either down the Red River or over its edges for about 40 miles, always with 37mm bursting over us. When we hit the confluence of the Red and Black Rivers, we left the river and flew over rice paddies for the next 25 miles to the SAM site. An EB-66 took a picture looking down on one of our flights and it was leaving rooster tails in the paddies. We started to take hits from small arms and .50- cal. equivalent automatic weapons as soon as we left the river. As we neared the SAM site, we came under fire from the 37mm and 57mm weapons that had been brought in to protect the site. We counted over 250 37mm and 57mm guns and a large number of automatic weapons around each site when we finally got the post-strike photography.

Jack Brown's flight hit the area with eight CBU-2s with all 19 tubes dispensing bomblets. I was number 3 in his flight and with my wingman was about 15 seconds in trail with him at the target. I was at 540 knots at 100 feet and the 85mm and 105mm guns were firing horizontally at us as we made the attack. The sound in the cockpit of those guns being fired as you flew over the site was deafening. The scene was surreal, the fire coming out of the barrel of the gun, forming a donut and the noise while all this conversation was going on made it difficult to stay calm. I got a little too low as I pushed up to above 600 and left part of my ventral fin on a berm surrounding a gun site, but it had no effect on the aircraft. Two had been hit and Lead was coaxing him to try and get over the next ridge before bailing out. Unfortunately, Walt Kosko, made it to the Black River, when he had to eject. Major Brown was trying to CAP Walt's position in the Black River, he had climbed a few thousand feet and I yelled at him to get back down. I saw Walt's chute/dinghy in the river. Brown decided that both Craw and Harris and their flights should go home and released them. He would stay for 30 minutes and see if Walt could be found. Walt Kosko was never recovered. Brown directed I contact control who put me in a racetrack pattern about 50 miles south of where a rescue effort for Frank Tullo was taking place for another 30 minutes. We were then released and headed to base. Our home base was in a thunderstorm and I was diverted to Korat with my number two man. He had been a spare that filled in a spot in my flight when one aircraft aborted. I didn't know him. He had delivered some aircraft from Yokota. After landing and parking, I noticed he was just sitting in his aircraft with the canopy open. I walked over to him. With effort, he came down the ladder and I introduced myself. He did not know me. He then said, "My God, are they all like this?" I said, "No, thank God, they are not." Craw and flight landed at Takhli and they counted holes. Of the twelve 563rd aircraft that went on the mission, two were shot down, nine had multiple holes, only one was not hit.

Billy Sparks said when I parked my bird, the first one up the ladder was Father Mac. The Father handed me a French 75, slightly warm, and blessed me. I told him that if he ever came up my ladder again, I would jump off and abort. He laughed, kissed my forehead, and said, "It worked, didn't it? Be thankful!"

Major Harris' flight dropped 24 napalm cans. Craw dropped 24 more into the mess. I heard Billy Sparks tell Craw that Kyle Berg's aircraft was on fire, then the aircraft slowly pulled up, rolled right and went in. Marty Case, who had gone through Cadets with Kyle, called, "Bailout! Bailout!" and then, "No way, he went in!" Captain Craw started to pull up through a hail of bursting flak to cover Kyle and both Case and Sparks yelled at him to stay down and get the hell out of Dodge. Craw stayed on the deck, accelerated to 600 and headed for the Black. Later we learned Berg had survived and had been taken prisoner.

Bad Day at Black Rock - by Bill Sparks

"It was easily the worst mission I ever had to fly. Wrong ordnance, wrong courses, horrible tactics, all topped by McNamara having printed the coordinates of our targets in the U.S. Times. Lesson: NOT ONE LEADER OBJECTED, AND NO ONE FELL ON HIS SWORD. I HAVE NEVER BEEN AS ANGRY OR FELT AS ABANDONED IN MY LIFE. WE WERE POORLY COMMANDED AND EVEN WORSE, WERE NOT TRAINED OR EQUIPPED. I THINK THAT THE FIRST SAM RAID EPITOMIZES THE WHOLE DAMNED MESS THAT LASTED SO LONG. For whatever it is worth I am sending my version of what I remember of that debacle. We actually lost six F-105s in less than three minutes, an RF-101C was shot down with the pilot killed while photographing the same site 2 days later. Of the 46 F-105s from both bases in the attack, we lost five of the six pilots flying #2 and one leader. I was so damned angry, I was spluttering. I am still almost as angry as I was then. Kosko, Farr, and Bartlemas were all killed. Berg and Purcell were alive, captured, and spent an eternity as POWs. A Rescue helicopter picked up Tullo from east of the Black River and took him to Laos. I had a major problem with the Thud losses that day. The F-105 community was so small that we either knew the drivers or knew someone who knew them. Jack Farr had been in the 8th Squadron with me for three years. Kyle and Walt were at Spangdahlem the same time. Purcell was from Louisville, my hometown, and Black Matt and I had been friends for over two years. It was a very bad day at Black Rock." - Sparky

The stories from the guys who were there are the brave and tragic aspects of this first SAM raid. But after 55 years, where these stories have been told and retold, I think it is time to also include the historic significance of what they did. SAMs changed air warfare. We had no way to deal with these beasts. The mission got the Air Staff's attention on how woefully deficient our ability to counter SAMs really was. Lesson: THE MISSION KICKED OFF AN EXPLOSION OF ANTI-SAM TECHNOLOGY PROGRAMS, ALL OF WHICH ARE STILL USED IN SOME FORM TODAY. They were tested at Eglin as the highest priority of all their testing at the time. Contractors and government agencies worked together, cooperatively, based on recognized urgency and trust. The first F-100F Wild Weasels arrived at Korat on 25 Nov 65. They proved the Wild Weasel concept by killing a SAM site less than a month later. Radar Homing And Warning (RHAW) for F-105s arrived in early December 1965. The first F-105F Wild Weasels got to Korat on 22 May 66; the first to Takhli on 4 July 1966. Shrikes, a Navy missile, became available to the Air Force in March 1966; ECM jamming pods in September 1966. This stuff worked but the crews who first took them into battle suffered severe learning curves.

How do you debrief an insane mission? Paul Craw said that he would never again allow anyone to dictate such a stupid set of rules. Lesson: I PROMISED MYSELF THAT I WOULD NEVER, EVER ALLOW ANYONE, REGARDLESS OF RANK, TO WASTE SO MANY FOLKS. I OWED IT TO THE PEOPLE I FLEW WITH TO TAKE BETTER CARE OF THEM THAN THAT. EVERY ONE OF US WOULD HAVE VOLUNTEERED TO GO ON A MISSION TO WHACK SAMS. TO BE THROWN AWAY BY IDIOTS IS ANOTHER THING.

The final straw occurred approximately a week after the mission when a 2nd Air Division O-6, with obviously no tactical experience, chaired a meeting with all the pilots who participated in the strike. He began the meeting by berating us and claiming we had not hit the target because as he stated, "...you let a little flak scare you off." As proof of missing the target, he threw up a slide of a BDA photo showing a perfect SAM site lacking any evidence of having been hit. An astute pilot in the audience questioned why the photo was dated two days after the attack. The O-6 responded with, "Heck, we didn't dare send in a recce right away, there was too much flak."

Lesson: IT WAS INDEED A VERY BAD DAY, ONE OF MANY THAT RESULTED FROM THE COMBINATION OF A DETERMINED AND CLEVER ENEMY, RULES OF ENGAGEMENT AND TACTICS DICTATED BY LEADERS WHO WERE DRIVEN BY FEAR OF ANNOYING OUR ENEMIES WHILE EITHER UNAWARE OF OR UNCONCERNED WITH THE OPERATIONAL REALITIES OF AERIAL COMBAT, PLUS OUR OWN YEARS OF UNREALISTIC TRAINING. Yes, it seemed that too many of our leaders were more concerned with promotion or political power than the conduct of the war or welfare of the warriors. "Leaks" of our plans, deliberate or otherwise, helped not at all and apparently continue today.

The reader will no doubt understand that the infamous "Fog of War" coupled with the fallibility of 55-year memories resulted in some variation in details in these accounts.

CHAPTER TWENTY-NINE

FROM FAT AND UGLY TO SLEEK AND POINTED

by Alex Wright

I can remember the day I got interested in flying like it was yesterday. My Dad had just taken my older brother and me to see "The Hunters" at the Temple theater in Meridian, Mississippi. It was a typical Hollywood flick about Korean War fighter pilots; bad plot, mediocre acting in spite of the cast, some outlandish stunts. But, it was the flying scenes that I remember the most. The flying scenes were amazing, absolutely amazing. I remember walking out of the movie house thinking to myself, "…one day I want to be one of those guys." And, 14 years later I became one of those guys.

My road to becoming a pilot was not a sure thing by any stretch. I went to high school and college in the turbulent 60s where anything that smacked of the military, much less the Air Force, was strictly taboo in the crowd with which I hung. I couldn't afford to take flying lessons and I didn't have any friends who were interested in flying. At times, I even forgot about how much I liked that movie and how much I wanted to be one of "those guys." But, that thought never left my mind, and in 1970, after graduating from college with a degree in political science, I needed a job.

The Air Force recruiter I saw had a line that was as long as the Santa Fe Railroad tracks from Chicago to Los Angeles: Go to pilot training, fly for the Air Force for five years, and then get out and become a real pilot and fly for the airlines. Oh, and be rich and never have to work but a couple of days a month. That sounded really good to me. I was on my way to fame and fortune. I could just see the buckets of money in my living room. Delta Airlines, here I come, just hold a place for me.

I took all the tests and scored fairly well. My recruiter was impressed, or so it seemed. "Son (he was probably my age, but liked to use that term), you are going to make a great pilot. Sign right here." And, sign I did. Wow! that was quick.

And, off I went. First stop, Lackland AFB, Texas, for Air Force Basic Military Training. I was the only guy in my group with a college degree, so I immediately became "college boy" to my Drill Instructor. He didn't like me, and I sure didn't like him. Think of the DI that R. Lee Ermy portrays in *Full Metal Jacket* and tone it down a few notches. When I graduated from BMT, he came up to me and said in a soft, condescending voice, "You won't make it through OTS (Officer Training School), much less Pilot Training." Well, thanks a lot for your vote of confidence, jerk. LESSON: SOMETIMES IN YOUR YOUNG LIFE, IN PURSUIT OF A LOFTY GOAL, YOU WILL MEET JERKS. THEY CAN TEACH YOU AN IMPORTANT LESSON - DON'T EVER BE LIKE THEM.

Next on the agenda was Air Force Officer Training School at the Medina Annex at Lackland AFB, Texas. And, I did make it through OTS. I graduated in the top 10 percent of my class as one of 15 Distinguished Graduates. I always wanted to go back over to main Lackland and find that SOB Drill Instructor, but my good angel convinced me not to do that.

I was assigned Undergraduate Pilot Training at Laughlin AFB, Del Rio, Texas. The day I drove along the highway from San Antonio to Del Rio and saw nothing but cactus and yuccas, I wondered what egregious sin I had committed to be sent to that corner of hell. But, the closer I got to the base I began to see airplanes, cool looking airplanes, white with pointy noses, flying fast, lots of them. Maybe this was not part of hell, but just purgatory.

I spent the next year in UPT purgatory, waiting to be sent along my merry way to Air Force pilot heaven. As we got close to graduation, I began asking seasoned Instructor Pilots what assignment I should strive for after graduation. Some said cargo planes, some said training, one even said bombers. Yeah, right. I had done well in pilot training, but I was not sure just how well until my Squadron Commander, a crusty old former F-100 pilot, said that I should consider fighters. That was a shock. Although I still admired Robert Mitchum and Robert Wagner from *The Hunters,* I certainly didn't consider myself in that esteemed category. Col. Mahaffey looked at me and said in his typical fatherly tone, "Son, if you choose an aircraft with more than one seat and one engine, you are making a huge mistake."

I took him at his word. I finished second in my class of 36 and that gave me the ability to choose my follow-on assignment. I chose an A-7D, a single seat, single engine fighter. That choice turned out to be the absolute best for me. My A-7 training took place at Davis-Monthan AFB, in Tucson, Arizona, which I thought was a cool place back in 1972 (more on Tucson later). The A-7 was a new airplane in the Air Force inventory, although the US Navy had been flying them for several years, and most of them were relatively new. The new ones smelled like new cars. I even got to pick a brand new one up at the factory, and, yes, it did smell like a new car.

After six months in Tucson, I went to my next assignment and the start of my tactical flying career in fighters in the Air Force. I spent time in Louisiana, Thailand, and New Mexico. I honed my skills in Louisiana, flew combat out of Thailand, and became an Instructor and Flight Examiner in New Mexico. Along the way I had several experiences that made me change my mind about the airline thing. I got hooked on fighters. I became the ultimate adrenalin junkie. Fighters gave me that charge that I never expected I would get from aviation.

My recruiter so many years earlier had omitted one very important part of his pitch to get me to sign up for the Air Force. He forgot to tell me that I just might like it. And, that was a huge missing piece of the puzzle. And, I didn't realize it until I got back from Thailand and became an IP in New Mexico. All of a sudden, I realized just how much I enjoyed passing along to other pilots what I knew. My last combat mission out of Thailand had not turned out so well, and I was bound and determined to pass along those lessons learned from that experience in hopes of preventing others from making the same mistakes.

In New Mexico, I spent all my efforts and time honing my skills as a pilot and as an instructor pilot. I wanted to become the best of the best. I took every opportunity I could to fly. I hung around the scheduling office and the operations counter all the time hoping to sandbag an additional mission. And, fly I did. One month I flew over 50 hours. Another time I flew 60 student missions in six weeks, two a day every flying day of the week for six weeks. All in all, while in New Mexico, I flew over 700 flying hours in just 23 months. And the bulk of those missions were 45 to 60 minutes long.

LESSON: TACTICAL AVIATION IS A DANGEROUS, UNFORGIVING BUSINESS. AN INSTANT OF INATTENTION HERE, A MOMENTARY LACK OF JUDGEMENT THERE, WILL BOTH KILL YOU IN A SPLIT SECOND. Without blinking an eye, I can name a dozen of my former fellow pilots that were killed for one reason or another. I can also name at least two or three dozen more who, like me, have suffered debilitating injuries or illnesses as a result of excessive G forces for prolonged periods of time (years), or from constant exposure to fumes, chemicals, or electromagnetic radiation. In spite of the military's best efforts to mitigate the hazardous effects of the tactical aviation environment those things exist and are as large a part of the hazards associated with tactical aviation as an enemy trying to shoot you down.

In my first eight years of flying, 10 of my fellow fighter pilot buddies were killed in fighter accidents. You read that right, 10. In a nine-month period in 1978 – 1979, four of my friends died in fighter crashes. And, several of them were very close friends, friends that were good and capable pilots.

Lesson: LIFE IS SO VERY PRECIOUS AND SO VERY TENUOUS. I CAME TO DETEST FUNERALS.

In 1977 the Air Force and I had a disagreement as to the best path my career should take. The Air Force felt that it was time to use my talents was as a staff officer. Needless to say, I disagreed. We couldn't come to an agreement. Consequently, I left the regular Air Force and headed to the Air National Guard where I could continue to fly and fly and fly.

And, fly I did. I took every opportunity to fly anytime and anywhere. I really liked it more than I realized at the time. I flew for two Air National Guard units between 1977 and 1984, a period during which I built both flying time and experience. I got to go to some exotic places and some really bad places. All of it was good and helped me become a better pilot: Turkey, Panama, The Netherlands, Canada, Spain, the UK, and all over the USA. I even got a T-shirt that read, "Join the Air National Guard, be a pilot, travel to exotic lands, meet exciting, unusual people, and kill them ... but only on the weekends." Our gallows humor was ever present.

And, then in the summer of 1984, something beyond my wildest expectations happened. I was selected to attend the A-7 Fighter Weapons Instructor Course. WOW! I didn't expect it, but I said yes about two seconds after I was asked if I wanted to go. The Fighter Weapons Instructor Course was the pinnacle of tactical aviation for Air Force fighter pilots. It is the school all fighter pilots ultimately want to attend. The course taught a fighter pilot how to be the best and how to teach others how to be the best - think of that awful movie, TOP GUN, without all the Hollywood BS, and in the Air Force, not the Navy. It was like that but a lot, lot better.

I signed on for a six-month course that was almost as intense as anything I had experienced up to that point in my flying career. I dove into learning as much as I possibly could about tactical aviation. I just couldn't get enough of what I was exposed to and required to learn. Weapons School was both mentally and physically challenging. A true test of my ability to learn, perform, and instruct others how to perform. I approached the challenge as a personal one and let nothing get in my way in the quest to do well. At the end of the course the reward for my efforts was, LESSON: SOMETIMES THE BEST REWARD FOR GAINING KNOWLEDGE IS TO PASS IT ON TO FUTURE GENERATIONS.

I must have done well because, after I graduated, Don Shepperd (the editor of this book) and Benny White (another Friday Pilot), offered me a job to return to Tucson and become an instructor in the very same school from which I just graduated. The decision process was a short one, and my family and I headed off to Tucson. Once again, my career took a path that would allow me to fly and instruct many more students in how to become much better fighter pilots.

For the next 14 years I had the privilege of teaching fighter pilots everything I knew about how to fly both the A-7 and the F-16. And, fly and instruct I did in a great place to fly. Tucson has some of the greatest flying weather in the world, some 300 days of sunshine each year. Plus, it is not a bad place to call home. We settled in and raised our family in a place that had managed to keep its small-town personality. Remember, I said in 1972 that this was not such a bad place. Once we moved here, I realized that I had been right back then.

I was privileged to instruct U.S. pilots, European pilots, Middle East pilots and Asian pilots. I instructed brand new fighter pilots, crusty old fighter pilots, pilots that had never flown a fighter before and pilots that had twice as many fighter hours as I had. It was a dream job for me. Not only did I impart knowledge to others, but I also learned a tremendous amount of stuff from my students. LESSON: EVEN WHEN YOU ARE THE INSTRUCTOR, STUDENTS CAN TEACH YOU MUCH. The students all had something to bring to the table and the symbiotic relationship I developed with them was mutually beneficial in so many ways.

I not only instructed students every day, I also got to do some pretty cool stuff a bit out of the ordinary. In the A-7 I was one of the unit pilots that flew weapons test and evaluation missions for new weapons that the Air Force was considering employing on that jet. I got to be part of the Infrared (IR) Maverick test, the 30mm gun pod test, the Durandal runway cratering rocket test, and others. In the F-16 I was a guest instructor in the Dutch Fighter Weapons School in The Netherlands. That participation on my part eventually helped encourage the Dutch Air Force to send its pilots to Tucson to learn to fly the F-16. Other countries were quick to follow the Dutch lead in that program. I also was an F-16 maintenance test pilot, Flight Examiner, and Chief of Safety. All of those jobs required me to fly, fly, fly. Life was good and filled with flying.

The F-16 also offered me the opportunity to hone my less than perfect air-to-air combat skills. I knew how to drop bombs. Hell, I was one of THE resident experts at that. But, I had to learn how to fly air-to-air combat in a jet that could do it better than any jet on the planet. Air-to-air became my passion and teaching it to others was a huge challenge for me. I wanted to be the best at air-to-air and be able to teach others that same skill. I took every opportunity to fly in the air-to-air arena. That was just what I needed at the time, a new challenge and a new skill.

At the time I flew the F-16 no other airplane in the world could outperform it in a dogfight. That was short lived as eventually the 5th generation fighter came along and surpassed the F-16, but it was great while it lasted. Plus, it had a pointy nose, unlike the A-7. LESSON: BUT, LET ME TELL YOU, NINE Gs WAS, OH SO PAINFUL EACH TIME I PULLED THEM. And, I mean painful.

That was the downside that I knew would catch up with me one day. The F-16 was not an old man's game. The air-to-air combat mission began to take its toll on my almost 50-year old body by 1997. I could tell it was beating me up pretty bad from the way my joints were screaming at me every day and night, especially my back and neck. So, in 1999 I made an extremely difficult decision to retire. I had to step away from flying so as to not hurt myself any further. By that time, I had flown single seat, single engine fighters for 28 years without a break. Very few individuals got to that point. But, I'll be honest, I was worn out. LESSON: SOMETIMES, YOU JUST HAVE TO KNOW WHEN IT IS TIME TO QUIT.

So, I hung my harness up for the last time. I was fortunate after retirement to get a job with the Boeing Company teaching academics and simulators at the same unit from which I had just retired. I knew everyone there and I was able to keep instructing new pilots, just without the flying, which was fine with me. My body needed time to heal. Plus, the job was here in Tucson and my wife and I could now begin to spend more time with our children and grandchildren. The other thing the job did for me was give the opportunity to get 28 years of "war stories" out to a new generation of fighter pilots. Life was good.

After I retired, I had the opportunity to reflect on just what instructing meant to me. I could not have had a better career path. I truly enjoyed that part of my flying career. Lesson: WHEN YOU FIND SOMETHING YOU ENJOY, STICK WITH IT. YOU WILL BE SO MUCH HAPPIER IN THE LONG RUN.

My retirement from the Air Force didn't last as long as I thought it would. In January of 2002, after the current war began, I got a call from a friend at the Air Force Personnel Center informing me that I was being recalled to active duty. Surprise, surprise, talk about a change in life once again. The good news was, I got an assignment to a job at 12th Air Force Headquarters here in Tucson. My wife was very pleased, as she was not about to move and leave our grandchildren. Had I been assigned anywhere else, I would have been going solo for sure.

I spent the next 45 months at 12th Air Force/US Southern Air Forces headquarters traveling to just about all of Central and South America. The job was very rewarding, but I didn't like the time away from home. I met lots of interesting folks, did a lot of very interesting stuff, and had a clear moral purpose each morning when I went to work. BUT...there was that separation thing.

The Air force finally released me back to retired status at the end of 2005, and I was really glad. I had over 32 years of service and was ready to have it over and done with. I was 57 and a half and I was tired.

I contemplated going back to work, and almost did, but shortly after I was released back to retired status, my wife became ill and would never recover. Kathy died of cancer several years later.

It took me a long time to climb out of the hole I dug after her death. I would probably still be there today had it not been for my friend, Benny White. One day in the fall after Kathy died, I got a call from Benny inviting me to join him and a group of retired 162d Fighter Wing pilots for breakfast. Reluctantly, I accepted. Going to that breakfast was a game changer. The other thing Benny got me to do was put down the shovel and stop digging. Thanks to his friendship and persistence, I slowly began to crawl out of that hole and rejoin the real world. I will always be indebted for that small, important gesture. Lesson: SMALL GESTURES CAN MAKE A BIG DIFFERENCE IN ONE'S LIFE.

My association with the Fighter Pilot breakfast folks led to my introduction to, and becoming a member of, the Friday Pilots. I would not be part of this group had it not been for my friends, Pete Carpenter and Bill Hosmer, two of the absolute finest gentlemen I have met on the face of the planet. Thanks, to you both.

I went back to work last December as the Director of a small privately funded aviation museum located on the grounds of the Pima Air and Space Museum here in Tucson. I never thought I would go back to work, but I was asked by two close friends and accepted. I didn't realize at the time this would allow me to get back into the swing of things and teach others once again. I get to tell museum visitors about the combat experiences of the 390th Bomb Group in World War II. My hope is we can preserve the stories of the veterans who served in this unit and keep their memory alive forever. Their dedication and sacrifice gave us the life we have today. Plus, we have a B-17 in our museum and not many museums can say that.

My flying career was filled with amazing moments of awe, sights that you can only get by being in an airplane, many of those sights, only by being in a fighter. Things like; seeing the curvature of the earth, or seeing the San Francisco Peaks covered with snow from over 300 miles away, or flying very, very low going really, really fast, or chasing the sun across the country and losing every time.

It was also filled with moments of absolute terror: things such as, just barely missing augering-in and actually hearing the sound of the afterburner echoing off the ground, or getting shot at, or passing another fighter head-to-head with your wingtips less than 10 feet apart, the closing velocity 1400 miles an hour or greater. Each one of those things can be deadly before you have time to react.

In my flying career I flew over 5000 hours in single seat, single engine fighters on over 3000 separate missions. I crossed the Atlantic or Pacific oceans 11 times in a fighter. I flew in all 50 states of the union and I flew in four of the seven continents, Africa, Antarctica and Australia being the ones I missed. And most importantly I trained over 300 students. I was so fortunate to be able to teach what I knew about flying fighters to that many fellow fighter pilots. I got to teach other pilots about aviation for over 21 of my 28 years flying. I could never have found a profession that I enjoyed more. I feel the same way that Jimmy Doolittle felt when he named his autobiography, LESSON: "I COULD NEVER BE SO LUCKY AGAIN."

And, I have had the privilege of meeting some of the finest individuals I know, people I can trust implicitly, men that are part of my extended family. All you have to do is look at the names of those that are part of the original book, "The Friday Pilots," and also this book, and you will know them all. I want to thank all of them publicly for allowing me the honor of knowing them.

So, what did aviation teach me? First of all, it taught me that life is precious and tenuous. It can be taken from you in a heartbeat, or in a long slow drawn out process. Either way the end result is the same. When you die it is time to move on to the next phase of your existence.

Aviation also taught me that when you find something you enjoy stick with it. I never looked back on my decision to stay in the military and continue to teach others. I realize how blessed I was to have been able to do that for as long as I did. Somewhere along my journey, instructing got in my blood and it never left. It made me happy to teach others what I knew about flying. It made me happy to know that in some small way my knowledge could help another become and stay a better pilot.

And, last but certainly not least, this one is for all my pilot buds, past, present, and future. Aviation taught me one final important lesson:

Lesson: NO MATTER HOW BAD ANY MISSION GOES…YOU STILL LOOK REALLY COOL TAXIING BACK IN.

ABOUT THE FRIDAY PILOTS

What happened to them after the Air Force,
the Army, the Navy and the Marines

Bob Barnett retired as a Colonel. He followed a POW dream of owning his own airplane business. He became a Rockwell Commander and Grumman American dealer and developed the business into a full service FBO. He sold the business and traveled extensively around Europe and the world. He was chief and only pilot for a silver/gold mine in Tombstone. He was hired by Flight Safety International as a simulator and ground school instructor and got his ATP and flew the Learjet. He then got a dream job living and flying out of Geneva, Switzerland. Bob was the Secretary Treasure of NAM-POW for five years and Vice Flight Captain and Flight Captain of the Daedalian "Old Pueblo" Flight. He was a founding member of the Friday Pilots group. His wife of 60 years, Anita, passed away in 2012. He has since met beautiful Suzanne, widow of a NAM-POW. They are enjoying life and traveling the world. He has a wonderful daughter, Lori, and four terrific grandchildren.

Bob Breault: After leaving the USAF, I entered the PhD Program at a "to be established Optical Sciences Center" at the University of Arizona. When I arrived in Tucson, in the Fall of 1969, they were digging the hole for a Center "to-be-built." I made arrangements to join the Air-Guard but that very month they put all their pilots on fulltime F-100 instructor duties to train pilots for Vietnam. I was sure I could not do both. I entered a new technology, "optics." After taking courses for two years, Dr. Roland Shack gave me a research position on the Hubble Telescope design and performance. I pioneered the concepts of scattered light that degraded optical instruments. There were no predecessors, so it was all open to my ideas. I redesigned the original NASA design and improved the performance of the Hubble by a factor of over 100,000. Since then, I have participated in the analysis of many (286) of the most renowned space-based sensors such as the Hubble Telescope, IRAS, DIRBE, IBSS, Cassini, Galileo, LIGO, most of the ground-based 8-meter apertured telescopes, and many of the military optical sensors. I have given numerous tutorials and have been Chairman of over ten conferences or symposiums in my field of expertise. I authored the first commercial Stray Light Analysis program called APART. I have also been instrumental in the design and fabrication and use of different devices to measure the scattering characteristics of surfaces. I received a Masters and then my Ph.D. in Optical Sciences in 1979. Upon graduation I created The Breault Research Organization. Forty years later, it still goes on. I have received several awards from NASA, the University of Arizona, and the International Optical Societies. I became a Fellow of SPIE, and OSA. I have worked with six Nobel Laureates one-on-one. Career three - about Feb. 1992 I was "drafted" unwillingly into regional economic development. I became a pioneer in the concepts of something, the Regional Economic Clusters processes and procedures. I founded the Arizona Optics Industry Association, a statewide organization dedicated to the development of the optics industry as an important economic resource to the state of Arizona. I became Chairman of the Board of Directors of the Governor's Strategic Partnership for Economic Development (GSPED), Board of Directors 1993-1994, 4TH R (Tucson Unified School District), Board of Directors 1993-1994 Greater Tucson Economic Council (GTEC) and many more. In 1997 I helped to found The Competitive Institute (TCI) in Barcelona to propagate the concepts of regional economic Cluster development. I have been a consultant or made presentations as a keynote speaker in over 38 countries, to two Presidents, two Prime Ministers, and fifteen countries' Cabinet Ministers. I lectured before over 110 countries economic development departments. I contributed many papers.

Frank Brown retired March 1996 from the Navy as a Captain. He started in the Hughes Aircraft Company Corporate office in Washington DC area working on cruise missile defense programs. In 2002, he transferred to Raytheon Missile Systems in Tucson initially as a business development director and then promoted to Director of Special Systems. In November 2011 he got a call from his former boss in Washington DC to come back working for him. In March 2008 Frank started his new job as Vice President, Business Development for Raytheon's US Navy and Marine Corps programs. It was a high visibility position with long hours, and he loved the job. In September 2008 was the beginning of a three-year battle with Non-Hodgkins Lymphoma. After this experience, he and his wife, Laurel, decided to move back to Tucson to be closer to their children. Raytheon made that happen with Frank becoming the Director, Advanced Air Missile Defense Programs. In August 2014 he retired from Raytheon after a 19-year career. Unfortunately, Frank had to deal with a second cancer which his participation in a clinical trial in July 2015 proved successful. Now in full remission and retired in Tucson, he enjoys taking cruises, doing some volunteer work and seeing his kids, grandkids and friends. He has also gotten back into his love of music, playing banjo in a Ragtime/Dixieland band and guitar in various Bluegrass jams.

Pete Carpenter retired as a Colonel and considered buying an east coast aircraft Fixed Base Operation. He moved to Tucson and got into real estate as an agent, then as a broker. He made commercial real estate investments and got into the restaurant/deli/catering business. His wife, Honeyjean, passed away, and he enjoys time with his daughter, Cricket, son-in-law, Raymond, grandson, Sebastian and lunch with his old flying buddies on Fridays.

Pete Collins retired after 21 continuous years in the cockpit of single seat fighters (with one-year solo in the O-2A in SEA) and practices law in Tucson with Gust Rosenfeld, the oldest law firm in the state. He has handled dozens of high-profile insurance cases, generally representing people and firms who have been sued in civil cases. He is listed in Best Lawyers in America and Super Lawyers. He has been Chair of the State Bar Trial Advocacy College and is on several non-profit boards. He is (still!) married to Debbie Munger Collins, with two great daughters, Courtney and Melinda, and four terrific grandkids, Hailey, Bode, Ashley and Colin. Two of them will be fighter pilots.

Kenneth S. "Ken" Collins retired in March 1980 as a Colonel from March AFB. In April 1980, He took a managerial position with California Microwave, Inc. Government Electronics Division in Woodland Hills, CA. He progressed from Program Manager of two classified programs, Rivet Kit (C-130) and Combat Sent (RC-135) to Business Development Vice President to Division General Manager/Vice President and retired again in 1999. He lived in Woodland Hills, CA from 1980 until 2018. He and his wife, Sandra formerly from Tucson, now reside in Prescott Valley and Tucson. He has two sons and two daughters, six grandchildren and six great grandsons. He has over 6000 flight hours in reconnaissance aircraft, RF-80, RF-86, RF-84F, RF-101, A-12 Oxcart/Black Shield (CIA) and the SR-71(SAC). 700+ flight hours in the A-12 and the SR-71. He was born in Leavenworth, Kansas on 5 February 1929.

John Dale accomplished "geezerness." Someone once said, "you can either be a pilot or grow up, but not both." I'm still a pilot, flying my 1947 Bellanca Cruisair which I restored 22 years ago. I'm now teaching my youngest son (57) to fly and he wants to learn the old way, the way I did, so in his 1947 Stinson it's déjà vu all over again! I stay busy keeping the old birds running well, giving checkrides and instruction at Ryan Airfield, and enjoying the companionship of fellow pilots, reveling in far past memories, (which are getting better) and thanking God that I never grew up. John Dale, Kid Aviator

Pat Halloran: After retiring from the AF in 1983 I headed for Riverside California where I had a beautiful home from a previous assignment and became very active in aviation through the Experimental Aircraft Association (EAA). I bought an unfinished midget racing airplane to complete and became President of the famous EAA Chapter One, which was located on Flabob Airport in Riverside. Flabob is a historical mecca for EAA's homebuilt aircraft activity and antique aircraft restoration business. Tom Wathen, who was the former sole owner of Pinkerton, the giant security organization, had a fascination for Flabob's historical aviation activity, so he bought the whole airport. He appointed me to the Board of Trustees of the newly formed Tom Wathen Foundation, a position I held for 30 years. He injected millions of dollars into facilities, expanded aircraft restoration programs and began building replicas of famous antique racing airplanes, his real love. I flew his beautiful racing replicas around the country to major airshows where they won many awards and were featured on dozens of aviation magazine covers. Two examples, which I flew exclusively for many years were the famous 1934 British de Havilland Comet Racer and the 1936 Schonfeldt Firecracker, formerly flown by Tony LeVier. We expanded plans for Flabob to include facilities dedicated to multi-faceted youth opportunity programs and STEM learning through an Air Academy for students aged 12 through 17. . .education through aviation. These programs were the seed for opening a free public charter high school with beautiful new facilities for 200 students on Flabob grounds.

Bill Hosmer retired from his Air Force career as a Colonel after 24 fulfilling years flying fighters. He continued flying for 12 years as a Cessna Citation jet demonstration pilot in Wichita, KS. He demonstrated the Citation all over the world on every continent except Antarctica. After full retirement, he and wife, Pat, moved "back home" to Montana and traveled as "Snowbirds" to Tucson where they eventually made their year-round home. Pat passed away of cancer in 2010. Bill has a new relationship with the sister of a West Point classmate, Elizabeth Russell Smith. They reside in San Antonio, TX.

Bruce Huffman: I finished my Vietnam tour, returned to the U.S. as a 2nd Lieutenant, became an Instructor Pilot and made a decision to leave active duty after nearly four and one-half years of devotion to my missions, my comrades and the country I love. My life continued an incredible journey of flying offshore in the Gulf of Mexico with Petroleum Helicopters. I met my lifetime partner, Beverly, in Jackson, MS. We would marry in 1974 and move our family to Iran, where I was a factory instructor for Bell Helicopter teaching in Jet Rangers and the Sea Cobra. Upon returning to the United States, we raised our two sons in Pleasant Valley, New York, which was neither a valley nor pleasant, while I rose through the ranks of the IBM Flight Department, eventually retiring after 20 years as a Flight Standards Captain. I finally caught the academic bug and completed my BS degree, cum laude, and earned my MS with a 4.0 GPA. I then went on to lead the Seagram Flight Department flying Gulfstream aircraft around the world before taking a role as the Managing Director of NetJets Europe based in Portugal. I held several non-flying as well as flying leadership roles in the business aviation community and developed a reputation for expertise in "regulatory compliance, aircraft completions, and avionics specifications." I started my own business, Flight Assurance LLC in 2009 and continue flying all models of the Global Express aircraft around the globe and assisting others with their regulatory needs, from our home in Tucson, AZ. I feel blessed at my age to have the health and ability to continue my passion for aviation and world travel, while being paid to enjoy both.

Terry Johnson finished flying fighters with the Air National Guard, became a production test pilot with Learjet, joined North Central Airlines which became Republic Airlines which became Northwest Airlines which became Delta Airlines. He raced sports cars for Mazda, Nissan and Chevrolet. Later, he and wife, Claudia, raced motorcycles. They are enthusiastic tennis players and enjoy their beautiful retirement home in the foothills of Tucson.

Tom Keck, a 1969 graduate of the Air Force Academy, concluded his distinguished 34-year career as a Lieutenant General in 2002. He was hired by General Dynamics Decision Systems as vice president of Business Development (BD), Air Combat Systems in Scottsdale. In 2003, he was hired as VP, Business Development for Raytheon Missile Systems. He retired from Raytheon in 2015 as VP BD, Air Force and NAVAIR systems. In 2009, Keck was inducted into the Rhode Island Aviation Hall of Fame. Tom and his wife Karen have retired in San Antonio under the Blue Skies of Texas.

Chuck Kennedy: After retiring for the third time, Chuck and his wife Pat moved to Tucson to be closer to their son and his family who live in the San Francisco Bay area. They spend their time with travel, visiting family, hiking, and volunteering with several not-for profits in the local area.

Barry "Knute" Knutson retired in 2001, moved to Tucson, Arizona to be close to family, enjoy the weather and outdoors. He consulted in the defense industry but primarily served as a "senior mentor" for the Marine Corps. He mentored and coached active duty commanding generals and their staffs. teaching operational planning and operational art. He also taught maneuver, aviation operations, operational planning and operational art at the Marine Corps University Quantico, VA. and the Army's School of Advanced Military Science at Fort Leavenworth, KS. He now enjoys raising his two adopted grandchildren. He golfs, hunts, fishes and enjoys his other six grandkids who all live in Arizona.

Marty Lenzini retired from the US Marine Corps with the rank of Colonel after a 26-year career. He joined Hughes Aircraft Company as a Project Manager in Missile Systems Advanced Programs working EO and RF missile sensors. During his 17 years with Hughes/Raytheon Missile Systems he served as Proposal Manager and Program Manager for several Programs such as EUROMAV, CASOM and Maverick. He finished his tour at Raytheon as the Senior Program Manager for Maverick International Programs having worked in almost every European Country due to NATO expansion and their desire for US Aircraft and Weapons. He is currently on the Board of Directors of the National DFC Society and Missile Systems Retirees Association. He is also serving as President of the Tucson Chapter of the DFC Society. Marty is enjoying life in Tucson with his wife Alice Ann as they try to balance their time between six children, 14 grandchildren, two great grandchildren and golf & pickleball.

Jim McDivitt was in the second group of U.S. astronauts. He retired from the Air Force and NASA in 1972. He was a Brigadier General and manager of the Apollo spacecraft program. He became Executive V.P. of Consumer Power Co. and later President of Pullman Standard, a railcar builder. Then, he became Executive V.P. of Pullman, overseeing three worldwide engineering and construction companies as well as the railcar company. He then joined Rockwell International as Senior V.P. of Strategic Management, later becoming President of Autonetics and finally retired in 1995 as Senior V.P. of Government Operations and International for Rockwell. He and wife, Judy, split time between Tucson and life on a Michigan lake in the summer.

Daniel E. Moore, Jr. is the son of a U.S. Navy B-24 (PB4Y) ace. Dan Jr. served as a U.S. Navy F/A-18 pilot for 29 years. An award-winning author, *Air & Space* Smithsonian Magazine featured Dan's "Night Terrors" in their Winter 2019 Collector's Edition of "CARRIER: City at Sea" – dedicated to all who have served on U.S. Navy carriers and to all who are serving today.

Chuck Ogren retired from the Air Force in 1983 after 20 years of service as a Lieutenant Colonel. He went to work for Hughes Aircraft Company at their Canoga Park, CA facility as a Program Manager in their Missile Systems Group. He moved to Tucson, AZ in 1995 when Hughes consolidated all of its missile activities. After managing a number of important missile system upgrades, he retired for a second time in 2013 after 30 years with Hughes/Raytheon. Since then he and Kim, his wife of 56 years, have enjoyed Tucson's great weather (they even like the hot season). They enjoy visiting with their four children and five grandchildren who are spread across the country. A key highlight of his leisure time is the weekly lunch with the "Friday Pilots."

Earl O'Loughlin retired from the Air Force after 37 years and returned to his home, East Tawas, MI. He pursued membership on corporate boards. At one time he served on eight boards. His passion was to hunt and fish and enjoy life with his wife and family. His travel took him hunting in Russia, New Zealand, Alaska, Canada, South Dakota, Michigan, Kansas, Georgia, Colorado, Texas, New Mexico and Arizona. He lost his high school sweetheart, Shirley, to cancer in 2003. He remarried an old friend, Thelma, and they enjoy splitting the year between Tucson and East Tawas. His four married children and 10 grandchildren love Thelma and life is good. He enjoys his farm in Michigan feeding deer, turkeys, and rainbow trout and Fridays with his buddies when in Tucson.

Phil Osterli: After retiring from UC, Phil and Linda departed the tarnished Golden State for the Evergreen state, settling in Poulsbo, Washington (Little Norway) where they explored the coastal waters of Puget Sound, the Canadian Gulf Islands and inlets in their boat "Nordic Spirit" with other members of the Poulsbo Yacht Club. As the years passed, the cold, wet winters caused them to start "snowbirding" via motorhome in the relative warmth of the Central and Southern California Coast, usually staying in military RV parks (gated communities with armed guards and golf courses) where they enjoyed a new group of like-minded friends. They also traveled to visit family scattered around the country, and attended numerous reunions re-establishing friendships from earlier times. After relocating to Arizona, Phil fortunately found the Friday Pilots, who graciously extended an invitation to join this impressive group of aviators. Always in awe of their valor, professionalism and accomplishments while serving our country, he looks forward to our informal Friday luncheons with these heroes!

Bill Pitts retired in 1994 as a Colonel after 26 years with almost 14 as an A-10 pilot. Following retirement, he was hired by UPS and flew there for 7 years. During that time, he and his wife, Ruthanne, started and built a multi-million-dollar commercial office furniture business which, at its peak, employed 25 people in 5 states. After 15 successful years, they closed the doors and fully retired. In 2014, Ruthanne died of a traumatic brain injury following a freak cycling accident. As you read in his latest chapter, "The Plan" had more in store. Through a series of unpredictable events, he met Frieda and after over two years of courting, they married in 2018.

They both love to travel and especially for fishing in Alaska each summer. From fighter pilot, to airline pilot, to business executive, to retired - WOW, WHAT A RIDE!!!

George Allen "GAR" Rose: "The rest of the story!" I retired from the USAF in January 1986, and was hired by a defense contractor in Tucson, AZ. My wife, Rebecca (Becky), was offered a lucrative job in Sacramento, CA, managing multi-family housing developments throughout northern CA. So, I became a camp follower for a brief time until it became obvious my talents for housekeeping and cooking were sorely lacking. The airline companies were hiring "experienced" pilots, so I joined an American Airlines regional affiliate operating in the west. Becky's career moves took us to San Francisco, Denver and Houston and I commuted to work ultimately at DFW. As I reached the 10 years of service point, the grind of the regional flying business and the commuting began to take a toll on my love of flight. The fun was gone, and each trip just became "a job!" My last trip as an airline Captain was in 2000. Until Becky's retirement I was a "kept man" and played golf, completed "honey do's" and became a landscaper and pool boy. We returned to Tucson in 2007 to our beautiful home (complete with a low maintenance landscape and a pool professionally tended) in the Catalina Mountain foothills. My son, Glen, and his wife have given us two wonderful granddaughters, Landry Jane and Willa Mae, to spoil. As "geezer hood" creeps upon us, we have moved into a retirement village in San Antonio from where we plan to continue our travels to be with friends and family. In residence here at "Blue Skies of Texas" are two classmates from pilot training, another Tucson Friday Pilot and one of my mentors, "Shock" Shockley. Recalling those "golden days of yesteryear" with this group is fun!! And two more lessons learned pop up as we share our stories, "IF WE'D KNOWN WE WERE GOING TO LIVE THIS LONG, WE'D HAVE TAKEN BETTER CARE OF OURSELVES," and often the phrase, "GUYS, YOU KNOW THERE IS NEITHER RHYME NOR REASON WHY WE'RE STILL ALIVE GIVEN OUR PAST EXPOLITS!"

Gene Santarelli retired as a Lieutenant General and Vice Commander of PACAF after 32 years having commanded a numbered air force, an air division and three wings in the U.S., Europe, and the Mid-East. He also served as Exec to the CSAF. He is one of five USAF Senior Mentors for general officers on command and control of air operations, a consultant to the defense industry, the State of Arizona and the cities of Tucson and Glendale, AZ. He has served as member and co-chair of the Arizona Governor's Task Force on Military Installations. He serves on several boards. He and wife, Kay, have been married 38 years and enjoy the Tucson climate from their beautiful foothills home.

Don Shepperd retired as a Major General and head of the Air National Guard. He formed his own consulting company, became a TV personality covering the wars in Iraq and Afghanistan for CNN for six years, served on several corporate boards and retired near his four grandchildren in Tucson where he and wife of 58 years, Rose, are mad University of Arizona Wildcat men's and women's basketball fans. He has six published books with many more in waiting.

Moose Skowron retired from the Air Force after 24 years. He went to work for Learjet as an independent test pilot for 26 years. He was a utility infielder flying production and experimental tests and demo and as an FAA Designated Engineering Test Pilot flying worldwide. His childhood sweetheart and wife, Margie, passed away and he lost an eye to cancer, but was able to fight with the FAA and get his commercial renewed. He just celebrated his 86th birthday and still considers himself one of the "the luckiest men on the face of the earth."

Jeff "Tico" Tice graduated from the USAF as a Lt. Col. In 22 years of active duty service, he flew over 3,000 hours in F-111, F-5, and F-16 jets. Following that retirement, he entered civilian aviation and flew for American Airlines amassing over 10,000 hours of flight time as a First Officer in the MD-80, Boeing 737, 757 and 767 aircraft on both domestic and international routes. He retired from American Airlines after 13 years. Tico has appeared on numerous television and radio programs including *Larry King, The Today Show*, and *60 Minutes*. He currently serves on the board of directors for the Marines' Memorial Foundation and is involved with several nationwide military-related charities.

Rob Van Sice retired from the USAF in 1994 and moved to northern Virginia to consult with Whitney, Bradley and Brown. In 1995 he was hired by Hughes Aircraft Company to work in Rosslyn VA. Raytheon purchased Hughes and in 1998, Rob opened the Seattle Raytheon office to support the Boeing/Raytheon Joint Strike Fighter team. In 2002, he moved to Raytheon Missile Systems in Tucson where he was an Engineering Director until retiring in 2008. He serves on several non-profit Boards in Tucson, travels extensively, and spends time with his grandchildren in Virginia. One of his weekly highlights is the "Friday Pilots" gathering.

Russ Violett went into the consulting business and worked with several major companies in marketing and management focusing on Saudi Arabia. He traveled monthly to the area. When companies removed personnel from management positions in Saudi for cause, he spent several weeks at a time living in the Mid-East filling those positions temporarily. After twenty years of consulting, he stopped traveling to spend more time with his family, wife, four daughters, their husbands and 31 grand and great grandchildren and play golf. He is active with and a member of the Board of Trustees of the Pima Air and Space Museum in Tucson.

Alex Wright retired from the Air Force as a Lieutenant Colonel after 32 years of service. In 2007 his wife, Kathy, was diagnosed with cancer and he spent the next three and a half years making sure she had everything she needed and wanted. After Kathy died in early 2011 it took a long time for Alex to climb out of that deep hole. Once out, thanks to his friend Benny White, Alex took up traveling again, mainly to the Hawaiian Islands and to the US National Parks. Alex also began volunteering with the Knights of Columbus and the Fisher House. He became a member of the Friday Pilots in the spring of 2015. Alex also became a docent at the 390th Memorial Museum that same spring, an independent non-profit aviation museum located on the grounds of the Pima Air and Space Museum in Tucson. In December 2019 Alex was selected to be the Executive Director of the 390th Memorial Museum. Although not looking for a job, Alex was all of a sudden back in the instructing business sharing with museum visitors the World War II combat story of the 390th Bomb Group. Alex spends time with his daughter and son and their families, all of whom live in Tucson. He also has found Nancy, a remarkable woman who gets him. Together they travel and enjoy what life has to offer.

EPILOGUE

The term "Flown West" appears more and more often in our emails. It is a term used by airmen. The sun sets in the west and the day ends as it is setting, and so too does a fallen pilot fly into the sunset at the end of their days. Twelve of our brothers from the Friday Pilots have Flown West. We will all follow. We grieved their passing, but treasure their memories. For us, they are still at lunch, smiling, laughing, telling their stories. It our firm belief that we will all join again in a different place - a true band of brothers.

GLOSSARY

This section contains a glossary of terms found in the stories and widely used by pilots:

AAA/Triple-A/Triple-A site - anti-aircraft artillery/anti-aircraft artillery site – enemy guns that shoot at aircraft

ABCCC/AB Triple-C - Aircraft that operated as Airborne Battlefield Command and Control Centers such as Hillsboro, Cricket, Crown, Panama, Waterboy et. al.

AB/Afterburner/burner - system of spraybars that inject jet fuel into the engine exhaust which is then re-ignited producing extra thrust

Abort/Aborting – to stop doing what you are doing immediately! i.e. "ABORT YOUR PASS!" or, "ABORT TAKEOFF!

AFSC - Air Force Specialty Code – personnel jargon for "job title"

AGL - above ground level. Refers to altitude above the ground, i.e. – 100 ft. AGL meant at 100 feet above the ground

ALO - Air Liaison officer - Air Force officer stationed with the Army to assist in coordinating air support

Ammo - ammunition

Alpha Strike Package - the package of fighters used to attack targets in the heavily defended Route Packages near Hanoi and/or Haiphong during the Vietnam War

Anchor - refueling orbit tracks flown by KC-135 aerial tankers, such as those over Thailand and the Gulf of Tonkin - Brown Anchor, Blue Anchor, etc.

Bailout - eject from the aircraft. In fighter aircraft the pilot ejects by pulling handles to fire the rocket-powered ejection seat

Barrier – arresting device installed at departure end of runway – cables to catch aircraft arresting hooks, now (Bak-9/12s). In the old days nets and chains were used

BDA - bomb damage assessment - the results of a strike, what the bombs hit

Bingo - pre-designated fuel level that warns the pilot to leave for home base, or the tanker

Break - a hard, high-G turn usually made to avoid gunfire, or a missile from an attacking enemy fighter, such as, "Olds 4, BREAK RIGHT!"

Briefing/Brief - the pre-mission session during which the pilots meet to plan the mission and receive information on the weather, latest intelligence, route of flight, etc.

Buffs – "Big Ugly Fat Fellows" - affectionate term for B-52s

Canopy - the parachute canopy. Also refers to jungle tree cover. Also the glass that covers the cockpit on a fighter aircraft that is opened for aircraft entry/exit

CAP/Capping – Combat Air Patrol - orbiting a location such as a downed pilot

CBUs - cluster bomb units - bomblets carried in multi-tubed canisters on wing stations of fighter aircraft and delivered at low altitude requiring flight directly over a target

Chatter - talk on the aircraft radio, as in, "Hold down the chatter!"

Chopper - a helicopter

Chute - parachute

Cong - slang for Vietcong - enemy soldiers

Counter – a mission over North Vietnam. Due to the high risks, a Vietnam tour was defined as one-year OR 100 missions over North Vietnam

Deadbug! - phrase shouted at beer call in an Officers Club. Everyone hits the floor. Last man standing buys the bar

DCO - Deputy Commander for Operations - Colonel on wing or squadron staff in charge of operations

Debrief - after mission sessions reviewing mission performance and mission results

Delta - the agricultural rice paddy area forming the southern-most part of Vietnam, fed by the Mekong River, often called the "Mekong Delta" area south of Saigon, now called "Ho Chi Minh City"

Delta Points - numbered geographic points on the ground over prominent geographic features used to designate locations, to abbreviate radio chatter and prevent enemy from knowing location of aircraft, e.g. "We are just west of Delta 60"

Delta Sierra – vulgar term referring to "dog poop" used normally to describe bad weather as in, "The weather is Delta Sierra today"

DEROS - date of rotation stateside. A pilot's return home date

Deskjockey - a non-pilot administrator such as a clerk-typist or staff officer

Dragchute - a parachute deployed from under the aircraft after landing by pulling a cockpit handle to assist with slowing the aircraft down

DMZ - Demilitarized Zone dividing North from South Vietnam during the war. The DMZ followed the Ben Hai River

DOD – the Department of Defense located in the Pentagon in Washington D.C.

Duckbutt – aircraft used to monitor overwater flights or support water rescues. In Vietnam the HU16 Grumman Albatross amphibian aircraft was used when appropriate

ECM/ECM pods – electronic counter-measures/pods to provide electronic jamming against ground radars

EGT - engine exhaust gas temperature (measured on EGT gauge in cockpit)

Eject - bailing out by pulling the ejection seat handles, firing the rocket-powered ejection seat, which subsequently fires the pilot out of the aircraft

FAC - Forward Air Controller, finds and marks targets with smoke rockets for bomb-laden fighters

Fast FAC - FACs who flew jets. In Vietnam Fast FACs flew F-100s and later F-4s with radio callsigns such as "Misty, Laredo and Wolf"

FCF - functional check flight - a test flight

Feet-wet/Feet-dry - operating over water, or over land

Flak/Flakbursts - smoke and shrapnel caused by anti-aircraft artillery shells exploding at pre-set times after firing. 37mm bursts were gray, 57mm, 85mm and 100mm were dark black

FNG - "Frigging" New Guy

Friendlies - the good guys. Used to explain the location of U.S. troops, i.e., "The friendlies are on the north side of the river"

FUBAR – Fouled-up beyond all recognition

G/Gs/G-forces/Pulling Gs - the force of gravity exerted on a pilot's body by turning the aircraft, or pulling on the control stick. "Pulling 4-Gs," means the pilot experiences feeling 4 X his body weight

GIB/GIBs - "guy in the backseat." The backseater in a two-place aircraft

Gomers - the bad guys - the VC and NVA

Groundpounder - a soldier, or non-pilot

Grunt - Army soldier

Guard or Guard freq - frequency 243.0 - the UHF radio frequency used for emergency radio transmissions and monitored by all UHF-equipped aircraft

Haiphong - the major port city of North Vietnam

Hanoi - the capital city of North Vietnam

Highdrags/Retards - 500 lb. finned/retarded bombs used to drop at low altitude

Hilton/the Hanoi Hilton - infamous prison used to hold American POWs in Hanoi

Ho Chi Minh - Ho Chi Minh Trail - named after the communist leader of North Vietnam who died 2 Sep 1969 - the series of roadways that led from the Hanoi/Haiphong area south through southern North Vietnam and Laos to Cambodia and South Vietnam to resupply Vietcong and NVA forces

Hook/Tailhook – large metal hook used during landing and takeoff emergencies to snag a steel cable that stretched across the runway to arrest the aircraft (like those used by Navy carrier aircraft)

Hootch - on base living quarters for pilots

HHQ - Higher headquarters

Hun - pilots favorite nickname for the F-100 aircraft

I Corps/"Eye" Corps - South Vietnam was divided into four Corps areas. I Corps was the northern-most Corps area closest to North Vietnam and the DMZ; II Corps was the Central Highlands; III Corps was the Central Highlands to Saigon; IV Corps the Mekong Delta area south of Saigon

IFR - instrument flight rules - in the weather - flying on instruments in the weather

In-country – referring to inside South Vietnam such as an "in-country aircraft checkout" or "In-country missions" meaning inside South Vietnam, rather than over North Vietnam

Intel/Intel Officer - intelligence/Intelligence Officer

Jink/jinking – turn/turning the aircraft randomly and unpredictably to confuse ground gunners and defeat aimed AAA

Jolly or Jolly Green - Air Force HH-53 rescue helicopters

Karst - geographic features, jagged limestone protrusions forming mountains, common in North Vietnam, Laos and Thailand

KIA - killed in action

Klick - slang for kilometer - 1,000 meters - .6 of a mile

Knots - measurement for airspeed - a "knot" is one nautical mile/hr., i.e. - 400 knots = 400 nautical miles/hr. A nautical mile is 1.15 statute miles. Jet aircraft cockpit airspeed indicators are in knots

Life Support - section in a fighter squadron that maintains the pilot support equipment and survival gear (parachutes, life rafts, survival radios, etc.)

Linebacker/Linebacker II – 1972 renewed air campaigns designed to force the North Vietnamese to the Paris peace table to end the war

LOC - lines of communication - refers to roads, trails, rivers, etc. over which men and material are moved

LPUs - Life Preservers, Underarm - the inflatable life preservers worn under the pilot's armpits. Used in case of over-water ejection

Mach – the speed of sound, roughly 666 knots or 766 mph, a mile in five seconds. Mach two is twice the speed of sound. "Breaking the mach," means exceeding the speed of sound

MANPADs – man-portable air defense systems - shoulder-fired IR, heat-seeking missiles. The SA-7 was first employed in Vietnam, now increasingly sophisticated models proliferate throughout the world

Mark - the white smoke cloud caused by the explosion of a white phosphorous marking rocket head fired by a Forward Air Controller and used to visually mark targets for attacking fighters

MAYDAY! - emergency radio call made to alert others that an aircraft is in trouble. From the French, "Venez m'aider!" meaning, "Come help me!" e.g. "MAYDAY! MAYDAY! MAYDAY! Ejecting west of Delta 60!"

MIA - missing in action - pilots, whose status could not be confirmed, were listed by DOD as "MIA"

Mike/mic/mike button - the microphone in the pilot's mask. The button on the throttle the pilot pushes to transmit on the radio

Mistys – Fast FACs that flew the two-seat F-100F aircraft over North Vietnam to locate and mark targets for bomb-laden fighters

Movers - any enemy vehicle that moved on the ground

MSL – altitude above mean sea level – the indicated altitude shown on the cockpit altimeter

Nape/napalm – thick, jelled fuel that was dropped in tanks and ignited to burn ground targets

nm - 1 nautical mile = 1.15 statue miles

NORDO - no radio - radio out

NOTAM - Notice to Airmen, an advisory message

NVA - North Vietnamese Army

O-Club - Officers Club

PACAF/PACOM – Pacific Air Forces was/is the Air Force component HQ for PACOM located at Hickam AFB, Honolulu HI. PACOM was/is the unified command HQ in charge of Pacific military operations located in Honolulu.

PCS - Permanent change of station - a military move from one base to another

PE - Personal Equipment - the flying and survival gear worn and carried by pilots and maintained by the squadron Life Support Section

Pickle/Pickle button/Pickling - to press the bomb button on the control stick, releasing a bomb or firing a rocket or missile

PIO - pilot-induced oscillation - usually caused by over-controlling the aircraft at high airspeeds

Pipper - the center of the gunsight on the pilot's windscreen. Used for aiming to fire guns, rockets, missiles or to drop a bomb

Pit/the Pit - the backseat of a two-place aircraft, as in "riding in the pit"

PJs - para-rescue crews that rode on the Jolly Green helicopters to rescue downed pilots

Playtime - the amount of time fighters have to work with the FAC on a target - limited by fuel, i.e., "We have 30 minutes playtime"

POL/POL storage area - petroleum, oil and lubricants, gasoline and oil

POW - Prisoner of War

Punchout/Punch - to eject (bailout) from the aircraft

R&R - rest and recuperation - a vacation - all military members in Vietnam got a one-week R&R during their tour, usually to Hawaii, Australia, Thailand or Malaysia

Recce - reconnaissance

RESCAP - capping (flying over) a downed pilot while taking part in a rescue attempt

RHAW/RHAW-gear - Radar Homing and Warning gear - electronic system that warned of radar lock-on by SAM radars or gunsites with visual symbols and audio sounds displayed on a cockpit gauge and in a pilot's headset. Modern gear is called RWR (Radar Warning Receiver)

ROE - rules of engagement - the rules established by HQ to be followed by all pilots while attacking enemy targets

Rolling Thunder - the air campaign over North Vietnam from Mar 1965 - Oct 1968

Route Pack/Route Package - North Vietnam was divided into six Route Packages - areas of operations. Route Pack 1 was the southern-most just above the DMZ. Route Pack 6 was divided into 6A (Hanoi) and 6B

(Haiphong). The Air Force had primary responsibility for RPs 1, 5 and 6A, the Navy, 2, 3, 4 and 6B

RPM - revolutions per minute - engine speed - i.e. "operating at high RPM" meant operating at high engine power. RPM was shown on a cockpit tachometer gauge

RT - radio talk - the conversations on a radio, as "Let's hold down the RT"

RTB - return to base - go home

Sabre Jet - nickname for the F-100 (the Super Sabre)

Saigon - the capital city of South Vietnam, now "Ho Chi Minh City"

Sandys – USAF A-1 (also called "Spads") aircraft used to escort Jolly Green helicopters and perform location of, protection for and rescue of downed aircrews

SAM/SAM site - Surface to Air Missile/Missile site

SAR - Search and Rescue mission

SEA - Southeast Asia, generic term used to include the countries of Vietnam, Laos, Thailand, Cambodia, and the Philippines during the Vietnam War

Secondary - an explosion of something on the ground caused by dropping bombs on it, such as ammunition, or POL

Seventh Air Force/7th AF – the HQ in charge of the Vietnam air war, located in Saigon at Tan Son Nhut Air Base

Shack - a direct hit, as in - Lead "shacked" the truck.

Sierra Hotel - vulgar term "Sh-- Hot" used by fighter pilots to denote something is good (hot), such as, "That was a Sierra Hotel job of bombing today"

Slicks - refers to un-retarded bombs with tailfins, i.e. 500 lb./750 lb./1000lb. "slicks," vs. 500 lb. "retarded" or "Snakeye" bombs

Slow FAC – FACs in slow propeller-driven airplanes such as the O-1 and O-2

SLUF - derisive nickname for the A-7 aircraft, Short Lille Ugly "Fellow"

Snakeyes - 500 lb. retarded highdrag bombs dropped at low altitude by fighters

SOF - Supervisor of Flying - pilot stationed on ground in command post to supervise flying operations

SPADs - propeller-driven A-1 aircraft used to escort Jolly Green helicopters on rescues

Steel Tiger - the air campaign over Laos

Strafe/strafing - firing the 20mm aircraft guns (30mm in case of A-10)

Super Sabre – another nickname for the F-100

Supersonic - faster than the speed of sound

Tallyho/Tally - I have it/you in sight

Tango Uniform - vulgar term used by fighter pilots meaning lying "breasts up," or dead, such as "Our radio is tango uniform"

Tanker - airborne KC-135 refueling aircraft equipped with drogues (baskets) or refueling booms. F-4s, F-105s and A-7s used "receptacle" refueling (tanker probe inserted into open aircraft receptacle). F-100 pilots inserted a refueling probe to a "drogue" (basket attached to fuel hose) to obtain fuel while airborne

TDY - temporary duty - away from home base

Three-man lift - Marine beer call trick. Strong man says, "I can lift three men off the floor at once." Three unsuspecting men lie flat on floor. Someone yells, "GO!" and audience pours beer over those lying flat

Thud – affectionate nickname for the F-105 Thunderchief aircraft

Tracers - illuminated rounds fired by AAA sites to allow gunners to track aircraft. Normally the ratio of tracers was 1:6 or 7

Truckpark - parking areas for trucks. Usually carved-out in fan-fashion at the end of a road to disperse vehicles, making them harder to hit by attacking fighters

Twenty mike-mike - 20mm ammunition for F-100, F-4 or F-105 aircraft guns

UHF - Ultra High Frequency radio - the radio frequency band on which all USAF/USN military aircraft operated. The Army aircraft and ground forces operated on VHF and FM frequencies

Unworkable - can't put in airstrikes, usually due to poor weather, i.e., "The weather is unworkable today"

Vietcong/VC - the Vietcong – indigenous enemy soldiers in South Vietnam

VFR - visual flight rules - flying in good weather

VR/VR-ing - visual recce/performing visual reconnaissance from the air

Warp-speed - refers to going fast

Warthog – affectionate term for the A-10 Thunderbolt II aircraft

Wheels-up - refers to raising the landing gear after takeoff

Wild Weasels/Weasels – aircraft equipped as SAM hunter-killers that provide strike force protection by locating SAM radars and firing homing anti-radiation missiles. F-100s were employed as early Weasels in Vietnam, later F-105s assumed the role, then F-4s, now F-16s

Willie Petes - white phosphorous smoke rockets fired by FACs to mark targets for fighters.

WOXOF – military weather acronym for "weather is - indefinite ceiling at zero ft, visibility zero in fog"

WSO – Weapons System Operator, the backseater (navigator) in a two-place fighter such as the F-4. Originally pilots were assigned to the backseat and called PSOs

ABOUT THE EDITOR

Don Shepperd is a Distinguished Graduate of the United States Air Force Academy. He graduated with the fourth class in 1962. He flew fighters in Europe and 247 combat fighter missions in Vietnam including 58 as an F-100 Misty Fast FAC over North Vietnam. He flew for the airlines and sold light airplanes in industry. He retired from the Pentagon in 1998 as a Major General and head of the Air National Guard with almost 5,000 hrs. in fighter aircraft. He formed his own consulting company and served on corporate boards. He covered the wars in Iraq and Afghanistan for CNN. He and wife, Rose, live in Tucson near their four grandchildren. He is an author and editor. His books can be found on Amazon.com

Other books by Don Shepperd

The Friday Pilots - ed. 2014, AuthorHouse, Bloomington IN

Bury Us Upside Down – the Misty Pilots and the Secret Battle for the Ho Chi Minh Trail – with Rick Newman, foreword by Sen. John McCain – 2006, Ballentine Books, New York, Presidio Press, a division of Random House, Inc. New York

Misty – First Person Stories of the Misty F-100 Fast FACs in the Vietnam War – ed. 2002, 1stBooks, Bloomington IN

The Class of '58 Writes a Book – A collection of original stories by the Class of 1958, Wheat Ridge High School – Wheat Ridge, Colorado - ed. 2008, AuthorHouse, Bloomington IN

Those Red Tag Bastards – their dreams, their lives, their memories - ed. 2012, AuthorHouse, Bloomington IN